# AID FOR
# JUST DEVELOPMENT

# AID FOR
# JUST DEVELOPMENT
## Report on the Future
## of Foreign Assistance

Stephen Hellinger
Douglas Hellinger
Fred M. O'Regan

## THE DEVELOPMENT GROUP FOR ALTERNATIVE POLICIES

LYNNE RIENNER PUBLISHERS • BOULDER & LONDON

Published in the United States of America in 1988 by
Lynne Rienner Publishers, Inc.
948 North Street, Boulder, Colorado 80302

and in the United Kingdom by
Lynne Rienner Publishers, Inc.
3 Henrietta Street, Covent Garden, London WC2E 8LU

**Library of Congress Cataloging-in-Publication Data**
Hellinger, Steve.
    Aid for just development: report on the future of foriegn assistance/
  by Stephen Hellinger, Douglas Hellinger, Fred O'Regan.
        p.      cm.
    Bibliography:  p.
    Includes index.
    ISBN 1-55587-121-6 (lib. bdg.)  ISBN 1-55587-122-4 (pbk.)
        1. Economic assistance—Developing countries.  2. Economic
  development projects—Developing countries.  3. Non-governmental
  organizations—Developing countries.  4. Project management—
  Developing countries—Decision making.  I. Hellinger, Doug.
  II. O'Regan, Fred.  III. Title.
  HC60.H38516 1988
  338.91'09172'4—dc19                                           88-4996
                                                                    CIP

**British Library Cataloguing in Publication Data**
A Cataloguing in Publication record for this book
is available from the British Library.


Printed and bound in the United States of America

The paper used in this publication meets the requirements
of the American National Standard for Permanence of Paper
for Printed Library Materials Z39.48-1984.  ∞

To those in the South
whose efforts to foster social change
continue to inspire our  work

# Contents

# Foreword

When I was president of the Inter-American Foundation, we published a book titled *They Know How*. "They" referred to the poorer people of Latin America and the Caribbean, whose development efforts the Foundation was dedicated to underwriting. The findings of the book—indeed, my entire nine-year experience at the Foundation—affirmed my earliest feelings gained from working among the people of the Third World that even the most deprived and humble among us is capable of determining his or her own needs and may possess great creativity and industriousness in organizing solutions to his or her community's problems.

I have also learned through the years that nothing is so important in the field of human relations as the respect we show one another, no matter the difference in wealth, education, or social status, and the dignity with which I believe all of us are entitled to live our lives. It is no wonder to me, therefore, that so many of our aid institutions have failed so miserably to curtail poverty and foster social change in the Third World. Most of the major aid agencies have operated on the principle that *we* know how, that *we* have the answers to the problems. These agencies have made it perfectly clear to the "targets" of their largess that there is no role for the poor and powerless in shaping and controlling their own destinies. Under such conditions, preserving one's dignity is difficult. Development is impossible.

Even in countries where there are free and fair elections,

limiting democracy and popular participation to the ballot box levies a heavy social cost. Wherever poor people are excluded from the daily discourse on matters that affect them, frustration and alienation are the inevitable results. In the Third World, whether or not these feelings are manifested in anti-American sentiment, U.S. policy goals are jeopardized by the social polarization and instability that fester in such pervasive dissatisfaction.

As the authors of this report on the future of foreign aid point out, the problems of aid and development have reached critical proportions. Billions of dollars of aid, provided on the basis of Northern short-term priorities, have helped build two societies in the South and an ever widening gap between the two. It is clearly time to rethink our aid strategies and to do so in conjunction with the people we say we are trying to help.

Over the past twenty years a number of major reports on aid, from Pearson to Carlucci, have been published. All suggest changes in focus or structure. None proposes a true partnership with the *people* of the South. *Aid for Just Development* is distinctive in that it makes practical, detailed, and at the same time far-reaching recommendations for restructuring aid institutions so that they can mold their programs according to local realities and the needs, interests, and efforts of those who live in them.

There are few who are in a position to write such a report. The authors' breadth of experience in the aid and development field is unique. As the founding directors of The Development GAP, they have worked with a wide range of organizations—from the World Bank and AID to private and voluntary organizations in the North, and from grassroots groups to government agencies in the South—and they have continually worked with Congress and other decisionmakers to translate this experience into new and better policy. They are not abstract theorists nor representatives of any of the many special interests in the aid field, but rather people with an ongoing, hands-on involvement who seek to give representation to the poor.

Long before it became fashionable to discuss possible links between microlevel and macrolevel development, The Development GAP was not only proposing such linkages but was already demonstrating in the field how they could be made. It has been at the forefront in helping to move the World Bank into consultation with the people the Bank proposes to assist. Without The Development GAP's extensive efforts, the autonomy of the Inter-American Foundation, and possibly the Foundation itself, would have been things of the past, and the African Development Foundation certainly would not have been created. The Development GAP has worked closely with popular organizations in the Caribbean, Latin America, and Africa to help reshape U.S. economic policy toward those regions. Above all else, it has helped set standards for the aid community and continues to challenge all those in the community to achieve and uphold them.

*Aid for Just Development* presents that challenge directly and unambiguously. Others might have been uncritical and allowed the reader to avoid confronting the mistakes of the past, as so many previous reports have done. A major strength of this report is that it does not permit us to do so. It forces us to reassess the very foundations of the prevailing aid paradigms, challenges us to construct a new paradigm that is based in Third World realities, and then offers us a concrete and creative development assistance structure that responds to those realities.

*William M. Dyal, Jr.*
President
St. John's College, Annapolis

# Preface

Over the past decade, The Development Group for Alternative Policies (The Development GAP) has worked with governmental and non-governmental development organizations in some thirty countries on behalf of a variety of development assistance institutions. We have also worked extensively in policy centers in Washington in an attempt to translate our experience into more appropriate aid policies. In both endeavors, we have been advocates of approaches that directly involve and serve the poor, that are responsive to their expressed needs, aspirations and efforts to shape their own future and that are predicated upon a recognition of their capabilities to do so.

In Latin America and Africa we have worked on developing projects that have demonstrated to the World Bank the viability and comparative advantages of involving non-governmental organizations as project designers and implementors. Similar efforts have taken us to Africa and the Middle East for the Agency for International Development (AID). For both donor institutions we have helped public agencies overseas to develop programs that involve and benefit non-governmental groups and associations of the poor. At other times we have worked directly with Third World groups, helping them to assess or develop programs and to identify sources of funding in the North.

The Development GAP's involvement with smaller donors has also been extensive. We have collaborated with a number of PVOs (private and voluntary organizations) on a variety of endeavors and have worked closely with PACT, a secular PVO consortium. A Development GAP co-director has served as chair of PACT's project selection committee. And serving as chair and then secretary of the Ecumenical Working Group on Africa, we have had the opportunity to work closely with a number of church development agencies, as well.

Our relationship with the Inter-American Foundation (IAF) dates back to 1973. It was while working there that The Development GAP's founders, formerly Peace Corps volunteers in Latin America and Africa, began contemplating the creation of an activist policy organization. Following its own establishment in 1977, The Development GAP provided various forms of assistance to the IAF through the remainder of the decade. Since political problems beset the Foundation in 1983, we have supported its efforts to maintain its independence and integrity. Meanwhile, The Development GAP has been intimately involved since 1975 in the creation of the African Development Foundation (ADF) and in the subsequent promotion of ADF's autonomy and its assistance mandate.

As reflected in the text of this report, our experience with some of these aid institutions has left us troubled about the course of the U.S. development assistance program. Our involvement with others, however, has shown us that a new and more promising approach can be taken. Meanwhile, in our collaboration with policymakers, it became apparent that common misconceptions about Third World local realities, as well as about the relationships between aid and development, have been paralleled by a strong desire to formulate a new assistance policy and program that would be streamlined and more meaningful to the lives of the poor.

We decided, therefore, to utilize the experience we gained overseas, and that gained from working on a range of aid-related issues in Congress, to develop and present an alternative aid paradigm that would have practical application. This report is the result of that effort. It is our hope that its analysis and recommendations for change in our country's aid program will be of assistance to policymakers and, consequently, to the Third World poor as well.

This report was prepared with support from the Ford Foundation, the Rockefeller Foundation, and the Presbyterian Hunger Program. To each of these institutions we are most thankful. We also want to express our appreciation in particular to Gary Sick, our program officer at Ford, who showed patience and confidence in our work. It should be made clear, however, that the opinions expressed herein do not necessarily reflect the position or policies of the Ford Foundation, the Rockefeller Foundation, or the Presbyterian Hunger Program, and no official endorsement by these institutions should be inferred.

We also wish to express our gratitude to our colleagues in the aid community in this country and Europe, to the people inside Third World development organizations with whom we have worked through the years, and to the many other people who shared their insights with us during the preparation of this report. We want to thank, too, the members of our Advisory Board, particularly Peggy Antrobus, Bob Busche, Corinne Johnson, Vic Johnson, Tony Lake, Bill Rau, and Sally Yudelman, as well as Ed Dela Rosa, Ted Owens, and Warren van Wicklin for their thorough and substantive reviews of the manuscript. Within The Development GAP, Blane Lewis deserves much of the credit for pulling together the material we have used. Tim Lake, Daniel Solomon, Karen Greg Elliott, and Diane Soles also helped us to put this report together. Finally, we owe a special debt of gratitude to Maggie Kennedy and Kathy Burks, whose efforts not only helped make this work a reality, but whose encouragement sustained us during periods when we needed it most.

# ONE

# Introduction
# and Overview

This report is about how the United States, through bilateral, multilateral, and non-governmental aid channels, can best promote equitable, locally defined, and self-sustaining development in the Third World. It is written from the perspective of those who have spent much of the past two decades working with institutions ranging from community organizations to the World Bank. In essence, it represents an effort on the part of The Development GAP to translate its experience with the Third World poor, development and aid organizations, and policymakers into an aid paradigm designed to underwrite the involvement and leadership of the poor in their own development, and thereby help foster long-term stability rooted in true self-determination.

In this endeavor we do not pretend to be apolitical. Indeed, development itself is a highly political process, pitting those lacking productive assets and access to productive inputs (as well as many of the basic necessities and amenities of life) against powerful forces in their own societies. Whether they address the matter directly or not, every proposal on aid or development policy at least implicitly establishes a position on the distribution of wealth, income, goods, services, and general economic well-being and, consequently, on the nature of economic and social relationships.

This is not to say, however, that our approach to these questions is either politically partisan or ideological. We have worked with representatives of both major parties and with people of all ideological stripes in seeking to fashion pragmatic, but just, responses to policy and programmatic issues. Our experience overseas and inside aid agencies has shown us that neither the traditional liberal approach of channeling large amounts of funds through Third World government bureaucracies nor the present conservative policy of maximizing the aid spent on the commercial private sector is effective. In fact, far more often than not these approaches have exacerbated, rather than helped resolve, development problems.

**THE FAILURE OF AID**

The conventional foreign aid strategies have failed to engender equitable and sustainable development largely because they have not corresponded to local realities. Inherent in these strategies is the belief that poverty can be successfully addressed in the Third World by outsiders—whether they be international donors, national public officials, or those in the business sector—lacking associations with and understanding of the poor and their communities. Causes of poverty are diagnosed, needs assessed, policies developed, and programs designed without consultation with the people who experience these problems every day and without whose commitment of time, effort, and other resources no program can be successfully sustained.

Indeed, a fundamental problem among many aid policymakers and even among some aid practitioners is the confusion of aid with development. An all-too-common perception is that development consists of a series of programs and projects that start and end with the provision and termination of aid. Too often, the poor are seen as a passive group—the "target population"—that receives the benefits of decisions made for their well-being in Washington, Paris, Nairobi, Quito, or any number of other policy centers to which they have no relationship or access. Development, in this view, takes place only when there is outside intervention: a supply of assistance to a public agency, a commercial bank, or another formal-sector institution that will apply resources on behalf of the poor. The more money, the more development.

The reality, of course, is very different. Development is a process of ongoing change at the local level. Individuals, families, and communities are continually planning, organizing, and acting to improve their lot, to gain control over their lives and their environment, or simply to survive under hostile conditions. Institutions, some hardly recognizable as such to outsiders, emerge to serve as vehicles for this activity. The major aid donors, however, usually bypass these institutions and their efforts, sometimes unwittingly undermine them, and effectively promote them only when they take the time to listen rather than direct.

A project that is implemented through an organization with which the local population is not involved will run its course and leave behind no basis for continued activity. The project will die and no follow-up activity will be stimulated if the local institutional capacity is not reinforced and expanded. Assistance for this mode of development does not generate self-sustaining change and is costly, misguided, and unfortunately, generally the rule.

We in the North have helped to create a modern institutional infrastructure in much of the Third World, an infrastructure that did not emerge from the local reality and that has little relationship to it. Our major aid organizations work through these structures because, being near mirror images of our own institutions, they are easily identified and accessible and often share short-term Northern interests. Furthermore, and perhaps more significantly, these modern structures provide development and project information of a nature and in a form that generally corresponds to the needs of their Northern counterparts rather than those of the poor. The size of these structures is also a factor in this regard, for they appear to have the capacity to absorb large sums of aid monies. Often, however, this capacity is in fact lacking.

This situation has helped to perpetuate the myth that the Third World needs and can effectively utilize even greater financial resources than it presently receives. Quantitative goals for aid funding, such as 0.7 percent of GNP, have been pursued without any practical demonstration of how this would be translated into more rapid, more extensive, or more relevant development among the poor. But aid agencies, consulting firms, commercial concerns, research institutes, and many other institutions have been built in the meantime upon this myth, and they are now part of the familiar landscape on Capitol Hill whenever foreign aid bills are debated.

### THE POLITICS OF AID

Yet, the needs of the aid industry alone could not sustain its expansion if aid did not serve broader interests. Aid's primary significance today lies in its policy leverage. As a tool of foreign policymaking, it has been used consistently by the State Department through The Agency for International Development (AID). In the economic arena, the current private-sector, Caribbean Basin, and African Economic Policy initiatives—and their counterparts within other bilateral and multilateral aid agencies—are examples of how aid is utilized to stimulate policy changes far more profound in their impact than what the field application of that aid could generate.

While the use of aid as a policy tool can, under certain circumstances, bring benefits to the majority of a country's population, the dangers are apparent. Those countries that followed the advice of Northern aid agencies and diverted agricultural resources to produce for export and to establish a modern industrial base have seen the prices of their commodities plummet, Northern markets contract, the cost of capital-goods imports steadily increase, the price of imported oil fluctuate dramatically, balance-of-payments problems intensify, and the cost of credit needed to cover these deficits only exacerbate them. Debt problems are rampant and in many places unmanageable. In much of Africa, countries that were once self-sufficient in food cannot feed their populations.

The common argument that this dire situation is the result of unpredictable changes in world economic conditions misses the point, for Northern-advocated development strategies have irresponsibly left Third World economies increasingly and precariously vulnerable to any changes that can, and do, occur in the international arena. If this were not bad enough, the policy advice that Third World governments receive today from the World Bank and other lenders remains fundamentally unchanged, encouraging them as it does to export their way out of their economic difficulties. Clearly, outside advice has done little for the long-term development of these countries.

It would be naive to expect that any country, particularly a world power like the United States, would place the interests of the poor majority in the Third World above its own. But it is equally foolish to think that one can pursue short-term self-interest in the Third World and achieve the long-term goal of sustained social, economic, and political stability. It would be wrong, as well, to believe that the enhancement of economic relationships between vested interests in this country and in the Third World will help the Third World poor. As witnessed in Southeast Asia, Central America, and Southern Africa, support provided through those who manage or benefit from systems that perpetuate inequities cannot succeed in closing the gap between the haves and the have nots. The consequences of the alienation and intense resentment that this widening gap breeds can clearly be profound.

At the same time, public support for foreign aid continues to languish. Polls show that while the majority of U.S. citizens favors aid in principle, a sizeable majority supports reductions in aid because it feels that most of our assistance does not reach the poor. A 1982 Gallup poll revealed that over two-thirds of the public is of the opinion that U.S. economic assistance benefits the rich more than the poor. The same poll demonstrated that there exists, overall, far greater support for aid among what Gallup calls the "elite public," or U.S. leaders, than among the general public (Chicago Council on Foriegn Relations, "Attitudes"). Five years later, another public opinion survey, conducted by Nancy Belden and the Strategic Information Research Corporation and published by InterAction and the Overseas Development Council, revealed that almost 90 percent of those interviewed from the general population believe that aid is largely wasted by the U.S. bureaucracy and frequently misused by foreign governments (Contee, Christine E., *What Americans Think*). Removed from the barrage of rhetoric from the protagonists for aid, the public appears to understand the realities of foreign assistance far better than do its leaders.

## MAKING OUR ASSISTANCE MORE EFFECTIVE

In the first place, money—or the lack thereof—is not a significant constraint on development. All too often, Third World agencies are overloaded with funds that they cannot effectively absorb and utilize. Most of the recipients are government institutions that have minimal or adversarial relations with the intended beneficiaries and have either no experience in, or commitment to, channeling aid funds for their use. Staff is generally inappropriate in its orientation, effective reward systems are not in place, and administrative procedures are normally more relevant to a more well-to-do clientele. In light of these limitations and local political realities, it is not surprising that most aid moves slowly (at best) out of the pipeline and serves the interests of those who are less than needy.

Every aid project officer knows the shortcomings of these institutions. But everyone also knows the institutional pressures at home to move funds. The effort to identify an institution that can design and implement a successful project may bring considerable benefits to the local poor, but it may not be as valuable to a donor organization seeking to justify a larger budget for the next fiscal year as is larger-scale, quicker funding through a far less appropriate institution.

If aid is to serve the poor, it must be applied judiciously. Its application cannot be determined by the institutional imperatives of aid donors, the debt position of commercial banks, the infrastructure requirements of investors, or the needs of other elite interests in the North and South. For all the rhetoric of the aid lobbyists—from the "poorest of the poor" to "basic human needs," from "employment generation" to "rural development," from "interdependence" to "private-sector initiative"—and for all the good intentions of other aid supporters, development assistance can often do far more to undermine equitable development than to foster it. Aid is not neutral. Its impact is a function of the institutions that utilize it and the circumstances in which they must operate. If the appropriate institutions cannot be funded or if they cannot operate freely, the poor will generally be served best by no aid at all.

Only when the fixation on the quantity of aid disappears can the quality of aid begin to improve. A country's development potential is only as great as the capacity of its development institutions, and any financial assistance that is programmed without this in mind is certain to have its shortcomings. Each institution has to be judged according to its demonstrated ability to promote equitable development. In those countries in which the government is not committed to this end, capable public institutions may be difficult to find. In such cases, institutions in the non-governmental sector usually constitute viable alternatives, as they are more likely to represent or directly work with poor communities and with disadvantaged groups, such as poor women, within those communities. Although such organizations, even in consortia, generally lack the size of public-sector institutions, their involvement as aid conduits can be far more productive.

Many private organizations do not, however, have such relationships with local groups, and thus their potential roles as intermediaries or facilitators are limited. In certain countries, there are few development institutions that legitimately and effectively represent the interests of the poor while demonstrating a capacity to manage development programs. Experienced Northern field officers are generally able to determine where these capabilities are present.

Where institutional development is still weak, there is a significant role that Northern organizations can—and at times, do—sensitively play in temporarily filling this programmatic and managerial gap while working to engender the required institutional strengths in the host country. EuroAction ACORD, a consortium of European and Canadian organizations, is an example of an institution that has played such a role effectively. Such interventions, however, should be the exception rather than the rule.

Whether the appropriate development institutions are public or private in a given country, long-term sustainable development can be fostered only if their capacities in the planning, programming, and execution processes are continually upgraded. This is a critical function of development assistance. Whether it be through program aid or project financing, support provided by aid donors in amounts and on terms compatible with the recipients' current institutional requirements, in conjunction with appropriate forms of training and managerial and technical assistance, can help build a strong foundation for meaningful development.

At present, however, our aid structures do not adequately correspond to the necessities of Third World development institutions. Private and voluntary organizations (PVOs), other non-governmental institutions (in Europe, as well as North America), and autonomous public institutions such as the Inter-American Foundation (IAF) and the African Development Foundation (ADF) play the role of supporting local-level development by assisting popular, broad-based membership organizations and other non-governmental organizations (NGOs). As the size and needs of the constituencies of these Third World institutions increase, however, and as the capacities of these organizations to handle loans and manage more sophisticated credit mechanisms develop, they require access to sources of mainstream financing. With such support generally unavailable from their governments and their commercial banking systems, the need for measured amounts of assistance from AID, the World Bank, and other major providers of aid is critical. The responses of those providers, however, in redirecting their aid have thus far been limited and disappointing, such funding being consistently marginal rather than integral to their mainstream operations.

As long as people's organizations and intermediary institutions that serve them are so marginalized, the relevance of foreign assistance to the needs of the poor will also remain marginal. Regardless of whether the conduit for aid is a public-sector, private-sector or "social-sector" (NGO) institution, its effectiveness is dependent upon its relationship with local-level organizations. Project success depends on local involvement, and that is activated and organized by local institutions, such as cooperatives, women's groups, peasant associations, and community and church organizations. It is not enough, however, that their role be confined to project implementation. Unless these organizations are involved—directly and through second-tier organizations that represent them—in the design and management of the program, the likelihood of misdirection and disillusionment is high.

In *Public Participation in Regional Development Planning: A Strategy for Popular Involvement,* published by The Development GAP in 1980 (see Appendix A), we pointed out that "...problems can arise in implementation due to the planner's lack of understanding of the 'dynamics' at play at local levels. A valid understanding of local and regional dynamics can only come about through communication between the planner and the public." We went on to emphasize "...the need to involve local populations, especially the poor, in determining the nature of projects and programs from which they are to benefit."

As far as the shaping of national development policy and programming is concerned, the absence of representative organizations from the planning process similarly deprives that process of its validity and virtually ensures that the interests it ultimately serves will not be those of the poor. Consultations, in particular, between aid donors and national governments have, as a matter of course, excluded such representation of the poor and have thus denied planners essential perspectives and input.

We recognize the dangers implicit in closer relationships between the major aid institutions and Third World NGOs. Extensive reporting requirements and efforts at co-optation and control are among the problems that the latters' Northern counterparts have already encountered in their own set of financial relationships. Yet, Southern NGOs and others involved in development on the ground are acutely aware that relatively small-scale funding to build a foundation for change or simply to support efforts at survival is no longer sufficient. The impact of the large aid institutions on Third World policies and programs and thus on the poor themselves has become so profound that these institutions must be engaged and their shortcomings addressed directly.

## THE NEED TO ASSUME A NEW POSTURE

The purpose of this report is to address these institutional shortcomings and to suggest fundamental changes in our development assistance structures that would help foster rather than inhibit the evolution of appropriate institutional capacity in the Third World. These changes, in turn, require a fundamental change in the posture of the aid community as a whole toward the poor, which must be reflected in a responsive approach to their organized initiatives. Implicit in this approach is not only a genuine respect for the capacity of the poor to manage their own development, but, perhaps more importantly, an appreciation for their understanding of their own circumstances, their knowledge of external constraints and internal capabilities, their creativity and their ability to define appropriate development paths for their immediate and wider communities.

To assume this posture implies the presence of a strong measure of humility, a trait found most often and most clearly in those members of the aid community who have lived and worked among the poor. In fact, it seems to be a rule of thumb that the less direct and sustained contact one has had with the poor, the more prone one is to impose solutions to their problems. New development theories are hashed and old ones rehashed but they rarely have any relevance to the lives of their subjects. The gap between the realities faced by the Third World poor and the perception of those realities on the part of an increasing number of aid officials and policymakers is expanding rapidly. Unless we in the aid community are able to recognize what we do not know and are willing to acknowledge that the "targets" of our aid, and not we, are the repositories of development expertise, we will experience another fitful quarter century marked by problems in the Third World at least as severe as the starvation, indebtedness, refugee stream, social polarization and political instability that now characterize parts of the world that have already received so much of our aid.

Those who perceive aid first and foremost as a tool in the pursuit of short-term foreign policy objectives and/or U.S. economic self-interest will likely find this treatise largely irrelevant to their concerns. Those who do not share our perception of development as a locally defined process of social change may find our arguments misconceived and misdirected. Those who are satisfied with aid's contribution to the well-being of the Third World poor

may find our analysis to be unduly cynical and our recommendations superfluous.  Nevertheless, we invite those inside and
outside the aid community, who are as disturbed as we are about
the inability of our development assistance to help foster meaningful
change and significantly improve the circumstances of the poor to
reflect upon our analysis and proposals and to give serious thought
as to how they might be modified, improved, and implemented in a
manner most beneficial to the marginalized populations of the Third
World.

In preparing this book, we decided to focus on those
institutions that, if fundamental changes were made, could together
form the core of an effective development assistance structure.  In
so doing, we of necessity left many institutions and programs not
central to our theme largely unaddressed.  Some are touched upon
briefly in Chapter 8.  Our general assessments of the regional
development banks, for example, are largely reflected in our
extensive analysis of the World Bank, but we do discuss a specific
Inter-American Development Bank program of relevance.  The
Peace Corps, though not essential to the potential success of the
proposed structure, is philosophically in tune with it and could play
a well-defined supportive role.  It is questionable, on the other
hand, whether the Overseas Private Investment Corporation (OPIC),
even with its development assistance mandate, can promote
development as defined in this book.  The Food for Peace Program
(P.L. 480) , as it is not an institution as such, does not fit into an
institutional construct.  While food aid is indeed a significant
element in our overall assistance program, we will leave its
treatment to those with far better knowledge of that field than we
possess.  For similar reasons, we defer to others on the matters of
disaster relief and refugee assistance.

It will also be noted that this book does not deal directly with
the questions of trade and debt, although they are clearly and
inextricably connected with foreign aid and the economic policies,
structures, and production that aid has engendered.  Their
significance and complexities merit far more comprehensive
expositions than can be afforded them in this treatise.  Similarly, we
address only peripherally the systemic constraints to the fundamental changes in aid structures prescribed in these pages, while
recognizing that they must ultimately be confronted by policymakers
interested in fostering such changes.

Nor is this a report about Third World development.  That is a
story best left to the people of the Third World to tell.  Rather, it is a

report about aid and how it can best be used to support the development efforts of those people. These pages are not replete with examples of aid successes and failures commonly found in texts on aid. Instead, we focus on the structures and characteristics of aid organizations in an attempt to demonstrate *why* aid fails or succeeds in fostering equitable development.

To this end, we do deal in depth with several institutions and related matters. Chapter 2 explains how and why the problems raised in this introduction have gone largely untreated by the foreign aid community and the many official reports commissioned to address them. In Chapter 3, the role of aid vis-à-vis development is delineated. The intrinsic shortcomings of the Agency for International Development are analyzed in Chapter 4, and a proposal for an external and internal restructuring is detailed. Chapter 5 takes an in-depth look at the two existing regional development foundations as the potential cornerstones of a restructured and reoriented official development assistance program. The need to enhance the performance, independence, and significance of the U.S. PVO community within the context of our aid program is the subject of Chapter 6. In Chapter 7, the shortcomings of the World Bank as a development assistance institution are explored, and recommendations are made as to how the Bank can become more relevant to the marginalized populations of the Third World. Finally, in Chapter 8, we integrate these institutions, in the roles we have prescribed for them, in a new structure designed to promote, in a cost-effective manner, more relevant, effective, and self-sustaining development throughout the Third World.

# TWO

# The Evolution
# and Perpetuation of
# —— Development Assistance

The past forty years have seen the emergence, growth, and consolidation of a multi-billion dollar aid industry. With land-grant universities, PVOs, consulting firms, and other special interests linked legislatively and/or programmatically with the aid program; with private companies reaping the benefits of aid-funded infrastructural development, investment guarantees, export credits, and procurement contracts; and with commercial banks receiving the cooperation of the international financial institutions amidst the deepening debt crisis, a powerful lobby has developed for aid.

Until relatively recently, a natural self-consciousness and political common sense prompted this constituency to publicly promote and to lobby for aid for the benefit of the poor rather than for self-interest. In the 1980s, however, even presentation has changed, to the point where the United Nations can issue a biweekly publication called *Development Business* and unabashedly market it with the advertisement that

> [S]uppliers of a wide range of goods and services are pursuing and winning big contracts in the developing countries—where project funding has reached epic proportions . . . not just for infrastructure and basic industries, but for agricultural projects, oil and gas, urban development sites, water supply and sanitation systems, education and health care services. To win your fair share of this huge and highly lucrative market, you need reliable information direct from the source. . . . This year [1986] more than $25 billion in loans is projected by just the World Bank and the IDB alone.

This rosy picture contrasts sharply with the message sent recently from Mexico by the widely respected economist, Gustavo Esteva. Having lived and worked among Mexico's poor for a decade, Esteva wrote in 1985 that externally defined development

> means to have started on a road that others know better, to be on your way towards a goal that others have reached, to race up a one-way street. Development means the sacrifice of environments, solidarities, traditional interpretations and customs to ever-changing expert advice. Development . . . for the overwhelming majority has always meant the progressive modernization of their poverty: growing dependence on guidance and management. . . . Around us, for a long time, development has been recognized as a threat. Most peasants are aware that development has undermined their subsistence on century-old diversified crops. Slum dwellers know that it has made their jobs redundant and their education inadequate. . . . Finally, the truly marginal groups know how it feels to be pushed, inch by inch, into the cash economy (Esteva, "Development," p. 78).

How have we reached this point? How is it that the development business has expanded so lucratively through the years while the circumstances of the Third World poor have deteriorated so dramatically?

**THE EARLY HISTORY OF AID**

The aid industry as we know it today began as the Second World War was coming to a close. A decidedly U.S. undertaking with significant British input, the Bretton Woods conference of 1944 established the International Bank for Reconstruction and Development as the long-term investment complement to the International Monetary Fund. The principal function of the World Bank, as the IBRD came to be known, was envisaged as the facilitation of private investment in Europe and in developing countries. Initial lending was directed toward the reconstruction of Western Europe, while the United States began to introduce political considerations into the Bank in effectively denying credit to Eastern European countries. The first loans for specific projects in the Third World were made to three Latin American countries in 1948 and 1949.

U.S. bilateral involvement in development has its origins in security concerns that existed during the same historical period. By 1948, the United States had established a number of large-scale programs to provide support for the reconstruction of Europe and parts of Asia. The largest of these programs, which set the precedent for large U.S. capital transfers overseas, was the Marshall Plan, spawned by the Economic Cooperation Act of 1948 and administered by the Economic Cooperation Administration (ECA). This act was amended in 1950 by the Act for International Development, which translated President Truman's Point IV proposal into the creation of the Technical Cooperation Administration (TCA) and a mandate ". . . to aid the efforts of the peoples of economically underdeveloped areas. . ."

In 1951, the Mutual Security Act replaced the ECA and TCA with the Mutual Security Agency (MSA) in response to the deteriorating political situation in the Far East. The program's economic development component was designed to utilize large sums of money to build up quickly  economic structures and political allegiances deemed necessary to fight communism. By 1954 the focus had shifted to India, Pakistan, and a handful of countries in the Near East for which a total of nearly $300 million (of approximately $600 million in MSA economic aid funds) was authorized under the act's new Development Assistance title. The emphasis of the aid program, however, was still on helping to maintain economic and political stability and on generally promoting short-term U.S. foreign policy interests. Furthermore, the International Cooperation Administration, which replaced the MSA in 1955, and its successor, the Agency for International Development (AID), have operated under legislation patterned after the Economic Cooperation and Mutual Security Acts, despite marked changes in the international political environment.

Meanwhile, the Senate established the Special Committee to Study the Foreign Aid Program, which commissioned a study by an MIT team headed by Max Milliken and Walt Rostow. The main conclusion of the study, which was published in 1956, was that economic aid, delivered through a comprehensive assistance program, could, if provided according to objective economic criteria, promote economic growth and thus constitute a weapon against the Soviet Union. Its authors' top-down development approach and cold war fixation have undoubtedly influenced subsequent legislation to this day. Their hopes, however, that such a program would yield success within twenty or thirty years, have been resoundingly dashed.

The application of objective economic criteria to aid decisionmaking requires the structural and operational separation of aid from the making of foreign policy. Yet, when in 1961 Congress authorized the President to implement the mandates of the new Foreign Assistance Act through a government agency, Kennedy directed his Secretary of State to establish AID within the State Department. In the meantime, a policy of expanded "tied aid," stimulated by U.S. economic problems and requiring the purchase of U.S. goods by Third World aid recipients, directly linked U.S. economic interests to the promotion of modernization strategies overseas.

## THE AID CONSTITUENCY

In fact, the trickle-down aid and development approach, which was in vogue for twenty-five years following World War II, was clearly consistent with the interests of several economically powerful and influential U.S. constituencies. Its underlying assumption was that major transfers of capital and sophisticated technology would quickly modernize the industrial sector, employ low-cost labor, increase incomes and demand for new goods, and enable substitution for imports while increasing exports. Industrial production would concentrate on goods in which the country had a comparative advantage in international trade, thereby utilizing local raw materials and stimulating their production while increasing incomes in that sector, as well as in industry. Cash-crop production for export was emphasized in the agricultural sector to cover the importation costs of industrialization. Foreign private investment was encouraged as a capital transfer mechanism and as a contributor to the national tax base.

The demand for modern skills and substantial financial resources inherent in this approach has made many large U.S. corporations natural adherents, promoters, and beneficiaries of the aid program. Aided by investment guarantees and support for Third World infrastructural development provided by the U.S. government, corporations have been in an enhanced position in their search for low-cost labor, natural resources, and new markets. U.S. companies in the export sector have also been supportive of a program that has promised an increasing demand for luxury, capital, and consumer goods.

In addition, rapid industrialization created a demand for credits from both host-country and multinational investors. Periods of economic stagnation at home, good returns on overseas lending, and anticipated "underwriting" by U.S. and multilateral public institutions made this development approach particularly attractive to U.S. bankers until the internal contradictions of the development paradigm promoted by Western institutions manifested themselves in today's Third World debt crisis.

The trickle-down approach has also been advantageous for many U.S. universities. Their research has generally concentrated on the problems of large-scale, capital-intensive, and advanced technological production, both in industry and agriculture, with which researchers in this country are familiar. Large consulting firms, engineering firms, shippers, and producers of farm and construction equipment have been among the many others to gain from externally designed development programs.

Legislative action has formalized several of these relationships by which our official aid program has consequently promoted the interests primarily, if not exclusively, of U.S.-based constituencies vis-à-vis those of the Third World poor. Chapter 1 of Part III of the Foreign Assistance Act of 1961, which, with its subsequent amendments, has guided U.S. foreign aid since AID was established, has directed the President to ". . . encourage and facilitate the flow of private investment to, and its equitable treatment in, friendly countries...[and] to utilize wherever practicable the services of United States private enterprise . . . to provide the necessary skills to develop and operate a specific project or program of assistance . . ." It has also directed AID to "encourage . . . the utilization of engineering and professional services of United States firms . . . in connection with capital projects financed by funds authorized" under the Foreign Assistance Act.

The Food for Peace Act of 1966 made it U.S. policy ". . . to develop and expand export markets for United States agricultural commodities." The Overseas Private Investment Corporation was authorized by Congress in 1969 (Part I, Chapter 2, Title IV of the Foreign Assistance Act) to ". . . mobilize and facilitate the participation of United States private capital and skills in the economic and social development of less developed friendly countries . . ." Under Title XII, Congress declared that ". . . the United States should strengthen the capacities of the United States land-grant and other eligible universities in program-related agricultural institutional development and research. . . ."

More recently, Congress has reaffirmed its support for U.S.

institutions within the context of Third World development, thereby generating dependencies upon, and constituencies for, the aid program. In 1978, it authorized that up to $10 million be provided as assistance ". . . to research and educational institutions in the United States for the purpose of strengthening their capacity to develop and carry out programs concerned with the economic and social development of developing countries." Since then, it has authorized that significant percentages of AID monies be provided not to non-governmental organizations (NGOs) in the Third World, but rather to their counterparts (PVOs) in the United States. Other legislation related to the Trade and Development Program and commodity import programs has been designed to assist a range of U.S. exporters.

Serving these U.S. interests has meant, of necessity, assuming a directive, rather than responsive, posture toward the Third World poor and their development interests. The trickle-down approach generally accommodated the former interests but rarely the latter. When applied to Third World economies, trickle-down has been characterized by its inability to foster equitable and self-sustaining development in those countries that have experienced a large increase in their GNPs through a strategy of rapid industrialization. Unlike Europe, which possessed the human and institutional capacities to absorb and effectively utilize at all levels of its societies the massive resource flows from the United States following World War II, most Third World governments have had to rely on a limited, elite skill and institutional base to put to use the large amounts of financing arriving from the United States and multilateral lenders. Furthermore, as most of the benefits from aid accrue to those who control the resource flows, the relative standing of the poor has declined as a result of this approach. Thus, dualistic economies and societies have often developed, leaving the majority of the population without the resources, capabilities, or opportunities to participate in or contribute to meaningful development, and consequently engendering social and political polarization and instability.

**DISILLUSIONMENT WITH AID**

In the late 1960s, both the U.S. executive branch and the World Bank commissioned reports on development assistance that, in their analyses and recommendations, did not depart substantially from the conventional aid approach. The task force appointed by President Nixon in 1969 and headed by Rudolf Peterson echoed, in its 1970 report, many of the viewpoints proffered two years earlier by President Johnson's General Advisory Committee on Foreign Assistance Policy. While the Peterson report suggested the promotion of popular participation, its emphasis was on the creation of an aid infrastructure—including the creation of a U.S. international development bank—that could provide the capital and technical assistance loans necessary to promote trade, investment, and economic growth in the Third World. It also suggested a predominant role in the delivery of development assistance for international lending institutions (Task Force on International Development, *U.S. Foreign Assistance in the 1970s*). Legislation based in part on the report's conclusions subsequently failed to win congressional approval.

While the Johnson and Nixon Administrations were assessing their aid policies, the World Bank's new president, Robert McNamara, was naming his own commission, headed by former Canadian Prime Minister Lester Pearson, to ". . . study the consequences of twenty years of development assistance . . . and propose the policies which will work better in the future." The Pearson report, issued in 1969, assessed aid not in terms of its impact on the relative or absolute conditions and capabilities of the poor, nor on its contributions to their self-development efforts, but rather on the basis of its contribution to savings, investment, and economic growth at the country level. Its recommendations centered on the expansion of aid, trade, and investment. The fostering of exports and an increased rate of capital formation should, the commission suggested, enable many of the developing countries to participate in the international economy as "self-reliant partners" by the end of the century (Commission on International Development, *Partners in Development*). The inequities in the control of economic resources among these "partners"—and within each country—were not addressed.

By this time, in the late 1960s, there was developing in the United States a general disillusionment with the government's aid strategy. While special interests underwritten by development assistance still constituted an aid lobby, polls were showing the public's increasing disenchantment with aid. The growing unpopularity of the U.S. involvement in Vietnam and the general budgetary problems of the government added to the increasing difficulties that aid bills were encountering in Congress. Whether or not development and military assistance bills were linked, development aid was gradually losing its hold on many policymakers, liberal and conservative.   Echoing the misgivings of some of his colleagues, Senator Frank Church, a member of the Foreign Relations Committee, took to the Senate floor to lay out the reasons for his opposition to aid in the fall of 1971, shortly before the Senate rejected that year's foreign aid authorization bill:

> I can no longer cast my vote to prolong the bilateral aid program as it is now administered. . . . [T]he present program is designed primarily to serve private business interests at the expense of the American people. . . . The oft-asserted lament that our foreign aid program lacks a constituency in the United States is just another of those myths we hold dear.  Actually, our bilateral aid program is . . . the source from which foreign governments borrow money on easy terms with which to buy goods and services from within the United States.  As such, it enjoys a lively constituency which exerts steady pressure on the government to keep the program going.

"Never yet," Church pointed out, "have we considered in full measure the possibility that the failure of aid is not technical and administrative but conceptual and political. . . . " Reactionary regimes, he contended in a subsequent magazine article, "value aid from the United States as a means of maintaining, not of abolishing, inequalities of wealth and power . . . . American economic aid is commonly used to promote industrialization programs which generate a high level of consumption for the privileged and little, if any, trickle-down  benefits for the dispossessed" (Church, "Farewell to Foreign Aid").

This disillusionment with aid spurred two fundamentally different reactions within the aid community.  One consisted of the initiatives taken by proponents of a responsive U.S. approach to participatory development, while the other was manifested by the repackaging of the current aid approach in order to build a broader aid constituency.

Title IX had been added to the Foreign Assistance Act in 1966 and represented a sharp departure from previous legislation.  It mandated that emphasis "be placed on assuring maximum participation in the task of economic development on the part of the people of the developing countries, through the encouragement of democratic private and local governmental institutions."  The impact of this legislation was negligible, however, as AID translated the mandate into marginal programs of support for this form of development and left its other operations otherwise unchanged.

In 1969, a few individuals from Congress, the State Department, and non-governmental organizations, disillusioned with the Alliance for Progress and AID's rejection of the principles and practices embodied in Title IX, drafted legislation, subsequently introduced by Representatives Dante Fascell and Bradford Morse, to create a new institution independent of the exigencies of short-term foreign policy and free of special economic interests. By 1971, the Inter-American Foundation (IAF) was in operation, providing relatively small amounts of money directly to poor people's organizations throughout Latin America and the Caribbean and, in so doing, pointing out a new direction for U.S. development assistance.

Recognizing the dwindling support for development assistance among U.S. citizens and their representatives in Washington, as well as the popularity of the ideals embodied by Title IX and the IAF, the aid lobby pursued a different course. A responsive and supportive stance taken by the major aid institutions to the development endeavors of the Third World poor would not do much for the U.S. exporters, investors, financiers, contractors, consultants, and other private interests underwritten by the aid program to date. Hence, the lobby was institutionalized in the form of organizations that promoted aid with idealistic-sounding language that hid their adherence to a top-down, directive aid methodology. The "poor majority," the "poorest of the poor," and "basic human needs" became part of a rapidly expanding aid vocabulary, but the donors still determined what those needs were and the poor remained the "targets" of their aid.

Rural development and employment generation replaced industrialization and increased savings rates as the foci of the aid community, but export-led growth, free trade, and the expansion of foreign investment remained the goals of the newly institutionalized aid lobby. These goals could be pursued in a "growth with equity" strategy as long as the aid institutions continued to define and direct the development process and as long as growth and the distribution of its benefits remained two separate functions. For this to be achieved, development planning, programming, and resource control had to remain centralized overseas in the hands of a public-sector and private-sector elite. In this very important sense, the aid proposals emanating from the liberal think-tanks in the 1970s differed little from their predecessors. The poor may have had more access to development resources, but (to the extent that aid monies did make their way down through institutional channels) they received those resources on the terms and for the purposes defined by people far removed from their reality, who had their own sets of interests.


## THE RAMIFICATIONS OF NEW DIRECTIONS

Unfortunately, this is the fate ultimately met by the New Directions legislation of the mid-1970s. Drafted and promoted in good part by individuals committed to enhancing poor people's control over their own development, the Foreign Assistance Act of 1973 directed that U.S. assistance support ". . . self-help efforts . . . and stimulate the involvement of the people in the development process through the encouragement of democratic participation . . . and [appropriate] institution building . . . . " Follow-up legislation in 1975 mandated that " . . . greatest emphasis . . . be placed on countries and activities which effectively involve the poor in development . . . . " In fact, much of Chapter 1 of Part I of the Foreign Assistance Act of 1961 was rewritten between 1973 and 1977 to reflect Congress's change of focus.

In practice, however, this change was of little consequence. In fact, it can be argued that New Directions, as applied by AID and by the multilateral lenders who followed U.S. policy directives, had as adverse an effect on poor communities as had larger-scale, trickle-down assistance efforts. International agencies and their host-country counterparts were now using aid to direct the reorganization of community life and were doing so without the counsel, much less the leadership, of the local residents. Not only did this open the door to a range of economic and social dislocations (e.g., the concentration of landholdings, the increased control of activities by men to the exclusion of women, etc.) that benefited local vested interests through which projects were often implemented, but it also made local populations vulnerable to outside political and financial manipulation. Furthermore, centralized decisionmaking and control has done little to foster capacity for self-sustaining development among the poor.

Moreover, the sectoral approach emphasized by New Directions ushered in a new generation of First World expertise in health, education, population planning, housing, rural development, employment generation, and a range of other activities that bore a relationship to basic needs. Universities, PVOs, and consulting firms rapidly developed and offered capabilities in these fields, not so much in response to demand from poor Third World communities as from the aid institutions themselves. And the latter found over time that they could utilize this demand to cultivate an expanding aid constituency and, ultimately, a useful dependency.

In essence, New Directions was a victim of the preexisting aid structure left unchanged by the new legislation. While the legislation addressed the objectives and functions of bilateral assistance, it did little to reorganize it or to make its directives operational. AID remained, like its predecessors, structured primarily to satisfy the needs of U.S. security, those of vested economic interests and, ultimately, those of its own bureaucracy. The direct participation and expressed interests of the poor, in spite of some good intentions and new rhetoric, remained operationally relatively low priorities. As long as AID remained an agency of the State Department, it was virtually inevitable that, in the midst of diverse and sometimes conflicting objectives, the antipoverty and long-term development concerns used to justify aid to the U.S. public would get short shrift.

In 1977, AID's new Administrator, John Gilligan, established a task force, chaired by Tony Babb, with a mandate to examine how the Agency should be organized to implement aid effectively and efficiently and to explore the organizational and personnel changes required to achieve Congress' New Directions objectives. The Babb report was the first public-sector study to recognize development as a bottom-up and participatory process and to recommend an internal reorganization, decentralization, and staffing modifications so that AID could provide assistance appropriately. Unlike the New Directions legislation, the report made the distinction between the "sectoral" and "participatory" strategies and proposed that greater authority and a far larger percentage of more culturally attuned staff be placed in AID field missions.

The task force also found that " . . . in practice, the 'voice for development' has too often been muted at the working level in confrontations between long-term development interests and short-term political exigencies." Then, abandoning logic and choosing to ignore the inherent nature of this conflict among objectives, the Babb report concluded " . . . that the organizational relationships between State and AID . . . are generally satisfactory" and suggested that the best way to advance development concerns " . . . is to nurture closer association between AID and State . . . " (Babb, *Organization*, V:2–3).

The Brookings Institute's *Assessment of Development Assistance Strategies*, prepared for the State Department at the same time as the Babb task force was completing its work for the AID Administrator, came to the opposite conclusion. Recognizing that the long-term effectiveness of development assistance " . . . is apt to be degraded when it overreacts to current political urgencies," Brookings recommended that a Development Cooperation Agency (DCA) be created as an independent agency reporting to the President and replacing AID. Brookings did agree with Babb that the principal U.S. aid agency should be decentralized in its structure and operations (Brookings, *Assessment*).

The Brookings study group was constrained, however, by its limited experience among the Third World poor. Failing to recognize the creative development endeavors in which the latter are constantly engaged and the alternative conduits in the Third World through which support could be channeled to them, it could define only two basic approaches to the alleviation of the "worst aspects of poverty": efforts to broaden productive employment and the provision of basic services and commodities. The Brookings group prescribed no role for the poor either in defining their own needs or in development planning. It recommended more aid without demonstrating that the institutional capacity yet existed in the Third World to handle it effectively. It suggested that development be fostered in middle-income countries through expanded trade and foreign investment, but it did not explain how the poor would thus benefit in those economies with a sharply skewed distribution of productive assets. Overall, despite its focus on "the poor majority" and "basic human needs," the Brookings report constituted a sharp contrast to the understanding and nonpaternalistic attitude of the Babb task force and a return to the conventional aid paradigm.

Meanwhile, Senator Hubert Humphrey and members of the Senate Foreign Relations Committee staff had also been giving thought to the reorganization of the U.S. bilateral assistance program. Their efforts yielded legislation in 1978 to establish the International Development Cooperation Administration (IDCA) as the centerpiece and coordinator of a new aid structure. The following year, executive orders and reorganization plans emanating from the White House made IDCA a reality, but by then it had been shorn of most of its power. As Brookings had proposed for a DCA, IDCA was nominally independent of the State Department, but bureaucratic turf battles had left it with few aid programs to coordinate. Furthermore, AID continued to exist, within IDCA, with virtually all its functions intact, and both institutions to this day maintain their offices inside the State Department.

For all its good intentions to divorce development assistance from short-term foreign policy and to promote the well-being of the poor, the Humphrey-IDCA initiative suffered from another shortcoming as well: like Title IX and the New Directions legislation before it, the International Development Cooperation Act failed to delineate the internal restructuring and operational procedures required to ensure the implementation of a fundamentally different approach to aid and development. Aid would thus continue to be programmed in a top-down manner and in a form determined by policy priorities often unrelated to poverty.

#### MORE OF THE SAME

This top-down approach also characterized the operations of the World Bank during the McNamara era (1968–1981) and beyond. McNamara's "poverty focus" notwithstanding, the Bank continued its heavy investment in large-scale infrastructure development and, to the extent that it did finance poverty-related projects, often exacerbated local inequities by failing to consult first with local residents and integrate them into project planning. Yet, virtually every official study, from Pearson to Brookings, recommended that a significantly larger portion of U.S. aid be channeled through multilateral institutions. Clearly, this strategy, to the considerable extent to which it has been implemented, has shielded our aid program from some of the vagaries of U.S. politics. At the same time, however, it has dramatically reduced the capacity for legislative oversight and the aid program's accountability in general.

Multilateral aid also received a plug from the Independent Commission on International Development Issues, chaired by Willy Brandt. The Brandt Report, published and presented to the Secretary-General of the United Nations in 1980, recommended an expanded role for the World Bank and the regional development banks and called for a significant increase in aid flows in general. The report also advocated liberalized trade and investment (Independent Commission, *North-South*). The Commission failed, however, to address, much less demonstrate, *how* these increased resources would indeed reach and assist the poor, *who* would manage them for whose benefit, *why* government-to-government aid arrangements should be expected to reduce poverty where they rarely had before, and *why* free-market forces would not concentrate investments in those countries in which governments suppressed labor unions and wages. Furthermore, the Commission did not investigate the relationship between aid and the deteriorating circumstances of the Third World poor over the previous generation. By avoiding these tough questions, the Brandt Commission, like the several prestigious commissions before it, did more to promote the well-being of the aid community than the well-being of those whom aid was supposed to assist.

It was not only commissions that had ignored these fundamental issues. By and large, aid officials and policymakers proved unwilling or unable to translate congressional mandates, such as Title IX and New Directions, into dynamic support programs for the development efforts of poor people overseas. With the notable exception of the Inter-American Foundation, few public-sector programs recognized popular organizations as the engines of development and relinquished to them control and direction of local economic activity. None included these representative organizations in national and regional-level development planning and programming, despite the fact that they are usually the only dependable sources of information about local-level needs, priorities, and capabilities. The creation and distribution of wealth, moreover, remained for the most part separate functions during this period, and thus aid continued, for all the rhetoric to the contrary, to contribute first and foremost to the well-being of the already well-to-do.

When conservatives assumed control of the White House in the 1980s, they also assumed control of an oversized, overly centralized, and inefficient aid bureaucracy, which had channeled billions of dollars through public-sector counterpart institutions it had helped to create throughout the Third World. With little self-sustaining development, as well as increased poverty and political and economic instability left in its wake, the liberal approach was open to criticism from the right.

The Heritage Foundation articulated this position constructively in a 1984 paper. It urged the United States to promote self-sufficiency overseas rather than "foster permanent dependency or create temporary institutions that collapse once American money is withdrawn." It lamented the involvement of the State Department and foreign policy concerns in the determination of U.S. assistance levels, as well as the fact that ". . . much of AID's attention has been focused on subsidizing U.S. businesses." It noted that ". . . many observers, including Congressmen serving on appropriations committees, tend to judge the success and failure of AID efforts by the amount of dollars flowing overseas. Thus, the agency is continually pushed to send more money abroad." The Heritage Foundation concluded that "money should not be proposed, appropriated, and spent if previous outlays have achieved little or nothing, or have even been counterproductive" (Butler et al., *Mandate for Leadership II*, pp. 370–372).

The Reagan Administration has, of course, been as guilty of these transgressions as previous administrations. Indeed, the Administration resisted the sharp cuts made in the FY 1987 aid budget by disillusioned and deficit-conscious liberals. While development and humanitarian assistance as a share of all foreign aid, economic and military, fell from approximately 50 percent to under 40 percent during Reagan's first term, the total amount of foreign aid almost doubled during that period. Furthermore, as then-AID Administrator M. Peter McPherson stressed in his March 1984 address to AID employees, AID continues to strengthen its relationship with the State Department, broaden and deepen its relations with U.S. universities, and draw upon the ". . . expertise available within U.S. business firms," while utilizing its Trade and Development Program to promote large-scale development through the involvement of U.S. industry (McPherson, "Message").

The Reagan Administration's commitment to the private sector in development and in its development assistance program—manifested in AID's policy directives, its large-scale private-sector initiatives, and its Bureau for Private Enterprise—is particularly striking in its fundamental conflict with the language, intent, and spirit of the New Directions legislation. Lacking the institutional autonomy that Congress bestowed upon the Inter-American Foundation, AID has easily been diverted from its congressional mandate and has returned openly to a trickle-down methodology, which concentrates resources in the hands of a relatively few well-to-do organizations and individuals in the private sector.

The promotion of private-sector involvement in development was also a recommendation of the latest official aid report, prepared in 1983 for the Secretary of State by the Commission on Security and Economic Assistance, headed by Frank Carlucci. The Commission's principal proposal, however, was the consolidation of most economic and military assistance programs under a new agency, which would report to the Secretary of State. In viewing economic development ". . . as the basis for meeting and forestalling threats to security" and translating its belief in "the complementarity of economic and military assistance" into a proposal for an institutional union, the Carlucci Commission wanted to return foreign aid to the structure of the Mutual Security Agency in the early 1950s (Commission on Security and Economic Assistance, *Report*).

The Commission also advocated the use of the Economic Support Fund (ESF) to further U.S. political and commercial objectives. The flexibility and usefulness of the Fund was recognized early on by the Reagan Administration and has since expanded far more rapidly than has funding for development assistance. Security Supporting Assistance had been retitled ESF by Congress in 1978, but it remained part of the International Security Assistance Act, and its application for development purposes has remained limited to this day. In 1980, the International Security and Development Cooperation Act combined military assistance, ESF, and development assistance legislatively, and contained security-oriented language that set the tone for foreign aid in this decade.

The 1980s have seen the occasional anomaly in the aid program, but these efforts to address the fundamental problems and inequities in the Third World have thus far had but a marginal impact. The Reagan Administration was unsuccessful in its effort to prevent the establishment of the African Development Foundation (ADF), but the ADF and its Latin America counterpart, the IAF, remain, as funders of participatory development initiatives, aberrations in the official aid field. The "Targeted Aid Amendment," which directed the President in FY 1983 to use not less than 40 percent of development assistance funds to ". . . expeditiously and directly benefit those living in absolute poverty," was well intentioned but lacked legislative teeth, as it simply called upon the AID Administrator to certify the Administration's compliance with the provision, which he subsequently did.

## LESSONS LEARNED FROM HISTORY

So aid, in effect, has come full circle without having addressed in any significant way the fundamental causes of poverty or the profound inequities in wealth that exist in much of the Third World. To the contrary, there has been no period during the forty-year history of U.S. economic assistance to the Third World when the vast majority of that aid has bypassed the privileged members of those societies. It is hardly surprising, therefore, that these funds have been used primarily to advance the economic and political interests of their relatively small elite, as well as counterpart interests in the United States. In this regard, there has been little difference in the way that liberals and conservatives have managed the foreign aid program since World War II.

This unfortunate history offers important lessons to be considered in the establishment of a new development assistance paradigm and structure that better serve the interests of the poor in the Third World.

1. Most policymakers see aid as a vehicle for promoting short-term U.S. economic and foreign policy interests.
2. Tied aid has linked U.S. economic interests directly to the promotion of modernization strategies overseas.
3. Many other special interests have been served by U.S. foreign aid legislation at the expense of the poor.
4. Serving these interests has necessarily meant taking a directive, top-down approach rather than a responsive posture toward the poor.
5. These same interests form an aid constituency that make fundamental changes in the legislation difficult.
6. Aid is all too often used to maintain inequalities of wealth and power, as the already well-to-do have controlled resource flows, allowing relatively few of the aid benefits to accrue to the poor.
7. Aid has been assessed too commonly in terms of the contributions it makes to improvements at the country level, including increased economic growth, rather than in terms of its impact on the conditions, capabilities, and self-development efforts of the poor.
8. AID's mainstream operations have rarely reflected congressional mandates to involve and assist the poor directly.
9. The aid lobby has employed idealistic-sounding language, which hides its adherence to a top-down, directive aid methodology, in order to attract well-intentioned supporters and move aid bills through Congress.
10. New Directions legislation has had little effect, as the poor have continued to receive aid on the terms and for the purposes defined by outsiders.
11. Decisionmaking and control remained centralized under New Directions, both in the North and in ineffectual Third World bureaucracies, thereby doing little to foster a capacity

for self-sustaining development.
12. The sectoral approach emphasized by New Directions has generated a new wave of First World expertise and thus a larger aid lobby.
13. New Directions did little to reorganize and decentralize AID and to make it responsive to the poor rather than to other pressures.
14. The legislation creating IDCA also failed to delineate the internal restructuring required and did not provide either IDCA or AID with the degree of autonomy required.
15. Despite the fact that the multilateral institutions have proven themselves equally incapable of assisting the poor, they have received an increasing share of U.S. aid resources.
16. The shift toward multilateral aid has reduced the capacity for legislative oversight and the aid program's accountability in general.
17. AID has not recognized popular organizations as the engines of development, nor has it included these representative organizations in development planning or programming.
18. The quantity of aid has too often been given greater importance than its quality and who controls and utilizes it.
19. AID's failure to appropriately implement its New Directions mandate has led to disillusionment with aid as an antipoverty tool.
20. Congress has allowed AID to promote a private-sector, trickle-down approach to development, despite its sharp departure from AID's New Directions mandate.

The relegation by major aid institutions of the interests of the poor to an afterthought in the promotion of Northern self-interest could not be depicted more clearly than it was recently in a 1987 AID newsletter. In that publication, titled "Foreign Aid: What's in It for You?," foreign aid is depicted as

> a sound investment that benefits both Americans and the people of developing countries. To make certain this investment pays off, programs are carefully planned and carried out by experts who know what works and what doesn't. Most of the talent and tools needed in an ambitious foreign assistance program come from American business and industry. That's why 70 percent of the money appropriated for direct, or bilateral, U.S. assistance is spent here, not overseas. . . . In addition . . . fully one-half of the

U.S. contribution to [multilateral development agencies] is spent on American goods. The benefits from foreign aid are shared throughout the nation. Businesses, research centers or universities in 49 states received foreign assistance contracts in 1985.

In light of the advantages that aid has brought special interests in the United States, it is not surprising that corruption in the use of aid monies is rife in the Third World. Host-country nationals witness firsthand the large expenditures made on U.S. and other Northern contractors and consultants in the name of development, and they observe the comfortable lifestyles of foreign aid officials in their country. They note the large disparity between the salaries of U.S. aid officials and those of most host-country nationals employed in counterpart agencies and in U.S. aid agencies themselves. Seeing the comforts that aid buys its providers, it is understandable that its recipients might have similar expectations.

Just as problematic is the effect relatively high incomes have on U.S. aid personnel. Management and staff of public-sector, multilateral, and many non-governmental aid agencies receive salaries that are considerably higher than the U.S. national average, despite their involvement in a field ostensibly devoted to the eradication of poverty. These salaries are unnecessarily high. Capable, committed, field-experienced individuals can be recruited for considerably lower yet still respectable compensation. High salaries have, as a rule, fostered more interest in job security and promotion than in the risk-taking that is an indispensable element in the provision of aid. In addition, the life-styles that these incomes have enabled most aid personnel to assume overseas have had the effect all too often of isolating aid officials from the people and the realities they must understand in order to do their jobs effectively.

If there is to be a change in the mode of delivery of development aid, there must be sustained contact between aid officials and grassroots development organizations. This is the level at which genuine development takes place, and these are the organizations that require support to make it happen. Awareness, understanding, and sensitivity are imperative on the part of aid personnel if grassroots organizations are to receive the appropriate types and amounts of backing at the appropriate moments in their evolution, so they can grow, thrive, and promote the interests of their members and constituencies with increasing effectiveness.

# THREE

# The Aid-Development Connection

Since the provision of assistance is but one element in what should be a locally initiated process of development, no valid analysis of assistance programs can be carried out without continual reference to development in the field. The relationship between aid and development can usefully be expressed by delineating the principal stages of both the development and development assistance processes, matching these distinct stages in parallel fashion, and demonstrating the interrelationship between the field process and the assistance process at each stage. It is on the basis of this understanding and analytical structure that criteria can be established for judging the effectiveness of a development aid program.

Within this framework, the development process may be viewed as consisting of three distinct parts or stages:

1. The identification and articulation of needs to be met and the formulation of plans to meet such needs
2. The implementation or execution of projects and programs to fulfill these needs
3. A learning process through which participants acquire knowledge, understanding, and specific skills which can be used to further their own development

These functions have their counterparts in the following aspects of the development assistance process:

1. The identification and selection of programs and projects to support, whereby the donor responds to expressed needs
2. The delivery of assistance, whereby aid is provided for the implementation of projects
3. The evaluation of projects, whereby the donor agency seeks to determine the effectiveness of both the projects it supports and its own methods of supporting them

This correspondence in function may be simply presented as follows:

| DEVELOPMENT PROCESS (Field) | DEVELOPMENT ASSISTANCE PROCESS (Donor Agency) |
|---|---|
| Needs Articulation and Project Planning | Project Identification and Selection |
| Project Implementation | Delivery of Assistance |
| Learning Process | Evaluation |

**PROJECT IDENTIFICATION AND SELECTION VIS-À-VIS BENEFICIARY NEEDS ARTICULATION**

Development is essentially a problem-solving process whereby unmet needs represent problems that must be identified, articulated, and then solved. Planning to meet needs is, simply put, the outlining of a solution to problems. The proper identification and articulation of needs, along with an appropriately formulated response with assistance to meet such needs, thus constitutes the most basic and important step of the development process. Misjudgments made at this stage (e.g., in assessing needs, selecting appropriate projects and policies, and determining means of support) are usually uncorrectable. This process must generate an enhanced institutional capacity to promote change if development is to become self-sustaining.

Local commitment is perhaps the most essential factor in the fostering of self-sustaining development. Authentic commitment is, in turn, most appropriately fostered through meaningful participation, since the most appropriate solutions to problems will arise from, and be best implemented by, those most directly affected by the problems at hand. Effective and meaningful participation in development begins with the articulation of needs by intended beneficiaries and requires their ultimate control over the process of planning to meet such needs. This point is essential, because, in practical terms, participant control guarantees the presence of a number of factors crucial to success. These include a local commitment to the long-term goals of the project itself, an appropriate "fit" or adaptation of economic and technical innovations, an appropriate (self-determined) distribution of economic and social benefits, a broad-based sharing of formal and informal project-related learning experiences, and reduced administrative costs through decentralization and local-level skill development.

Development assistance programs and organizations may therefore be judged effective to the extent that they:

1. *Focus upon the promotion of programs and projects that clearly demonstrate central elements of beneficiary participation in, and direction of, development processes.* These processes would include the identification of needs to be met, the establishment of methodologies by which to meet expressed needs, and the implementation of projects themselves. In accordance with this criterion, projects supported by foreign assistance organizations should, first of all, display concrete and democratic participatory mechanisms. Hence, project selection criteria of a technical nature, though important, would not be the primary consideration in the choice of projects to support.

2. *Approach the identification of projects in a responsive rather than initiatory manner.* In this perspective, once the element of participation is verified the actual expression of needs to be fulfilled and the means of fulfilling them would remain primarily the responsibility of the beneficiaries and not that of development assistance organizations. Aid agencies would therefore be expected to play only a minimal role in identifying and designing projects. Their most appropriate posture would instead be one of *responding to requests* for assistance from indigenous organizations and institutions.

3. *Institutionalize direct contact by aid program officials with local-level and intermediary organizations* to verify participatory mechanisms and directly assist in assessing needs.

Increasingly, the overly centralized and inflexible patterns of modernization—reinforced in the Third World by conventional development assistance programming and private investment—have served to limit the options of the "poor majorities" to either negotiating their survival in the "modern sphere" or remaining desperately poor. Being ill-equipped to compete successfully for the material benefit of a modernization process insufficient in its scope to support their growing numbers, and being severely limited in their access to productive resources, the world's poor face a dilemma of increasingly critical proportions. A central challenge in the field of development assistance must therefore involve the expansion of options to this segment of the world's population so as to provide the poor the real possibility of satisfying their needs through a self-initiated process.

There are two major strategies by which this challenge can be successfully translated into action. The first involves the influencing of policy decisions in the Third World so as to foster greater social and economic equity. The second involves direct support to projects and institutions that inherently promote social and economic change. Given that external assistance is but one factor in the development process, resources must be allocated in a manner that complements policy and programmatic activity in the Third World in support of broader social, economic, and institutional change.

Development assistance programs and organizations may therefore be judged effective to the extent that they:

1. *Assist projects which, in turn, form a pattern in support of broader, structural changes beyond the parameters of the particular projects themselves.* In this sense, assisted projects would in large measure address broader issues such as income distribution; continued access to resources by the marginal populations; increased learning, confidence, and self-esteem among beneficiaries; and the ongoing institutionalization of participation by the poor in decisions that affect their lives. This consideration should become an integral part of project-selection policies, as isolated endeavors receiving limited assistance cannot be expected to have an impact on entire social and economic systems.

2. *Support innovative, participatory projects that have methodologies that can be transferred, through natural communicative processes, to other development settings.* Given the limited potential impact of direct project support, this type of replicability provides

the most efficient and effective multiplier factor in expanding development options and opportunities among the poor in the Third World.

3. *Condition the provision of assistance to large intermediary institutions, including central government agencies, upon the willingness of these entities to promote broad and systematically equitable development policies and programs.* Adherence to this criterion would require a commitment on the part of governments to strengthen or establish mechanisms through which the "poor majorities" could affect decisions related to their own needs. Popular organizations, as they possess a first-hand knowledge of the local reality, would be expected to participate in national development policymaking and programming (See Appendix A).

4. *Support the emergence of locally organized and controlled development institutions throughout the Third World.* More than a generation of experience has demonstrated the inefficiency and ineffectiveness of most large national and international intermediary organizations in promoting self-development endeavors at the local level. Continued, long-term reliance upon such intermediaries may, if they remain fundamentally and structurally unchanged, be counterproductive for marginal populations as they pursue the goals of self-directed development. At the same time, locally controlled development organizations may represent the only feasible means through which the poor can effectively plan and initiate their own development processes.

The diverse requirements of projects signal the need for maximum flexibility in assistance programming. The successful implementation of such programs involves the decentralization of the delivery of our assistance in order to reach numerous self-development endeavors and institutions and to respond effectively to the expression of diverse human needs. Decentralization is further impelled by the fact that the needs of these local participatory development endeavors vary greatly according to region, culture, project type, relative level of sophistication, and physical environment.

Development assistance programs and organizations may therefore be judged effective to the extent that they:

1. *Reliably analyze projects and project backgrounds* in each case to determine the project's potential to meet the distinct needs of both the particular region and the project beneficiaries. Such

analyses would include specific reference to such factors as:

(a) The participatory mechanisms of the organization or project in question

(b) The institutional linkages with the broader socio-economic system enjoyed by that institution, particularly in terms of its real or potential authority to leverage increased access to necessary resources at the international, national, or regional level

(c) The feasibility of the technical and organizational aspects of the project, in terms of the sociocultural (ethnographic) orientation of the people to be involved

(d) Its potential for achieving self-reliance and self-sustainment

(e) Its potential for promoting self-learning among participants

(f) Its ecological soundness, in relation to the immediate ecosystem

2. *Render a thorough account of distinct program factors that may have a negative impact upon local populations as a result of ill-planned endeavors.* Such impact analyses would specifically include assessments of:

(a) Possible economic and social dislocations (e.g., displacement of traditional jobs and industries by new economic activity, the destruction of homes and traditional agricultural lands by urban and rural construction projects, etc.)

(b) The possible concentration of land holdings brought about by the effect of new infrastructural projects on land value, speculation, and taxation

(c) The possible exacerbation of imbalances in wealth and power within traditional communities through channeling funds to narrowly based endeavors

(d) The possible intensification of control by decision-makers related to development activities, particularly those in which women are primarily engaged

(e) Other possible damage to the local community, cultural, and environmental fabrics

3. *Assign field staff who are well experienced at the community level in the Third World to identify and assess requests for support.* Often the most crucial factors in assessing local endeavors must be discerned intuitively rather than intellectually. Such factors would include, for example, the true level of commitment to the project within the community, the degree of representativeness of the

organization, and the quality of project leadership. The assessment of such factors is an experiential and not an academic exercise. This criterion emphasizes on-the-ground experience, rather than technical and academic training, as the primary credential of those involved in project identification and selection.

4. *Utilize decentralized decisionmaking processes in project selection.* Given the specificity of factors, details and, consequently, the assessment of participatory projects, centralized decisionmaking, far removed from the field, runs the risk of unreliability. Thus, decisions regarding project support are best made as close to the immediate setting as possible and by competent and experienced staff to whom sufficient authority is delegated. It also follows that the overall structure of our development assistance agencies would display measures of decentralization congruent with the specific assistance requirements in all stages of the development assistance process.

## THE DELIVERY OF ASSISTANCE VIS-À-VIS PROJECT IMPLEMENTATION

Self-development should, of course, be self-implemented. During most of our aid history, projects receiving our aid have been supplied with relatively high levels of capital and technical and personnel assistance. Basic responsibility for the implementation—and eventual success—of projects has been seen to rest more with donor and intermediary entities than with the participants themselves. While short-term technical and economic success has, at times, been achieved, these successes have not been matched by the inherent adaptation and diffusion of economic and technical innovations by and among local populations that are required for long-term self-sustainment. Furthermore, sustained personal commitments to what are essentially foreign phenomena have not been forthcoming.

As noted earlier, if self-sustained betterment in the quality of life among those most in need is the legitimate goal of development, effective development assistance is more essentially a matter of quality than quantity. That is to say that the *manner* in which the essential factors of development are transferred and then accepted and adapted by beneficiaries is as significant to success as the transfer itself. Rather than the imposition of Western-styled modernization upon traditional societies, this means the sensitive extension of support to Third World populations in their attempts to build development upon the traditional social and economic strengths they inherently possess.

Development assistance programs and organizations may therefore be judged effective to the extent that they:

1. *Deliver assistance on a "hands-off" basis that appropriately complements ongoing or emerging self-development endeavors in the field.* In this perspective, assistance is nondirective and delivered in response to specific requests from local development endeavors, rather than being initiated by development assistance agencies. Accordingly, the assumption of any role central to a determination of the outcome of assisted projects would not be consistent with this criterion.

2. *Channel assistance directly to the poor through democratic development institutions whose roots extend into the local community fabric.* Since assisting self-development through centralized mechanisms has limited sustaining potential, development financing should favor local-level endeavors, rather than indirect, large-scale programs and projects. Thus, greater numbers of smaller grants and loans should replace larger, less numerous capital outlays.

3. *Assist local groups in gaining the resources and leverage necessary to control their own development processes.* The fostering of local self-reliant development can break dependency relationships, including reliance upon foreign capital assistance.

Assistance being provided directly to self-development efforts with catalytic intent must be appropriately suited to specific local settings and projects. This entails correct determinations of the *types* of assistance to be provided, the appropriate *levels* or *amounts* of assistance extended, and the *timing* of the delivery of such assistance.

Emerging development endeavors and institutions, for example, do not usually require large amounts of financial assistance, but they do need it quickly and in proper combination with other inputs if they are to survive and grow. In all cases, *overfunding* of projects is a constant problem, since the over-availability of external resources can quickly sap continued commitment to self-reliance at the local level and alter the relationship between the institution and its constituency.

Development assistance programs and organizations may

therefore be judged effective to the extent that they:

1. *Exhibit sufficient flexibility, in terms of both structure and function, to reach numerous and diverse local development endeavors quickly and with appropriate types of assistance.* The decentralization of assistance processes will not, in and of themselves, increase development options among marginal populations unless smaller, more adaptable packages of assistance can be delivered before self-initiated endeavors wither and die due to lack of support. The delivery of such support requires the ready availability of a diverse arsenal of financial, technical, and other assistance mechanisms. Most importantly, this criterion would require that these mechanisms be utilized in response to specifically determined needs and not in an inflexible, preprogrammed or preplanned manner.

2. *Extend financial support at levels that reflect, in all cases, a reliable determination of the absorptive capacity of the project or institution in question.* Often, viable participatory organizations at the regional or community level in the Third World lose vital democratic characteristics through overly accelerated growth and technical diversification beyond the grasp of local participants. External assistance should complement ongoing activities without overwhelming them with financial or technical support.

3. *Base the provision of assistance upon a reliable determination that (a) local resources are being mobilized to the maximum extent possible in support of the project or program in question and that (b) such resources are not in fact sufficient to provide fully for the execution of the endeavor.* An examination of assisted ventures should reveal significant matching contributions—either material or "in-kind"—on the part of local participants. This determination should also take into account national resources external to the project or community in question but necessary to the sustainment of that project. It would follow, as well, that development assistance help provide the means by which project participants can gain access to other necessary financial and technical resources and services.

Although the provision of nonfinancial assistance, particularly in the areas of management and technical training, remains crucial to the process of self-development, a reconsideration of the purposes for which, and methods by which, those types of assistance are proffered is required. Technical assistance in the conventional aid framework has usually been taken to mean the exportation of technical information, hardware, and personnel to the Third World. The direct results of this export process have usually proven to be not only short-lived, but also disruptive in many cases, especially in those involving traditional populations. Technical assistance is far more appropriate when it emphasizes the building upon, rather than substituting for, local skills and resources. It therefore follows that the main thrust of technical assistance must be one that complements inherent technical capacities.

Development assistance programs and organizations may therefore be judged effective to the extent that they:

1. *Place the responsibility for the planning, control, and execution of the technical aspects of development squarely in the hands of beneficiaries.* Where external technical assistance is required, participants are in the best position to assess and select its most appropriate source, either locally, if at all possible, or externally. Accordingly, assistance in this area would remain responsive to technological requirements as expressed by project participants, supplying information and offering technological options upon request.

2. *Plan and deliver technical assistance—including the introduction of technological innovations at the local level—in a manner which is both complementary of, and congruent with, cultural, economic, organizational, and technological factors in place at the local level.* Assistance in this regard should thus be specifically designed to complement and build upon existing knowledge, resources, and technologies. The provision of technical assistance, therefore, should not constitute a process in which local, especially traditional, communities are encouraged or required to accept technologies not directly adaptable to prevailing social and economic activities. Such planning and analyses should also thoroughly address the possible negative impacts made upon the communities in question by the introduction of inappropriate technologies.

3. *Assign directly to development projects, upon beneficiaries' request, technical or managerial advisors who are qualified both technically and interculturally.* That is, such personnel, while being technically competent, should also exhibit skills and experience in local languages and cultures as some indication of sensitivity and respect for the people involved in assisted projects. Experience in the Third World has demonstrated clearly that sensitivity and

commitment—though difficult to assess—are critically important in fostering self-enablement among developing populations through non-directive assistance.

## PROGRAM AND PROJECT EVALUATION VIS-À-VIS THE LEARNING PROCESS

While the necessary and important processes of *learning* on the part of participants in development, on the one hand, and project and program *evaluation* on the part of donor agencies, on the other, are similar in logic and function, little attempt has been made to relate the two. Conventional learning and evaluation by Northern developmentalists have emphasized the analysis of inputs, outputs, and gross economic indicators through the utilization of lengthy and expensive *ex post facto*, hypothesis-testing techniques. The complexity of this process has precluded a high degree of involvement by project participants in both the selection of evaluative criteria and in the implementation of the learning process itself. This situation has engendered considerable chagrin among many Third World developmentalists, who increasingly complain that the learning process in the development field is principally a means of putting more books on Northern shelves.

While consideration of project output remains important, a valid understanding of self-development impels the examination of the *process* which lies between inputs and outputs—that is, the *dynamics* and *self-generating* factors of development itself. Since development is a human process, new knowledge and understanding of its dynamics must be based upon the experience of those most directly involved. Thus, the meaningful participation of intended beneficiaries in self-learning and evaluative processes is of crucial importance both to their own development process and to external attempts to understand that process and more effectively support it.

Development assistance programs and organizations may therefore be judged effective to the extent that they:

1. *Incorporate participant learning processes as integral and continuous components of assisted projects at each of their stages*—from the identification and articulation of needs to project planning and implementation. Learning mechanisms should be specifically designed and adapted to local situations and projects,

but in a consistent, simple, and logical manner. For example, an evaluative system could simply be based upon the meeting of project objectives that have been articulated by the participants in the planning process. Basically, such a learning process could be established upon the following questions: Are we accomplishing what we set out to do? What factors—both internal and external to the project itself—would seem to account for this?

2. *Carry out research and evaluation activities which proceed from and are based upon the learning experiences of project participants in the field.* This would apply to efforts undertaken by the agencies to determine their own effectiveness in delivering assistance, as well as to attempts to further understand the essentials of the development process.

3. *Support the establishment of direct and continued contact between researchers, program and project participants, and other developmentalists in the South and North.* This would serve to facilitate a two-way learning process and enrich the quality of both Third World development policies and programs and development assistance programming.


## INSTITUTIONAL LINKAGES

Development assistance, in the appropriate form and magnitude and at the appropriate time, is often critical to the successful completion of the development project cycle. Its misapplication, on the other hand, can undermine ongoing development efforts or, at the very least, undercut local control over them and thus leave behind no capacity for generating change. In such cases, which arise all too frequently, no aid is again the preferable option.

This is true not only of the relationship between the processes of development and aid but between the sets of institutions which carry them out, as well. With the support of small Northern donor organizations, some of the many grassroots initiatives taken in the Third World have developed into ongoing organized efforts. Some of these unfortunately lose their sense of original purpose and their effectiveness because of overfunding or excessive control by their Northern counterparts; other incipient organizations never become more than extensions of these Northern aid institutions, with their roots far from penetrating local reality.

Some, however, do evolve, with or without foreign support, into mature organizations, which serve as important vehicles for community organizations, women's groups, church organizations, precooperatives, peasant groups, and other people's organizations often serve as models that are replicated in other communities. Through the federation of some of these organizations and the emergence of new organizations to service others, a critically important institutional capacity has developed over the past generation at sub-national and national levels throughout the Third World—in some areas more rapidly and extensively than in others.

What characterizes the significant and successful intermediary organizations is the capacity not only to provide services needed by grassroots groups but also to induce social change. This is accomplished by bypassing local elites and working directly with the poor, and by serving as a conduit of expression for the latter in communications with policymakers. Examples of such intermediary organizations include:

- BRAC (Bangladesh Rural Advancement Committee), a Dhaka-based organization focusing on intergrated rural development and community self-reliance, which has established nation-wide health and banking systems and which lobbies on behalf of the poor with government
- MDA (Manicaland Development Association), a Zimbabwean regional development program, whose board is elected by the people of the region and which promotes the economic development of former tribal trust lands through the provision of support in the areas of food production, irrigation, marketing, and price negotiation
- Maison Familiale, a nation-wide Senegalese intermediary organization whose member groups elect and control the board and receive assistance in project management, book-keeping, food production, water supply, preventive health, and related educational and organizational activities
- CIDIAG (Centro de Investigación y Desarrollo Integral de Autogestión), a Peruvian service organization with grassroots people serving on the board, which provides technical and managerial assistance to large and small self-managed enterprises and manages integrated rural development programs
- WAND (Women and Development Unit of the Extra-Mural Department of the University of the West Indies), a Barbados-based center for coordinating and promoting women's activites in the Caribbean and for promoting the interests of women in national development planning, which has

strengthened women's organizations through training in community organization and assistance in project development

These organizations and many others like them have emerged from, or responded to, local-level reality and are considered legitimate by those they claim to represent. Their credibility, in the North as well as in the South, emanates from this legitimacy and representativeness and from their proven ability to provide extensive assistance and to foster change, often in difficult environments.

While much of this capacity is, indeed, non-governmental, some of the constructive response to grassroots organized activity has come from public institutions, as well. More often than not, this governmental involvement is to be found among municipal and provincial authorities, but enlightened national agencies in some countries have also recognized that public programs cannot be effectively planned and implemented without ongoing relationships with local organizations. It is often more practical, however, for public agencies to deal with second-tier organizations in the non-governmental sector than to try to work directly with many grassroots groups.

Unfortunately, these second-tier organizations have generally found both government and the commercial banking sector in their countries unresponsive to their need for resources. The expanding constituencies of these representative federations, facilitator service organizations, and other intermediary institutions make increasing demands for the credit and other services that these organizations provide. On their part, these institutions have generally matured over time, developing strong administrative capabilities and the ability to manage increasingly more sophisticated credit mechanisms and programs and larger amounts of funds. At this point, the resources of the smaller international aid organizations become insufficient. With funds from domestic institutions generally unavailable, some of the Third World's most effective development organizations have looked to the larger international aid agencies for the scale of financing that their constituencies require. To date, however, this support has rarely been forthcoming.

Herein lies the paradox, indeed the tragedy, of the foreign aid business. At one level, indigenous organizations continually emerge and, often by attracting outside support, develop into potential vehicles for constructive and pervasive change in their societies. Relatively small amounts are spent at this level, but the impact has been profound and the development knowledge accumulated expansive. At another level, however, billions of dollars are spent on Third World institutions that have no link to the local reality and no capacity to respond to it. U.S. policymakers inside and outside the major aid agencies operate on the premise that, while the efforts of small aid and development organizations are "nice," the focus of major agencies must be elsewhere if they are to have a significant impact on Third World development. Operating on this premise, and in the vacuum that forms when one ignores the insights gained over time at the local level, the major donors have, indeed, had a significant—and deleterious—impact.

The more enlightened policymakers and aid programmers recognize that far more development knowledge resides among organizations operating at the grassroots than within the major donor institutions and their large counterparts overseas. Many of them, however, value primarily the small donors' sectoral knowledge and expect to apply an enhanced understanding of health, housing, or rural development, for example, in their spheres of operation. They have failed to learn the principal lesson that those working at the grassroots have to offer: that development assistance is no better than the institutions that utilize it.

# FOUR

# AID and the Need
# for a New Structure

As addressed in Chapter 3, the contribution that foreign aid makes to self-sustaining development is a function of its responsiveness to the institutions and activities of poor people. Ostensibly, virtually all aid institutions exist to help the poor, directly or indirectly, and it is on this basis that most seek to establish their legitimacy and their constituencies in the public arena. Yet, as shown in Chapter 2, our principal aid agencies were established for very different purposes, and they operate today in pursuit of several non-developmental goals. In the case of the Agency for International Development, U.S. foreign policy objectives, trade and investment interests, the state of the country's economy, and a variety of special interests strongly influence its bureaucratic behavior.

These influences drive AID to limit its range of organizational choice overseas and to manipulate the project environment in which it operates. In this context, even the best-intentioned project officers, committed to the support of meaningful development for and by the "poor majority," face internal structures, operational procedures, and reward systems geared to promote objectives related primarily to expansionary and survival interests of the AID bureaucracy.

The opportunities that these officers have to work with the poor have diminished further as aid is used increasingly as leverage to exact policy changes by Third World governments. The most visible manifestation of this change is the large increase in economic support funds in recent years, but this shift can also be seen in AID's growing desire to "de-projectize" the use of its development assistance funds and to exert greater policy leverage through program lending.  Defining the latter not as support for a collection of projects but rather as undesignated funding unrelated to specific development activities, AID is seeking to use its influence more directly at the macro level.

To the extent that AID moves away from project lending, it moves further from contact with local-level realities.  Although the New Directions legislation mandated a close relationship between AID and the poor, AID has shown itself to be incapable, as structured and organized, of complying successfully with that mandate.  Private and voluntary organizations (PVOs) and the Inter-American and African Development Foundations, buffered by their relative independence against some of the external forces that influence AID, have increasingly taken on this responsibility and public funds to fulfill it.

Clearly, all project responsibility cannot be left to these organizations.  There remains a critical role for the principal U.S. bilateral aid institution in providing significant support to effective development organizations as they evolve into mature institutions. It is also critical to the attack on Third World poverty that policies promoted by AID be informed by the people who live in, and understand, that poverty, rather than by outside "experts" and interests whose primary goals may not be those of the poor.

This can only be accomplished by providing AID with far more autonomy than it presently enjoys.  It is clear that Congress, since the days of the Vietnam War, has not been trusting of the executive branch's utilization of appropriated aid funds.  Its fears are well founded, as the Administration in recent years has made clear that the well-being of the poor is not the primary determinant of the allocation and application of aid funds.  In 1983, for instance, the chair of the Administration's Development Coordination Committee explained in his annual report that, in the previous two years:

> U.S. interests in a particular region or country, due to the country being a source of important raw materials, the location of substantial U.S. private investment, or the scene of actual or potential destabilizing conflict, have been given greater importance as criteria for the allocation to countries of all forms of U.S. assistance, including development assistance (*Development Issues*, p. 175).

Congressional apprehension about the effects of external political and economic pressures has been manifested in a range of regulations and reporting requirements that have, according to the Office of Technology Assessment, substantially increased AID's already extensive paperwork and bureaucratic constraints (OTA, *Continuing the Commitment,* p. 10). Congress, of course, has also been part of the problem, as its members translate their constituents' interests into non-developmental policy.

### CREATION OF AN AUTONOMOUS STRUCTURE

The ability of Congress, the White House, the State Department, and other government agencies to divert AID from its development assistance mandate would be circumscribed if AID were structurally protected from day-to-day interference by these bodies. The establishment of a restructured, independent AID by Congress, along with an appropriate policy framework, would thereafter enable Congress to limit its involvement to appropriations and oversight functions. Assured that the possibilities of politicization by the executive branch were limited, members of Congress could at the same time use the autonomy of AID as a basis for resisting the myriad of extraneous pressures brought to bear on them.

Congress has already established precedents in the creation of independent organizations in the international field. The Overseas Private Investment Corporation (OPIC), the Inter-American Foundation, and the African Development Foundation (ADF) are examples of institutions that have been created by Congress as public corporations with their own boards of directors. The IAF, in particular, is an example of the viability and resiliency of such a structure. Its founding legislation, like that of OPIC and the ADF, mandated that the President nominate people from both the private and public sectors to its board and that their terms be staggered. The intent was to prevent effective policy control by any given Administration. While nominal control of the board has been gained by the White House during the mid-1980s, its difficulty in dictating policy is testimony to the internal structures, operating principles, and staff that the first dozen years of structural and *de facto* independence enabled the IAF to establish, sustain, and build upon.

Similar structures exist in other industrialized countries. The Swedish International Development Authority (SIDA), which is in charge of preparing and implementing Sweden's bilateral aid program, is governed by a thirteen-member board of directors named by the government. In Canada, the International Development Research Centre (IDRC), which was established in 1970 as an autonomous institution with government funding, is controlled and directed by an international board of governors. The British aid system includes a number of special scientific units that also operate autonomously.

The autonomy needed by an aid institution to enable it to effectively underwrite self-determined development rather than Northern interests was absent from the International Development Cooperation Administration when it was created in 1979 as the new U.S. aid superstructure. While a principal intent of the reorganization was to remove the U.S. bilateral aid program from the control of the State Department by making IDCA's director directly responsible to the President, IDCA was not provided with an independent governing board that could protect it from politicization.

In the end, IDCA has become little more than a paper organization, representing just another layer of bureaucracy between AID and the State Department. By 1981, the Center of Concern was already reporting the failure of IDCA to remove AID from the foreign policy arena. AID officials were even then acknowledging the arbitrary and unilateral action by the State Department to which AID could be and was still subjected (Schmidt, et al., *Religious Private Voluntary Organizations,* pp. 20–21). Indeed, despite the existence of IDCA, the Foreign Assistance Act still places ultimate responsibility for economic assistance in the hands of the Secretary of State.

Upon assuming office, the Reagan Administration moved to dismantle IDCA. It was only the AID Administrator's desire to achieve greater access to the White House by assuming the leadership of IDCA, as well, that saved that institution from extinction. AID's internal memoranda on submissions to Congress soon were void of any reference to IDCA, but referred frequently to clearances required of the State Department. By the end of the first term of the Reagan Administration, The Development GAP could find few at AID who had heard of the aid superstructure, including those, in one instance, who worked less than ten yards from its small office in the State Department building.

The restructuring of AID from an agency of the State Department or IDCA into an autonomous public corporation (perhaps known as the Administration for International Development) would require the creation of a board of directors appropriately designed and composed to serve as an effective shield against politicization and special interests. Board members should be experienced in Third World matters and committed to protecting and promoting the mandate and autonomy of the institution. A nine-person board, elected to six-year staggered terms, would ideally consist of:

- The four presidents of the Inter-American and African Development Foundations and of a new Asian development foundation and PVO-support foundation, who would be able to provide guidance to AID in the identification and support of representative and effective development organizations
- One current and one former cabinet member, at least one of whom shall have been Secretary of State, in order to provide guidance on foreign policy matters relating to the new AID
- Two non-governmental leaders recognized for their intellectual and moral leadership, such as the head of an ecumenical church body and a university president
- A Third World representative, possessing U.S. citizenship, who has worked directly with poor communities overseas in development activity, to ensure the injection of a "reality factor" into board deliberations

While the President of the United States would nominate the board members (whose nominations would be confirmed by the Senate), the board's chair should be selected to a specified term by the board itself, so as to minimize the possibilities of politicization by the White House. He or she would be chosen from among all the board members, with the exception of the two cabinet members, so as to ensure a development rather than foreign policy focus by the institution.

## AID FOR NON-DEVELOPMENTAL PURPOSES

While the creation of an independent public institution is a prerequisite for the promotion of long-term, sustainable development relevant to the needs and circumstances of the poor, there is at the same time a place for aid that can be used in pursuing political objectives. Presently, the Economic Support Fund is the principal source of funds used explicitly for that purpose. The 1983 report of the DCC chair explained that the "criteria for the country allocation of the Economic Support Fund are related to political and security considerations: financial assistance is offered on the basis of U.S. security interests, in an effort to maintain or achieve the political and economic stability of governments favorable to (or at least not hostile to) the United States . . ." (*Development Issues*, pp. 175–176).

While there is plenty of room for discussion and disagreement over the wisdom of pursuing a range of foreign policy goals, with or without the use of foreign aid, it is clear that political aid should be designated as such and controlled and managed by institutions not engaged in the promotion of development and anti-poverty activity. This means that, under the present aid structure, those ESF resources utilized for developmental purposes should be the exclusive responsibility of AID, while those allocated for political purposes should continue to be programmed elsewhere in the State Department. The latter, which possesses a limited understanding of development, should be prohibited from utilizing ESF monies to influence development policy. Local currencies generated by the ESF program should be utilized by an autonomous AID only if no conditions were attached and if AID were not accountable to the State Department for their use.

The majority of ESF loans and grants are provided as balance-of-payments support and for commodity import purchases. The remaining portion is utilized as development project funds, and as such have been frequently misallocated. A 1983 study by the General Accounting Office revealed that AID officials in twelve of the twenty-nine countries surveyed were concerned about the recipient country's ability to absorb ESF resources (GAO, *Donor Approaches*).

Egypt is a classic example of this imbalance between development resources and development capacity. The commitment by AID of approximately $1 billion per year has driven AID officials to plan

> big, expensive projects to get rid of a backlog in cash. But the projects have been bogged down in interminable delays. Many have not worked properly when completed. Some of those that did work have already started to break down. . . . Hermann Eilts, [former] U.S. ambassador to Egypt and a chief architect of the effort, conceded recently that no thought had been given in

advance to how much Egypt could absorb or how much money should be spent. . . . "We always had more money than we had projects," Elits said. "Instead of the program being designed by projects, we had an amount of money we had to find projects for." [F]rom the start, the aid program was shaped not by Egyptian needs but by U.S. foreign policy and economic interests, and Egyptians are increasingly aware, and resentful, of that (Phelps, "An Aid Plan Gone Awry").

Meaningful development cannot be fostered if the State Department is allocating aid on a political and security basis. For U.S. aid to have a positive impact on development, all project aid must fall within the development assistance account and AID must be in control of both policy and administration. The clear differentiation in the roles of the State Department and AID, which would be greatly facilitated by the transforming of AID into an autonomous public institution, would go a long way toward enhancing the credibility of our development assistance program overseas.

A similar and parallel change must also be made in the structure of the present aid legislation. The integration of military assistance, ESF, and development assistance in a single foreign aid bill in recent years may, as some claim, have enhanced the chances of congressional approval of the development assistance program. What is certain, however, is that the inclusion of development support with security-related aid muddies the waters and both sullies the reputation and compromises the integrity of the U.S. development aid program.

The task force headed by Tony Babb addressed the consequences of this link in its 1977 report to the AID Administrator:

> The U.S. public does not understand very well what AID is doing, what foreign assistance is, or why it is important. Americans are basically altruistic and have historically been prepared to support humanitarian programs, particularly when the people who benefit can be identified. But, faced with the great diversity of programs identified by the media as "aid". . . the public becomes understandably confused and ready to view aid with a jaundiced eye (Babb, p. V–14).

The development assistance program should stand and be judged on its own. Should that happen, the likelihood is that a streamlined, independent institution devoted exclusively to the provision of support directly to the poor would attract the support of a large majority of Americans.


**BASES FOR ALLOCATING DEVELOPMENT ASSISTANCE**

The autonomy of a new institution would enable it to make decisions regarding the allocation of funds on a development instead of a political basis. The Center of Concern, in its 1981 report, pointed out that most of AID's development budget was apportioned to U.S. client states, which included those with repressive governments. It concludes that:

> [W]hile there is an unquestionable need for assistance in those countries, much of their poverty is the result of an unequal distribution of wealth perpetuated by an entrenched ruling class, corruption, and oppressive governments that are not willing to share the benefits of development with all of the people. Consequently, most of the U.S. aid does not reach the countries' poor, but is absorbed by the elite, who use the aid for their own aggrandisement (Schmidt, et al., p.38).

A government's efforts to narrow the wealth and income gaps between the rich and the poor should be the principal factor in determining the allocation of bilateral aid funds to Third World public institutions. Additional evidence of government concern for the less privileged segments of the population are free-functioning and democratic labor unions, producers' organizations, community associations, and other popular organizations, as well as the right to establish such institutions. Furthermore, there should be evidence that those to be affected by programs and projects supported by U.S. aid participate in their planning and implementation.

These and related standards should be stated explicitly as policy by the new AID. Those governments which meet these standards would be eligible for assistance; those that do not would be aware of the changes they would have to make to qualify for support. At the project level, AID, as stressed in Chapter 3, must select the most capable implementing institutions from among all public and non-governmental organizations if project effectiveness is to be maximized. Where national and local governments are not promoting equitable development, the institutional choice should be made within the non-governmental sector, if such organizations are free to serve their constituencies. If a government were to oppose this action, AID should withhold funding from that country rather than invest in a public institution that would use its assistance to perpetuate inequities. Furthermore, those governments that refuse to permit the new bilateral aid organization to operate in their countries should also be denied political aid from the State Department. As some of the worst poverty exists in the Third World countries with the highest per capita incomes, aid should be available to institutions in all countries, regardless of the latters' income levels.

## UNTYING AID

The new aid institution should also be freed, to the maximum extent possible, from congressional mandates relating to the purchase of U.S. goods. The United States has not been the major practitioner, among the industrialized countries, of tying aid to such purchases, but still the larger portion of AID's budget is so tied. It is understandable that the United States would feel compelled to pursue this practice as long as nations such as the United Kingdom, Canada, France, and West Germany formally and informally tie most of their aid. The cost of this practice in development terms, however, is high. Such purchases retard self-sufficiency which, if enhanced, could reduce long-term foreign exchange costs. Even more significantly, they distort local development patterns through the introduction of inappropriate technologies and techniques.

The Office of Technology Assessment, in its 1986 report on the Sahel, reflected on this problem:

> Congressionally mandated AID requirements to use American equipment have proven ineffective in stimulating new markets for U.S. goods, a major objective of such measures. Meanwhile, they have complicated and even hindered project operations. Delivery time of U.S. equipment has been long, and inoperative U.S. vehicles, pumps, and other equipment litter the Sahel for want of spare parts, maintenance skills, or operating funds. . . . In addition, these "buy American" requirements have led to use of inappropriate capital-intensive technologies. . . . So-called "tied aid provisions" for equipment and technical assistance have greatly increased the total cost of aid, and, from the perspective of the Sahelian recipients, greatly diminished its value to them (OTA, *Continuing the Commitment* p. 105).

When development assistance is untied, local costs may in principle be financed up to 100 percent. Local production and regional trade can be stimulated rather than retarded. Recurrent costs can be financed to the extent necessary. Labor-intensive programs, more appropriate to the circumstances of most Third World countries, are more likely to be generated if aid monies need not be expended on foreign imports.

While many argue for tying aid on the basis of its contribution to economic well-being at home, tied aid, as OTA discovered in the case of aid to the Sahel, generates little in the way of permanent markets for the donor country. Maurice Strong, first President of Canada's aid agency, CIDA, has contended that new markets are not developed by requiring people to buy goods—at as much as 25 percent above internationally competitive prices—that they will not buy when they have the freedom to choose (Freeman, *Political Economy*, p. 32). Strong's contention that aid is not trade-creating is supported by a number of studies. Some advantages are gained in the short-term by individual exporters, but the advantages to the donor country's economy are questionable. A German aid official told The Development GAP that, even if all German aid were officially tied, it would produce only a 0.7 percent increase in German exports. Furthermore, the extra aid required to subsidize these purchases is a drain on the taxpayer and a very expensive manner of creating jobs in the donor country.

It seems self-defeating, therefore, to promote aid, as some organizations have done, by trumpeting the trade gains made by a relative few in the U.S. export sector, while the U.S. taxpayer grows increasingly disillusioned with the ineffectiveness of aid overseas and its costliness here. A far better approach would appear to be to give preference in the use of aid monies to the purchase of appropriate goods and services at relatively low prices in the aid-receiving country and from other Third World countries. Aid would be tied to the purchase of U.S. exports only where Northern resources are required and the United States can offer a product that is competitive in terms of price and relevance. A monitoring capacity should be established in the executive and legislative branches to oversee this policy.

## PROGRAM AID VERSUS PROJECT AID

As mentioned earlier in this chapter, it is important that a restructured AID not divorce itself entirely from project activity. AID can provide development institutions with significant amounts of financial support on relatively soft terms at key moments in their evolution, and these organizations, in turn, provide AID the contact with the local reality that it requires for effective policy planning. The balance between project and non-project, or program, aid must be determined on the basis of a number of factors: the trade-off between a degree of policy leverage and a degree of control over the micro-economic efficiency and success of projects; the relative importance to the national development process of changes in the policy context and constructive activities at the project level; the generally more staff-intensive nature and higher administrative costs of project support; the capacity of recipient country institutions to manage and "projectize" aid funds; and one's philosophy regarding the intensity of the involvement of the donor in the development process.

Program aid has different meanings to different people and different donor institutions, but can be viewed as falling within two general categories. One is non-sector-specific assistance representing a cash transfer for balance-of-payments support or, for example, for commodity imports or structural adjustment activities. In this case, policy changes leveraged as a result of the aid should be informed by organizations representing the poor, and the local currencies generated by the sale of the dollars should be managed by local institutions that have incorporated the poor in the design and implementation of development activities. The other form of program aid relates to assistance provided to one or more institutions in a particular sector for the purpose of, for example, facilitating specific policy or management reforms, the importation of required goods, or the upgrading of a capacity to identify, design, and execute projects. This type of program support should be provided only to those public institutions that have demonstrated through previous project work a proclivity for responding to the expressed needs of the poor.

Most Northern donors have emphasized some form of program support, usually incorporating long-term sectoral planning, and have left the responsibility for project identification, development, and management to the recipient country. These donors point to the lower administrative costs related to this approach as a major reason for its adoption. These costs are not, however, always lower than those of project aid. Responding to a 1983 GAO report, AID official John Bolton suggested that the study had ". . . exaggerate[d] the management benefits of non-project assistance . . ." and had "overlooked some of the 'hidden' management costs normally associated with non-project assistance (e.g., administration of local currency generation, economic expertise required to promote policy reform usually related to non-project assistance)" (GAO, *Donor Approaches*, p. 91). The OECD has similarly reported that more administrative time is needed, in some cases, to prepare, implement, and monitor non-project aid than project aid (OECD, *Compendium of Aid Procedures*).

There is no question, however, that program aid enables the movement of larger amounts of financial support at a lower per-unit cost and that its policy leverage is greater than that of project aid. These are clearly factors in AID's recent interest in more program lending, as it has sought to promote private-sector activity and to alter its low status among major bilateral donors at the start of this decade in terms of the ratio of financial commitments to staff size.

European donors favor program aid not for enhanced policy leverage but rather because it makes it possible for them to play a *reduced* role in the recipient country's affairs. The Swedes, in particular, have integrated their assistance as much as possible into the recipient's development plan, while seeking to promote independence and self-sufficiency by moving away from a rigorous pre-appraisal of project activities. SIDA has found, however, that weaknesses in project preparation in some of the least developed countries have necessitated an increase in its direct involvement. The Dutch have also adopted a more programmatic approach in order to increase the development responsibilities of the recipient country. Part of this strategy hinges on the identification of an appropriate implementing institution to which its aid agency can make a long-term commitment. The British, like the Swedes and Dutch, recognize the problems of accountability inherent in program aid and its suitability only for those Third World countries capable of administering it.

In the final analysis, a mixture of program and project aid is most appropriate. A restructured AID should provide program aid on a multi-year basis to those governments that have exhibited a commitment to a form of development that directly involves and benefits the poor; these recipients might be designated "program" countries, as is done by Canada and some European countries. This status should be denied to those countries whose governments are determined by Congress to be violators of human rights. AID should make project aid available on an institution-by-institution basis where such a commitment does not exist. The implementing institutions should be chosen from the public and private sectors on the basis of their experience in participatory development and their capacity to manage funds. The degree of latitude that an institution exercises in applying aid funds to discrete projects should be a function of the confidence that AID gains over time in the former's development capacity.

A long-term investment in a capable and developmentally appropriate institution with which a relationship of mutual trust has been developed, rather than individual project funding, is clearly the most effective and efficient vehicle for achieving socio-economic progress. This approach should be pursued wherever possible, particularly in the non-governmental sector and in conjunction with agencies of governments which are actively engaged in promoting development that is truly equitable. As the latter are, lamentably, the exception to the norm, a strong case can be made, on a developmental basis, for either a fundamental change in AID's clientele or an emphasis on project aid. William Sommer, who served in three Asian countries as an AID official, addresses this point directly. "If past experience is any guide," he suggested in a 1982 article, "only project action will have a measurable effect on some of the poor. Programs and country strategies, because of their emphasis on management and because they must deal with client-state bureaucracies, are unlikely to meet with much success" (Sommer, "Rescuing Aid," p. 18).

**THE NEED FOR GREATER DECENTRALIZATION**

Recently, AID officials have expressed the opinion that the Agency cannot promote project work and that it is not structured to do so. In fact, AID has never made the internal structural and operational changes necessary for compliance with its New Directions mandate to assist the poor directly. As long ago as 1977, AID's Babb task force urged the Carter Administration to "set AID's house in order." With its credibility thus reestablished, AID could then work with Congress "to effect the legislative changes necessary for carrying out a more responsible yet flexible assistance program" (Babb, p. v).

Babb warned that the Agency had become top-heavy and cautious, as well as over-centralized in terms of decisionmaking and the location of personnel. Unfortunately, little was done to rectify the situation. AID officers continued to be rewarded not for the support of projects that helped the poor but for the design of those that helped move money.

Both Judith Tendler and Coralie Bryant, among others, have written on the internal hierarchy that pressure from outside the Agency has created. This hierarchy is found both in Washington and at the level of the field mission, where it is reflected in the type of development that is supported. Where risk taking is not rewarded by supervisors, and the expenditure of funds is, the project officer is more likely to select a large project operated by an established institution than a smaller participatory project run by an organization unknown to him or her and AID.

Much has been made of the life styles of AID's field staff, many of whom receive housing, services, and other perquisites that they do not have at home. The high cost of this aside, a more serious consequence of what Bryant calls the "mission village" is the separation of AID officials from the common people of the country, not just socially but at work as well (Bryant, "Organizational Impediments," pp. 3–4). In its report on the Sahel, OTA observed that most members of the AID community "live in prosperous enclaves within capital cities" and that their life style "increases the perpetual gap between them and the rural poor (OTA, p. 102). When added to their paperwork, the pressure to move money, and the uncertainties of the project environment, the enclave mentality all too often leads AID personnel to avoid projects created by the poor and to generate projects from within the mission instead.

This does not mean that there are not capable and dedicated personnel who would be more effective and more satisfied if they were to be working within a different type of system. Such a system would have to be considerably more decentralized than AID is today. With missions in dozens of countries and with the majority of its direct-hire employees (including host-country citizens) overseas, AID is already more decentralized than any other Northern bilateral aid agency. It is still top-heavy, however, with personnel in Washington performing project-related functions best carried out in the field, orchestrating the administrative work that leaves mission personnel (as well as aid recipients) buried under mountains of paper, and in other ways doing their best to comply with the myriad of often conflicting directives and interests emanating from Congress and other institutions.

**PROBLEMS IN THE PROJECT CYCLE**

With Congress expecting AID-supported projects to promote special, non-developmental interests while remaining consistent with its with a set of internal checks and reviews that produce a lengthy and cumbersome project cycle. AID's statutory checklist of issues which must be addressed during project development reflects both the breadth of Congress' interests and the intensive internal review that AID feels it necessitates. In order to be responsive to Congress, which controls its future, AID/Washington has imposed upon itself enormously complicated procedures which make it difficult for the field missions to be responsive to the poor. This lack of responsiveness is reflected in at least two ways: in the long delays by AID in providing support and in the nature of the projects that are ultimately assisted.

The longest delays occur during the project-design stage of the project cycle, which features frequent exchanges between the mission and Washington to sort out questions that must be satisfactorily addressed. These take up a great deal of field staff time that could be spent far more productively. Project development consumes approximately two years on average from identification to approval, and as much as three years in total can pass before operations commence. AID has of late decentralized some project approval authority to the field in an effort to address this problem.

AID has for some time had programs through which certain funding could be secured more rapidly. In the particular case of a relatively small project in Kenya in the promotion of which The Development GAP was involved, funding was provided via AID's Accelerated Impact Program. In spite of the program's name, fourteen months passed from the time the project proposal was submitted to the time that the project agreement was finally signed. In its 1985 report on this experience, The Development GAP reflected on the delays that continually developed:

> These project-development problems within AID cannot simply be blamed on project staff, as almost all personnel carried out their responsibilities without major delays. Rather, the problem appears to lie in the project-development system itself. The number of distinct steps that must be undertaken to fund a project—ranging from the submission of pre-project notification for Congressional approval to the numerous communications between the field and Washington on project document review—renders the system both burdensome and time-consuming. This is compounded by the number of offices and personnel involved in the project development and review process (AID, *PISCES II Experience*, Vol. II, p. 70).

According to AID's Office of Evaluation, poor project development is the major reason for delays in the implementation of AID-supported projects (GAO, *Donor Approaches*, p. 58). The study concludes that projects are judged on criteria unrealistic in terms of implementation and are approved as long as they are  well articulated and presented in the proper form.  OTA notes that AID favors the designer and obligator of funds over the project implementor and manager.  This leads to ."..a bias toward large-scale, complex projects, with inadequate attention to field realities. . . . " (OTA, p. 103).

While these realities could be accessed through the involvement of local organizations and the participation of local populations, the demands of the present project cycle and the pressure to expend funds discourage such risk taking among AID staff.  The length of the project-development process also leaves staff with little time at the end to observe the actual product of their efforts in operation. Hence, commitment, follow-through, learning, and accountability suffer.

The pressures faced by project officers are also partly accountable for the economic and social dislocations that frequently take place locally as a result of AID-supported projects.  These are often not taken into account during project design because of AID's generally limited contact in-country beyond that with government officials and the local elite.  Even when these problems appear during project implementation, missions are reluctant to delay the project any longer by asking headquarters and Congress for approval for project modifications.  The recent delegation of greater authority to the missions by the AID administrator will help some in this regard, but many, particularly larger, projects will remain problematical for local populations.

**CONSTRAINTS ON DECENTRALIZED DECISIONMAKING**

In 1977, at the time the Babb report was prepared, 64 percent of the direct-hire U.S. workforce was based in Washington.  According to the Babb task force, this was primarily the result of decisions to increase the use of contractors in implementing overseas projects and to increase the role of AID/Washington in project review, approval, and management (Babb, p. IV–4).  The task force urged a reversal of this trend, so that the field officers would have far more substantive responsibility.  It recommended to the AID Administrator that it shift "major responsibility for program content, implementation, and evaluation from headquarters to the field offices, i.e., to the spot where expertise on individual country needs and capacities is greatest, where operating problems can best be evaluated in terms of local conditions, and where early signs of program and project difficulties can best be detected" (Babb, p. A5–2).

The model that the Babb team recommended featured stronger field missions, decentralization of authority to regional bureaus over all services not needed in common by those four bureaus, and smaller central bureaus for policy, coordination, and management services. At the mission level, there would be more staff, serving longer tours of duty, with each being in close collaboration with host-country beneficiaries and responsible for all phases of the project cycle. Meanwhile, there would be a moderate staff decrease in Washington, as greater responsibility was delegated to field missions and centrally planned and implemented programs were cut back.

This decentralized model represents a definite improvement over AID's previous operational structure and was apparently a basis for some of the changes made within AID during the 1980s. Beginning in 1981, AID has—in some regions faster than in others—decentralized authority to the field over the approval and amending of smaller projects and over the approval of contractors. The standard tour of duty has been lengthened and steps have been taken to increase the proportion of staff in the field while staff in Washington is reduced by attrition. Approval of Country Development Strategy Statements has been made a multi-year exercise in order to reduce the burden on mission staff, which now submit annual "Action Plans." Communication between missions and Washington regarding project identification documents has also been reduced.

Some major problems in field operations have yet to be overcome, however, in large part because they are inherent in the aid system as presently structured. Increasing amounts of AID's budget are being programmed for political reasons in Washington rather than developmental purposes in the field. This has not helped to revive a sagging staff morale. Nor does the continuing push within the Agency to move money so as to justify new appropriations desired from Congress and to satisfy foreign policy exigencies, especially in countries where the institutional capacity for managing development cannot absorb such expenditures. With new projects and project ideas still being generated from

Washington and with the bulk of program and project funding still requiring Washington's involvement, mission staff will remain overworked, unresponsive to the poor, and removed from local realities. Meanwhile, their dependency on consultants, PVOs, and other U.S. intermediaries, will, of necessity, continue.

Congress showed its wisdom in the 1970s when it gave AID its New Directions mandate, but it failed to provide the Agency with the autonomy and structure required for its compliance. As discussed above, an aid institution that is unshielded from outside influences will organize itself internally to respond to those influences rather than to the intended beneficiaries of the aid and to the realities of their environment. The Babb task force recognized this in concluding that a model considerably more decentralized than the one it recommended should be adopted by AID in the future, should AID gain greater independence. Until that happens, however, congressional initiatives to make AID accountable to the poor, no matter how precisely and well articulated, will meet with, at best, very limited success, just as they have over the twenty years since Title IX's participatory mandate was enacted.

Therefore, it must be stressed that the impact of the changes recommended below is closely tied to the relative autonomy that AID might attain and exercise. It would also be contingent upon the transfer of the administration of political and security-oriented economic support funds to the State Department, leaving a smaller and leaner institution dedicated solely to supporting development activities.

### PROPOSALS FOR AN INTERNAL RESTRUCTURING

As the Babb task force and OMB suggested, the size of the planning and support bureaus in Washington should be substantially reduced and their activities severely circumscribed. No specific policies, programs, or projects for implementation in the Third World should emanate from Washington, but instead should be developed in each country mission or regional office, where local realities can inform them. The Washington policy-development office should be structured to enable a continual review and synthesis of diverse regional experiences, views, and learning and, based upon this, the development of a broad policy framework. Once and for all, the aid community could rid itself of the need to respond to policymakers' latest fad, whether it be "basic human needs" or "private-sector initiative," microenterprises or cooperatives, non-formal education or health, foci that may for awhile be in vogue but which may have little relevance to site-specific circumstances.

This would mean the elimination of functional accounts within AID. An end to programming by sectors would enable the overseas offices to support activities truly relevant to the needs of each particular society, to provide assistance for integrated endeavors, and to respond rapidly to evolving needs and opportunities. AID favors such a change, but, until AID is effectively independent of non-developmental influences, Congress must maintain and exercise the authority to define the fields of the Agency's investment. In the meantime, minimum levels of expenditures should be established in specific social and economic sectors, with 20 to 30 percent of appropriated funds left unearmarked to provide some flexibility for the field missions.

Just as the principal role of the mission should be to provide support to development activities in a responsive fashion, the main role of AID/Washington should be to assume a similar posture vis-à-vis the mission. This, in essence, amounts to turning AID's present internal structure upside down, so that the inputs that move the system would enter from the base and compel responses as they make their way up through the hierarchy. Similarly, research should not, by and large, be done by AID/Washington to be shared with the missions. Instead, headquarters should be gleaning the experiences gained in-country and sharing this learning with policymakers here and with AID mission staff worldwide.

On each continent, AID should have from one to three regional offices, depending upon the number of country missions. The former should be small and should provide administrative and logistical support; their programmatic responsibilities should be limited to only occasional reviews of projects to ensure their consistency with AID's mandate. Between the regional and country offices there should be established sub-regional or "cluster" offices, where AID's principal programmatic responsibility would be centered. These intermediary structures would group countries by their proximity and their ecological and ethnological similarities. They would be designed to facilitate and upgrade development planning, project review, and learning.

Country missions should be physically separate from U.S. embassies, just as AID headquarters should no longer be housed in the State Department, in order to ensure autonomy. While there should be a core staff in the capital city, most of the mission staff should be organized in small groups and based in provincial centers. This would put AID far more in touch with local realities than with local elites, generate more policy leverage from below than from above, reduce living costs and other overhead expenses while not necessarily creating hardships for employees, and foster greater responsiveness to the more marginal segments of the population. These recommendations are not dissimilar from those made by the Babb task force ten years ago. It reported then to the AID Administrator that "project implementation personnel should be located as close to the project site as local circumstances permit," and that AID field missions should pay ". . . less attention to support of creature comforts and amenities for its employees . . ." (Babb, pp. III–15–16).

A staff decentralized in-country would be in far better touch with ongoing and potential development initiatives and with local institutions. It could assess the legitimacy and effectiveness of institutions, particularly those that do or could play a role in national development programs. This could be done in conjunction with colleagues from other provinces at regular meetings at AID's central office. Staff could build upon the funding of smaller donors by providing support for endeavors undertaken at a multi-village or regional level while helping to generate greater development capacity. It could also stimulate contact and learning among local organizations located in different provinces.

It should be clear, however, that the success of a decentralized staff depends heavily upon the experience and qualities that the staff brings to the job. Given the proper institutional framework, decentralization can be effective if project officers have been in touch with life at the local level and are instinctively responsive to pressures from below. If these officers are not sensitive, however, to the needs, limitations, and capabilities of local populations and their organizations and to the environments in which they must operate, direct contact with them can do far more harm than good. Overfunding, co-optation, unnecessary exposure to political risks, and other problems that can be created by staff with inappropriate experience can do irreparable damage to even the strongest of organizations. Presently, AID has too many people working overseas who, while skilled in other areas, do not possess the local-level development experience required by this approach. Until there is a change in this situation, it would be a safer and still effective strategy to limit decentralization to capital cities and to establish mechanisms that enable staff to receive local information from indigenous NGO personnel on the ground.

Each AID mission should also have on staff in the capital a few people with a multi-disciplinary knowledge and a deep understanding of that particular country. That staff should provide support when requested by field personnel and should serve on a project review board. This exercise should be facilitated by their understanding of the social and economic dynamics of the country and the relationship among the various projects, programs, and policies.

In many cases, however, secondary reviews and final determinations on funding and funding policy should be made in the cluster office. It is here that AID's most experienced and knowledgeable staff should be based. The proximity of the countries in each cluster would offer that staff a firsthand view of virtually all projects and facilitate the transfer of learning across national lines. Technical expertise that cannot be afforded at the mission level should reside in these offices. On occasion, AID's regional offices and headquarters should review projects to ensure consistency with AID's mandate; these reviews should include several annual or biannual on-site assessments in order to ensure accountability.

Such a restructuring of AID would, if outside influences were minimized, enable the maximally effective application of objective criteria to institutional program and project appraisal. Ideology and new orthodoxies would be eliminated as determinants, as people who daily experience the development problems would be in a position to guide AID decisionmakers. Suggested criteria for the funding of Third World projects are listed in Appendix C. A fundamental criterion would be the participation of the intended beneficiaries throughout the project cycle. In 1980, AID anthropologist Alice Morton responded in an in-house memorandum to AID officials skeptical about this approach. Morton explained that such participation, through more appropriate institutions than those normally involved by AID, can actually speed up rather than retard project development and, far from being necessarily equated with small-scale funding, can generate a broad base for significant national development activity.

## PLANNING AND BUDGETING

Participation and consultation would also mark AID's various planning processes. AID's field personnel would participate, along with representation from the country's popular organizations, in AID's own program and policy planning sessions. This planning would also incorporate well versed representatives from U.S. PVOs, other Northern NGOs, and U.S. regional foundations. With their involvement, AID could formulate country assistance plans based upon projections of the capacity and needs of effective development institutions that might receive AID support. It would often be the work of these smaller funders in the identification and strengthening of institutions that AID would be building upon when it funds mature local organizations.

These foundations and PVOs might also help AID establish a participatory process for formulating the positions that it takes with government in national-level "policy dialogue." To date, the policies that have been fostered by AID overseas have generally reflected only the interests and perspectives of a small elite in this country and in the host countries. Without consultative mechanisms that enable a communication between policy planners and local populations, policy dialogue is doomed to failure as a development tool. Accordingly, regular meetings, perhaps on a quarterly basis, should be held with local groups to elicit their input.

AID's country budgets should be established on the basis of its participatory planning process, and unutilized funds would ideally be carried forward from year to year. This would enable AID to maintain a responsive posture throughout the fiscal year instead of having to spend and perhaps misallocate funds because of a deadline that had no relevance to local development realities. While Congress is not normally receptive to this approach, it might be willing to make this concession to a bilateral development assistance organization with, at least in the short- and medium-term, a significantly reduced budget.

A restructured AID could operate for some time with a considerably smaller budget, because its funding would be based upon the still limited absorptive capacity of appropriate development institutions and not on external, non-developmental factors. Investments in large and ineffective government agencies would be replaced with support for more democratic institutions in the public and non-governmental sectors. AID could play an important role in building up the capacity of these institutions over time. Costs would also be cut as a result of the recommended streamlining of AID and relocation of mission personnel outside of the capital cities. Furthermore, local procurement of goods and consultant services would greatly reduce AID's expenses.

### EFFECTIVE USE OF HUMAN RESOURCES

A new bilateral aid institution would have to make better use of available personnel than AID does today. The GAO pointed out in 1983 that most of AID's projects were carried out through contractors, and this has remained the case. The GAO likened the role of AID's overseas officers to that of "travel agent" providing logistical and administrative support to contractors. It concluded that a reduction in this support would free AID field staff to assume a direct development assistance role (GAO, p. 73).

OTA's Sahel report stressed the high costs associated with U.S. contractors. It pointed out that the short-term nature of such consultancies reduces institutional learning within AID, just as it does the personal commitment to the long-term success of projects. OTA also bemoaned the reliance on outside contractors at the expense of a more significant role for host-country personnel:

> AID also hires local staff, but this pool of expertise is poorly tapped. Local staff often are the informal institutional memory of AID missions, but they are usually occupied with routine work and are infrequently used to help with program development and management. This wastes the potential their special perspective could offer and misses an opportunity to increase their skills in a form of internal institution-building (OTA, p. 101).

For the same reason, preference should be given to the contracting of local consultants and other Third World firms and individuals, whose expertise is often more relevant than that of their Northern counterparts. Whether it be in the area of research, project development, implementation, or evaluation, the strong bonds that have developed over the years between AID missions and U.S. consultants must be loosened to allow Third World institutions more control over the identification and selection of contractors.

In this regard, the prominent role of U.S. universities, in particular, must change. The Babb task force noted that the land-grant approach, promoted by Congress and AID, is an example of a strategy that is uniquely American and not directly transferable. It criticized U.S. universities for often being

> merely "body shops" for AID projects without substantive involvement in project formulation or sufficient concern with providing the best personnel for implementation. At times the campus experts have concentrated more on strengthening their own academic knowledge of development subjects rather than on adapting and applying to LDC problems the knowledge they already possess.

The task force urged AID and the universities". . . to adapt to the process of helping LDCs find their own development paths" (Babb, pp. V–7–8).

U.S. universities can effectively provide this assistance by working collaboratively with Third World universities, research institutes, and development organizations to upgrade prevailing local and traditional methods and techniques and to assist in their dissemination, adaptation, and application in other sites. The U.S. academic community might also make a significant contribution to development efforts within the United States by providing a vehicle for the "reverse" transfer of the many creative technologies and methodologies employed at the local level overseas.

Over the past ten years, U.S. government studies have repeatedly recommended that full-time AID staff, rather than U.S. consultants, assume major responsibility for development assistance functions. The Babb task force also emphasized that ". . . project design and implementation must be done by people who understand the problems of the poor and who can provide the proper professional advice. AID needs . . . planners," its report continued, "with an ability to work with cultural, social, and economic systems of developing countries" (Babb, p. IV–9). As the task force stressed, these people should be located as close to the project sites as circumstances permit.

Little action on those measures has been taken by AID since Babb submitted his task force's report to the AID Administrator in 1977. OTA recently reported that AID's effectiveness in the Sahel is constrained by internal factors that often render its contact with beneficiaries and counterparts inadequate. "Cultural and linguistic barriers, far beyond French language skills, face AID staff and contractors. . . . While dialog is difficult enough at the level of national development agencies, the communication gap increases at the village level . . ." (OTA, p. 102).

According to AID insiders, some progress has been made in this regard in recent years, as the Agency has hired more people who have served in the Peace Corps or who have had similar experience living and working among the poor. There is no reason, however, that such local-level experience (perhaps a minimum of one year) should not become a requirement for employment with AID. Tens of thousands of Americans now have such a background and thus possess an understanding of Third World realities that others lack. Indeed, entering the aid and development fields without an extended hands-on experience is much like practicing medicine without the benefit of a residency.

The stationing of AID personnel in provincial centers will, in fact, far more likely attract individuals who have lived in poor communities. These Americans can even be recruited locally, bringing firsthand knowledge of local conditions to the AID mission; further education in specific technical areas could be provided by AID. Their lower expectations in terms of salary and local amenities would help to reduce the high cost, for which AID has often been criticized, of maintaining employees in the field. For those already on AID staff, their relocation to provincial sites (and retraining where necessary) would provide them with a critically important perspective that they may have hitherto lacked. Those who do not wish to move so close to the development process would leave openings for the "new blood" for which AID observers have called for years.

## CONGRESSIONAL RESPONSIBILITIES

Because the foreign aid bill is one of the few tangible handles that the principal foreign affairs committees have on international policy, its passage has become a priority item. Similarly, the White House is generally more concerned in the end with having a foreign aid program, which it can use to advance its policies, than with many of the specifics of the bill. The result is usually a series of compromises reflected in legislation (if, in fact, legislation can be passed) that, in advancing both developmental and non-developmental objectives, is fraught with inconsistencies and contradictions. Each new amendment to the now mammoth Foreign Assistance Act of 1961, either, depending upon one's viewpoint, clarifies AID's mandate or adds to the confusion.

Guy Gran, a leading world-systems analyst, captures this problem in his review of AID's legislative mandate:

Following the paragraphs of participatory rhetoric in Section 102, there are twelve principles enumerated which are supposed to be applied to achieve the development objectives of the preceding paragraphs. It is no wonder the Executive Branch is confused. Some of the principles do not logically relate to the goals and, in fact, would contribute to antithetical goals. In addition many of the principles are mutually conflicting. An Executive Branch official can find any policy guidance desired if he or she reads long enough. . . . [A]id legislation, misconceived or contradictory, has created myriad opportunities for donor agency officials to pursue whatever policy is convenient (Gran, *Development by People,* pp. 47–49).

Furthermore, Gran explains, it is clear to the executive branch that Congress does not insist upon the application of some of the principles. Nor does Congress explain either how to apply these principles or how to translate its policy statement promoting participatory development into the design, implementation, and evaluation of projects (Gran, pp. 49–51).

Clearly, a new Development Assistance Act is required that, in addition to authorizing the creation of an autonomous bilateral aid institution—the Administration for International Development— defines its mandate in simple, short, and unambiguous terms. Through this legislation Congress would, as mentioned earlier, establish a policy framework within which AID would operate. It would also exercise its oversight function and receive notification and summaries of all projects supported, but it would not involve itself in the review and approval of programs and projects. This would be left to those more experienced within the new development assistance administration. Congress would maintain, of course, extensive and direct influence over the non-developmental aid program that would be operated by the State Department. This program would ideally take the form of an agency, as AID is at present, and would be required to report to Congress as diligently as AID does today.

For all AID's reporting, Congress has not been able to effectively exercise its oversight responsibilities. Committee and subcommittee staffs are too small, overburdened with other issues, and, for the most part, inexperienced in hands-on aid and development work to ensure that AID fully and faithfully follows its mandate. While the General Accounting Office has been effective in monitoring some aid flows, it has not, by and large, demonstrated a strong capacity in the monitoring and assessment of support programs for participatory development. The Office of Technology Assessment, on the other hand, has demonstrated such a capability, but would have to undergo some changes to enable it to play a more significant role in this area. The upgrading of OTA's capacity and the establishment of an aid oversight subcommittee in each house of Congress, staffed with people experienced in participatory development, would help to keep AID more accountable to the Third World poor and the U.S. taxpayer until a new aid structure is established.

**RECOMMENDATIONS**

1. Congress should pass a Development Assistance Act, authorizing the  creation of an autonomous bilateral development assistance institution known as the Administration for International Development (AID). As an independent government corporation, the Administration would be structurally protected from day-to-day political interference. Congress should define the new institution's mandate in simple, unambiguous terms and establish a clear policy framework. It should thereafter limit its involvement to appropriations and oversight functions.

2. The Administration's mandate should be strictly developmental in nature. Clarity of purpose and structural independence would enable the new institution to make funding decisions on a developmental rather than political basis, to underwrite self-determined development processes, and to promote long-term, sustainable development relevant to the needs and circumstances of the poor.

3. The new Administration should have a board of directors that is able to serve as an effective shield against politicization and special interests. A nine-person board, elected to six-year staggered terms, would ideally consist of the presidents of three regional development foundations and a new PVO foundation; a current and former cabinet member (including a Secretary of State); two non-governmental leaders, such as the head of an ecumenical church body and a university president; and a Third World representative possessing U.S. citizenship who has worked directly with poor communities overseas. While the President of the United States

would nominate the board members, the board's chair should be selected to a specified term by the board itself from among all the board members, with the exception of the two cabinet officers, so as to ensure a development rather than foreign-policy focus by the institution.

4. Aid for political and security purposes should still be provided, but it should be designated as such and kept separate legislatively and administratively from development assistance. The State Department should control and manage those Economic Support Fund resources designated for non-developmental purposes and should be prohibited from utilizing these funds to influence development policy. AID should determine and control the application of ESF development assistance money, as well as all local currencies generated by the ESF program as long as it is not accountable to the State Department for their use. Rather than continuing to integrate military assistance, ESF, and development assistance in a single foreign aid bill, Congress should allow the development assistance program to stand and be judged on its own.

5. AID should utilize a mixture of program and project aid. It should provide program assistance on a multi-year basis to those governments and agencies thereof which have exhibited a commitment to a form of development that directly involves and benefits the poor and a capacity to promote it; these recipients might be designated "program" countries. This status should be denied those countries whose governments Congress determines to be human-rights violators. National-level policy changes leveraged by the transfer of program aid for balance-of-payments and related purposes should be informed by organizations representing the poor, while local currencies generated by the sale of dollars should be managed by those local institutions that have incorporated the poor in the design and implementation of development activities.

6. Those countries not designated as "program" countries should receive project aid on an institution-by-institution basis. The new bilateral aid institution should build upon the work of U.S. PVOs and regional development foundations by supplying significant financial support on relatively soft terms to effective local NGOs as they evolve into mature institutions. It should assist both public- and private-sector institutions in accordance with their experience in participatory development and their capacity to manage funds.

7. AID should select the most capable implementing institutions from among all public and non-governmental

organizations if project effectiveness is to be maximized. Where national and local governments are not promoting equitable development, the institutional choice should be made within the non-governmental sector; if government were to oppose this action, AID should withhold funding from that country rather than invest in a public institution that would use its assistance to perpetuate inequities. Repressive governments on the left and right should be refused aid, but support for NGOs in all countries should be considered a viable option if they are free to serve their constituencies. Those governments that refuse to permit AID to operate in their countries should be denied political aid from the State Department. Aid should be available to institutions in all Third World countries, regardless of the latters' income levels.

8. A government's efforts to narrow the wealth and income gaps between the rich and the poor should be the principal factor in determining the allocation of bilateral aid funds to Third World public institutions. Additional evidence of government concern for the less privileged segments of the population are free-functioning popular organizations. Furthermore, there should be evidence that those to be affected by programs and projects supported by U.S. aid participate in their planning and implementation. These and related standards should be stated explicitly as policy by the new AID.

9. As parts of a smaller and leaner AID, the planning and support bureaus in Washington should be substantially reduced in size and their activities severely circumscribed. No specific policies, programs, or projects for implementation in the Third World should emanate from Washington, but instead should be developed in each country mission or regional office, where local realities can inform them. The main role of AID/Washington should be to assume a responsive posture vis-à-vis the field missions within a broad policy framework.

10. On each continent, AID should have regional offices, which should be small and provide administrative and logistical support. Their programmatic responsibilities should be limited to occasional reviews of projects to ensure their consistency with AID's mandate.

11. AID's principal programmatic responsibility should be centered in subregional, or "cluster" offices, established between the regional and country offices. These intermediary structures would group countries by their proximity and their ecological and ethnological similarities. The proximity of the countries in each cluster would offer staff a first-hand view of virtually all projects and facilitate the transfer of learning across national lines. In many

cases, they would be responsible for secondary project and programmatic reviews, as well as final determinations of funding and funding policy. Technical expertise that cannot be afforded at the mission level should reside in these offices.

12. Each country mission should have a small core staff in the capital, including people with a deep understanding of that particular country. They should provide support when requested by field personnel and should serve on a project review board. Most of the mission staff should be organized in small groups and based in provincial centers. They should assess the legitimacy and effectiveness of institutions, particularly those that do or could play a role in national development programs, and build upon the funding of smaller donors by providing support for endeavors undertaken at a multi-village or regional level.

13. Prior local-level field experience should become a requirement for employment at AID. The stationing of AID personnel in provincial centers should attract individuals who have lived in poor communities. Present staff willing to continue with the new aid institution would gain critically important development perspectives through their relocation.

14. AID's field personnel should participate, along with representatives from each country's popular organizations, in AID's own program and policy planning sessions. This planning should also incorporate well versed representatives from U.S. PVOs, other Northern NGOs, and U.S. regional foundations. With their involvement, AID could formulate country assistance plans based upon projections of the capacity and needs of effective development institutions that might receive AID support.

15. The new AID should also call on these smaller Northern organizations for assistance in establishing a participatory process for formulating its positions for its "policy dialogue" with government. Regular meetings should be facilitated with local groups to elicit their input.

16. AID's country budgets should be established on the basis of its participatory planning process, and Congress should allow unutilized funds to be carried forward from year to year. Investments in large and ineffective government agencies should be replaced with support for more democratic institutions in the public and non-governmental sectors, with the level of funding based upon their absorptive capacities. Such a funding shift, a streamlining of AID, and the relocation of mission personnel should allow for smaller AID budgets in the short to medium term.

17. Congress should eliminate the functional accounts to allow the new aid organization to respond faithfully, rapidly, and comprehensively to evolving needs and opportunities. Until AID attains an independent status and freedom from political interference, however, minimum levels of expenditures should be established in specific social and economic sectors, with sufficient unearmarked monies left for purposes of flexibility in funding.

18. AID should also be freed, to the maximum extent possible, from congressional mandates relating to the purchase of U.S. goods. Preference should be given in the use of aid monies to the purchase of appropriate goods and services at relatively low prices in the aid-receiving country and from other Third World countries. Aid should be tied to the purchase of U.S. exports only where Northern resources are required and the United States can offer a product that is competitive in terms of price and relevance.

19. Preference should be given to the contracting of local consultants and other Third World firms and individuals so as to more consistently tap more relevant expertise. Third World institutions should also be allowed greater control over the identification and selection of contractors. Similarly, U.S. universities should assume a less direct role and should work collaboratively with a range of local institutions in supporting, upgrading, and drawing upon local knowledge and techniques.

20. Congress should establish aid oversight subcommittees in each house and/or upgrade the oversight capabilities of the Office of Technology Assessment so as to hold AID more accountable to the poor and U.S. taxpayers until a new aid structure is created.

# FIVE

# Foundations for
# a New Aid Structure

As discussed in Chapter 4, the establishment of a restructured AID as an independent public institution with its own governing body is not without precedent in the U.S. development assistance community. Late in 1969, Congress, frustrated by its inability to make AID responsive to the poor in Latin America, authorized the creation of the Inter-American Social Development Institute (ISDI). The Inter-American Foundation (IAF), as ISDI was renamed in 1972, celebrated in 1986 fifteen years of operations, during which time it provided over 2,000 grants in support of the development activities of some 1,700 non-governmental organizations in Latin America and the Caribbean. The IAF's success provided a model for the creation of the African Development Foundation, which was established by Congress in late 1980 and commenced operations in 1984.

The IAF has made significant contributions to the development of poor communities, and the ADF, in its infancy, is beginning to do the same. Just as important, their efforts, responsive as they are to the undertakings of the poor themselves, represent to the people of Latin America and Africa a respectful recognition, on the part of the U.S. government, of their right, need, and capacity to define their own development and forge the future course of their societies. As such, these regional foundations constitute a model upon which the operations of the entire U.S. development assistance program should be fashioned. At the same time, the work of these relatively small risk-taking public funders to identify and strengthen local institutions should, ideally, be built upon by AID and other large aid organizations.

The very existence of the IAF and ADF is a surprise to many people in the Third World who did not believe that the United States government could separate its short-term foreign policy interests from its support for development. The founders of the two institutions clearly understood that their independence from the pursuit of non-developmental objectives depended upon a structural autonomy. The creators of the IAF had witnessed the failure of AID to use the Alliance for Progress program to assist the organizations of the poor, as well as AID's translation of Congress' Title IX initiative into endeavors on the periphery of its mainstream operations. They recognized that a congressional mandate to help the poor would, in and of itself, have limited impact on an aid institution that was not protected from external pressures. Hence, the establishment of ISDI (IAF) as a public corporation with its own board of directors was essential.

### FORGING INTER-AMERICAN FOUNDATION INDEPENDENCE

Yet, the provision of an independent structure and a developmental mandate is not sufficient to ensure that a new institution will faithfully pursue that mandate, much less achieve its objectives. The IAF's founding legislation established a seven-person board of directors of which four were to come from the private sector and three from government. Although they were to serve staggered six-year terms to prevent politicization, there was no way to prevent the White House from nominating a board (to be confirmed by the Senate) that was dedicated to pursuing the Administration's foreign policy agenda. To the credit of the Nixon Administration, it did not do so. As Robert Mashek relates in *The Inter-American Foundation in the Making,* initial opposition from the Administration to ISDI and efforts by the White House personnel office to name board members on the basis of political patronage were overcome by National Security Council (NSC) staff members (Mashek, *Foundation,* pp. 21–23).

In the summer of 1970, the President nominated a board of seven Republicans to govern the new institution. What characterized the nominees far more than did their party affiliation, however, was their commitment to the mandate and integrity of the IAF, their familiarity with the context in which the Foundation would function, and, perhaps most importantly, a recognition of the limitations of their own knowledge. As people of stature and integrity unmotivated by private gain or personal political advantage, the original board members (and most of their successors) took the responsibilities of their new unpaid positions seriously. Led by its chair, Augustin Hart, Jr., the board provided a framework and a protective shield within which the management and staff of the IAF could focus on the problems of Latin America and the Caribbean rather than those of Washington.

As important as the board was to the success of the Foundation, the IAF would have struggled to assert its independence were it not for its congressional sponsor, Rep. Dante Fascell. As chair of the House Subcommittee on Inter-American Affairs, Fascell understood from the beginning the nature and significance of this initiative urged by his advisors. He adroitly forged bipartisan support for it, repelled the Administration's efforts to thwart it, and secured $50 million in multi-year public funding that would, in spite of subsequent OMB interventions, facilitate the Foundation's planning. In addition, Fascell has not, from the IAF's inception, intervened in its internal operations and has opposed all efforts to do so or to use the Foundation to promote special interests.

The third critical factor in the Foundation's success was the selection of its president. Aware of the limitations of their knowledge of the field, desirous of identifying the best possible person for the job, and committed to preventing political interference from the White House and other sources, the board hired a management consultant firm to conduct a search for candidates. In the end, the board chose William Dyal, Jr., although no board member had known of him previously and had made no inquiries into any political party affiliations he might have. This selection was a reflection of the professionalism of the board and, as the future would demonstrate, constituted a great leap towards the fulfillment of the Foundation's mandate.

The board had taken several months to refine the new institution's mandate, select its chief executive officer, and establish a framework for operations. It was time well spent. In May 1971, the board officially set the policies and guidelines for the organization's operations. It committed the IAF to supporting the change process in the region within each country's cultural patterns and traditions through the implementation of a program aimed at generating a more equitable distribution of income and greater opportunity for participation. The Foundation would be responsive to the region's needs as perceived by its people and as evidenced by their actions, rather than as defined by U.S. groups and individuals. Support would be provided only to Latin American and Caribbean autonomous non-governmental organizations, which would be responsible for their relations with their governments. The IAF would operate openly, but would not solicit government support or approval of projects or institutions.

The principal criterion for selecting projects would be their probable effectiveness in fostering structural changes and institutional development, and thus the IAF would respond to endeavors with such promise rather than focus on particular sectors or program categories. The board gave priority to innovative social development projects and encouraged experimentation through pilot projects. The Foundation would educate itself by evaluating these endeavors and determining what lessons could be derived from them. It would facilitate the flow of information among projects so as to foster the replication and adaptation of projects.

Mashek explained the significance of this unique board posture:

> With these decisions, the ISDI directorate radically altered the terms by which governmental agencies dealt with their clienteles. It put severe restraint on its own exercise of the power that accompanies the purse. It held the responsibility to make choices in funding. However, it decided to support programs planned by others, along broadly defined criteria, without interference in the design or the implementation. While other entities may have professed to do the same, their criteria were so specific as to be impositional. ISDI virtually foreswore the kind of programming and planning by which a bureaucracy decides what it, and by extension others, should do. ISDI's "program" was to be not so much what it was doing but what others, outside its control, were doing to build better lives for themselves (Mashek, p. 46).

## STRUCTURING FOR RESPONSIVENESS

An organization dedicated to the support of participatory development and social change endeavors will be only as successful as its staff is adroit at identifying and building confidences with community groups and popular organizations. As the IAF was not in the business of creating its own program, it was fully dependent on its project staff to provide the inputs for in-house analysis and review. More than a few people had warned that there simply were not enough viable local development organizations in Latin America for the Foundation to succeed in its mission. Most of these people had never worked at the grassroots. The IAF hired people who had such experience, people of sensitivity, and, most importantly, decentralized responsibility to them, demonstrating a trust that fostered risk taking and intensive, successful searches for creative initiatives.

Dyal explained that, as incoming president of the Foundation, ". . . I knew I wanted listeners, people who were open and could identify with others . . . I wanted a balance between cultural sensitivity and toughmindedness . . . people who could sit in the ambassador's office in the morning and talk to him and who then could get into a jeep or climb on a mule and in a few hours be in a campesino's house and be equally at home there" (Breslin, *Development and Dignity*, p. 13).

The IAF became an exciting and creative workplace. That it has remained so for so long and through an intense political trauma is in good part due to the Foundation's original staffing pattern and decisionmaking structure. Project staff traveled to the field on a regular basis, as it continues to do, returning with proposals from organizations with which they had become familiar. The proposals were reviewed and discussed by the regional team, composed of the IAF's representatives for the countries in a particular geographic region. It was at this level that most of the decisions on funding were made, because it was at this level that the Foundation's greatest expertise on a particular grant resided. For a particularly creative period during the IAF's earlier history a program director reviewed most projects with the regional team in an effort to enhance the consistency of decisionmaking and to achieve breakthroughs in understanding about social change. Only funding requests over a certain level were sent to the president and the board for approval, who relinquished this responsibility as the Foundation quickly matured.

Through the years the IAF has funded a wide array of initiatives at the community, regional, and national levels, as it has sought to engender a dynamic and an institutional base for constructive nonviolent change in the hemisphere. It has provided its grants to organized groups, small and large, so that this basis for change will be in place after project funding has expired. The IAF's grantees have ranged from small groups of peasants involved in self-help activity at the community level to national-level organizations that provide support to many such initiatives. The Foundation has supported projects backed by conservative businessmen and others by progressive priests where they have left direction and control of the development initiatives in the hands of the participants.  The fact that the IAF funded in Chile during both the Allende and Pinochet years and in Nicaragua before and after 1979 is a reflection of both an absence of ideology from its funding and its appreciation of peoples' needs and struggles under all forms of government.

Nor has the Foundation given preference to any particular sector or field of activity.  Because it has understood that the solutions to development problems must emerge from the people themselves if meaningful change is to occur, the IAF has remained responsive to them throughout its history while ignoring the latest fashions in development continually defined by the aid establishment.  Similarly, it has understood that learning should be based not on experiences in specific sectors but rather on lessons drawn by development organizations on the processes of development and social change, institution building, and an appropriate role for outside assistance.

The Foundation's responsive, respectful, and low-profile approach and the quality of its funding has earned it the respect of the people in the region and bipartisan support in Congress.  This support has been enhanced by the IAF's relatively low overhead. By concentrating its resources in the program area and streamlining its non-essential functions, it has been able to maintain its overhead at between 10 and 20 percent of its overseas funding during virtually its entire history.

## THE DEFENSE OF AUTONOMY

This is not to say that the Foundation has not had its problems. Particularly during the height of dictatorships in Latin America, it has had to use all its skills in asserting its independence in funding. Some U.S. ambassadors, accustomed to controlling all aspects of U.S. public interaction on their turf, have also challenged the Foundation's independence.  At home, it has had to fight its political battles without the constituencies that other aid organizations have cultivated through the use of the purse strings.  It has reserved its funding for the poor in Latin America and the Caribbean and expanded its funding base for a period of time by negotiating the unconditional use of, and control over, local currency reflows from Alliance for Progress loans.

Although it was not apparent at the time, the Foundation's most serious problems began in 1978 when the Carter White House named as the new board chair a Democrat formerly prominent in the aid field. He, in turn, oversaw the selection of a clearly identifiable Democrat as Foundation president in 1980. The new president showed himself to be highly capable and did nothing himself to politicize the Foundation. Yet, his appointment angered the critics and enemies of the IAF and set a dangerous precedent that would lead to his forced resignation three years later and plunge the Foundation into crisis.

A major shortcoming in the IAF's board structure is that, with three public-sector seats turning over with a change in Administrations, the White House could gain and exercise control of the seven-person board within two years. By late 1983, the Reagan White House, lacking the internal constraint present during the Nixon years, had done just that. The Reagan appointees on the board, steadily increasing their majority, have spent the ensuing years in an unsuccessful effort to tie the Foundation's funding into the Administration's foreign policy agenda.

There are several reasons for its failure to do so. First, and foremost, the Foundation staff, particularly its project personnel, have maintained a high level of professionalism and commitment under the most trying of circumstances and have held the IAF to its mandate. Second, supporters on the outside, including The Development GAP, have, through Congress and the press, brought public scrutiny to bear on the board's efforts. Finally, and perhaps most significantly for this treatise, the very structure of the Foundation has made it difficult for even its board to divert it from its mandate. Unlike AID, whose lack of autonomy exposes it to non-developmental interests in this country which effectively dictate from above the responses of its bureaucracy, the IAF's operations are driven by the inputs (i.e., participatory project proposals) that enter from below. The responsive posture and decentralized decisionmaking structure adopted by the Foundation at its inception have reinforced this fundamental strength. Together, they make the IAF an important model for other development assistance institutions.

## THE BIRTH OF THE AFRICAN DEVELOPMENT FOUNDATION

The success of the Inter-American Foundation and the potential significance of a counterpart institution for Africa led the founders of The Development GAP in the mid-1970s to explore the possibility of establishing such an organization. Its significance lay both in the impact that it could have among the poor in Africa and in the second cornerstone that it would represent in the building of a more responsive and relevant U.S. bilateral aid program. The Development GAP hoped that its creation would constitute a vehicle for the education of policymakers about the transformations required in the U.S. aid structure. Just as importantly, a public institution that supported what Africans were defining and doing for themselves could help establish relationships of mutual respect and trust at a time when the profile of the United States in Africa was beginning to rise.

In late 1975, the IAF put The Development GAP in touch with individuals in the long-term planning unit of AID's Africa Bureau who had been contemplating a similar initiative. Following consultations, and with the subsequent encouragement of the Senate Subcommittee on Foreign Assistance, The Development GAP took responsibility for the development of the concept and its translation into a concrete reality. By 1977, legislation had been produced mandating the establishment of the African Development Foundation. During the first half of the year, the bill was introduced by Representatives Don Bonker and Cardiss Collins and by Senators Edward Kennedy and George McGovern.

In drafting the bill with congressional and AID colleagues, The Development GAP drew upon the IAF's founding legislation, refinements in its mandate made subsequently by its board, lessons learned from a half dozen years of IAF operational experience, and the differing realities of the African development context to shape a clear and precise mandate for the new Foundation's leadership. In so doing, care was taken to restrict ADF support to African organizations (the IAF had been deluged at its start by requests from U.S. PVOs), specifically those that, as the legislation designated, are "representative of the needs and aspirations of the poor . . ." for the principal purpose of fostering ". . . local development institutions and the support of development efforts initiated by communities themselves." The legislation directed the ADF to ". . . give priority to projects which community groups undertake to foster their own development and in the initiation, design, implementation, and evaluation of which there is the maximum feasible participation of the poor."

In order to reduce the potential, exhibited in the case of the IAF, for the politicization of the board of directors, the ADF legislation authorized that two, rather than three, members of the seven-person board be officials of the government. As events would subsequently demonstrate, even this arrangement is no guarantee against politicization by the Administration that nominates all seven members of the original board. With the exception of a $250,000 per project ceiling being placed on individual ADF grants, no substantive changes were made in the original legislation. While opposing this restriction at the time, The Development GAP later recognized its importance in lowering the political profile of the initiative.

### BASIS FOR A NEW RELATIONSHIP IN AFRICA

To provide the substantive rationale for the legislation, The Development GAP prepared and published a report during 1977 that was later reissued under the title of *The African Development Foundation: A New Institutional Approach to U.S. Foreign Assistance to Africa.* Unable to convince funders of the importance of consulting Africans on the ground about the need, nature, and potential viability of the ADF, The Development GAP interviewed a number of African ambassadors to the United States, among the many people consulted for the study. Their uniform enthusiasm for the proposal undermined the contention of ADF opponents that African governments would not permit a public aid organization to operate independently in their countries. The short history of the ADF in Africa has since demonstrated that governments, if kept apprised by the ADF of its activities, are, in fact, appreciative of the non-directive and sensitive funding posture of the Foundation.

The Development GAP report emphasized that any attempt to establish mutually respectful relationships in Africa must:

> (1) recognize the unparalleled diversity and transitional nature of the present African situation; (2) honestly represent, both in deed and attitude, a recognition of the competence and responsibility of the African people to determine . . . their own state of affairs; and (3) entail . . . development assistance geared toward the search for authentically African models of development (O'Regan, et al., *The African Development Foundation*, p. 7).

"The importance of the self-development process in Africa," the report continued, calls for a new mode of foreign assistance which incorporates the insights of our past experience into the attempt to build upon the inherent strength, stability and competency of the African people. Such initiatives must take shape as part of a reorientation of our African development assistance programs—a reorientation based upon a number of underlying considerations of particular relevance to that continent.

First, we must place much greater emphasis on the processes of social development, i.e., on the development of the human resource and organizational capacities needed to understand, adapt, control, and carry out the economic and technical aspects of development per se.

Second, we must greatly diversify both our approach to the delivery of assistance and the types of assistance offered so that they correspond to the diversity of settings and approaches encountered in self-development projects in Africa.

Third, we must *directly reach* and *assist* innovative and forceful initiatives and institutions which will enhance the self-sustainment of indigenous development efforts.

And fourth, since we lack significant experience in this approach to development in Africa, we must discover both the diverse methods of self-development and the most suitable means of supporting them. These discoveries can only come about through an experimental "learn as you do" process and an increasing awareness of our own ethnocentric values (O'Regan, et al., *Foundation*, pp. 16–17).

The ADF is now translating these words into reality. Its approach, from the perspective of Africans, contrasts sharply and refreshingly with the sometimes patronizing attitudes and style of the aid establishment. These attitudes were reflected recently in the Report of the Committee on African Development Strategies, which contended that "[t]here is a new mood of realism in Africa—a willingness to enter into a tough analysis of past mistakes and present confusion, a sobriety that verges on humiliation." Africans, the report continues, "are looking, frequently Westward, for new ideas" (*Compact*, p. 11).

Contrary to this claim and that of early skeptics that there were few local organizations for an ADF to fund, the most innovative and significant development ideas and activities have been emerging from the local level and from a new generation of experienced and dedicated young Africans. The ADF, like the responsive funders within the North American and European NGO communities, is supporting this creativity, and may find, as the IAF did when it became well known across Latin America, that the very existence of a supply of funds can stimulate new grassroots initiatives and an increased demand for those resources.

**OBSTACLES TO THE RELATIONSHIP**

Although the ADF has a natural constituency among the people of Africa and its mandate is consistent with citizen preference in this country for the provision of aid directly to the poor, it has not received active support in the aid community or in policy centers. The reasons for this reflect some of the deep-seated problems in the development assistance field, problems encountered through the years by the IAF as well. When legislation appeared that reserved all ADF grants for African development groups, few U.S. PVOs supported it despite the benefits it might offer their African counterparts. Similarly, the sections of the bill that placed decisions regarding procurement, technical assistance, evaluations, and research in the hands of grantees and other Africans, cost the ADF an active constituency among exporters, contractors, consulting firms, universities, and other research institutes. OMB opposed it because it could not see that it represented, in the long term, a potential cut in aid rather than an increase. The State Department did not wish to have a U.S. public institution in Africa that it could not force to comply with its foreign policy agenda. AID quietly opposed the creation of a new institution which reflected on its own inability to deliver assistance to grassroots initiatives.

In Congress the situation was somewhat different. Fears and mistrust among different groups slowed the movement of the bill, as did the absence of a large active lobby and the preoccupation of the Senate Foreign Relations Committee with a series of major foreign policy issues. Yet, the decentralized, low-cost, direct-aid approach promised for the ADF, bolstered by the track record of the IAF, was appealing to congressional liberals and conservatives alike. Through the efforts of Don Bonker, with the backing of Cardiss Collins and her staff, the ADF legislation gained support. This support was adroitly broadened and galvanized by Rep. William Gray III after he and Bonker reintroduced the bill in 1979. With a coalition of Democrats and Republicans behind it and with the active support of the House Africa Subcommittee staff, the ADF proposal became part of the 1981 foreign aid bill. With the passage of the latter in December 1980, Congress had authorized the Foundation's establishment.

The process of winning congressional approval was long, intense, and arduous, but the legislation had emerged unscathed. Three more years were to pass, however, before the ADF became a reality, as the Reagan Administration attempted to prevent its establishment. Twice the White House tried to rescind the Foundation's entire appropriations and both times it was rebuffed by Republicans and Democrats. By 1983, the still nonexistent ADF had accumulated $4.5 million for future use. House members next had to send a warning to AID to put an end to its programmatic planning for the ADF and to leave that function for its board of directors. Finally, the White House delayed almost three years in nominating a board. It is clear that, given the absence of language in the ADF legislation setting a time frame for board nominations, those delays might have lasted much longer were it not for the persistence of some congressional members.

The White House did, in fact, finally nominate board members in 1983, but it did so on a purely political basis. While Congress could not prevent this, the Senate could have rejected the nominations. It did not do so. As a result, the ADF had a board whose five private-sector members had virtually no Africa or Third World development experience among them. Not recognizing this limitation, bowing to political pressure, and rejecting advice to seek professional assistance in the search for a president, the board chose for that position a person without aid, development, or managerial experience but with conservative Republican credentials. If the White House had wanted the ADF to fail, it could not have chosen a better script. The situation inside the Foundation quickly became politicized and deteriorated rapidly. Finally, outside intervention to force changes in the ADF leadership was required to save the Foundation itself.

This experience reflects two unfortunate realities. One is that any given Administration, if it is intent on doing so, can quickly politicize a new public aid organization, its statutory autonomy notwithstanding. Second, the creation of a truly independent institution geared specifically to help the poor overseas and the subsequent protection of that independence demand constant vigilance.

## PROGRESS IN THE EARLY YEARS

While the IAF was a victim of politicization efforts at the same time as was the ADF, the latter had not had the benefit of time in which to establish itself. The IAF had built a strong internal structure and decentralized systems of decisionmaking and had established relationships with organizations throughout Latin America and the Caribbean. The ADF had none of this in 1984 and thus was extremely vulnerable. Furthermore, lacking the track record and therefore the reputation of the IAF, the ADF did not have the broad constituency in Congress that the IAF had built. The ADF continues to face this situation today, and it will take time and a low-key but intensive effort to build up a record of high-quality funding in order to generate the support that it needs.

The ADF has also suffered for its early funding experience. With its first fiscal year virtually behind it before its internal crisis could be resolved, the Foundation felt that it had to make some rapid funding decisions in order to establish a measure of credibility. It had to do so, however, without having done the groundwork that has served the IAF well. Some of its early decisions reflected this. Fortunately, however, the ADF had been appropriated most of its funds on a "no-year" basis and thus could carry the unused portion forward to the next fiscal year.

The second ADF president, Leonard Robinson, Jr., possessed the experience that his predecessor had lacked, and he quickly moved to professionalize the organization. The Foundation has closely followed its congressional mandate, responding to grassroots development activity and supporting institution building in Africa, while relying upon African expertise and rebuffing U.S. special interests. The ADF is facilitating cross fertilization in learning among its grantees and broadening the scope of its funding to encompass a wider array of African-defined initiatives. To the extent that it continues to expand its funding beyond strictly economic activities and to assert its independence vis-à-vis the State Department and AID, the ADF's credibility and significance in Africa will also continue to increase. Unlike the IAF, it has taken the early step of contracting local field staff, a decision that is probably more fitting in the case of the ADF, given the development conditions and travel demands in Africa. It would be consistent with the ADF's philosophy for it to place a number of African grantees on its advisory council, as suggested in its legislative mandate. Finally, with its internal systems in place, the ADF will have to reduce its non-program overhead costs if it is to live up to its billing as a streamlined organization and expand its support base in Congress.


## LESSONS LEARNED FOR ASIA

The IAF and ADF have encountered serious difficulties during their histories, but both remain today the most effective official conduits of development assistance to the poor that the United States has ever had. As risk-taking organizations, they have, indeed, made mistakes in project selection and will continue to do so, but these errors have also been a basis for learning.

Supporters of the IAF approach had used five years of Foundation operations, and lessons learned from them, as arguments and bases for the development of a counterpart for Africa. Now a dozen more years have passed and, while the ADF experienced a difficult birth and infancy, it has survived and has begun to establish itself in Africa. Meanwhile, AID is moving away from project support and is now further removed than ever from the local level. Even a new, restructured, and autonomous aid administration would not be geared to provide the type of quick, small-scale support that regional foundations do. Clearly, a vehicle must be established that can effect the transfer of this type of support to parts of the Third World not served by the two existing foundations.

An Asian and Pacific Development Foundation (APDF) would be such a vehicle. Sixty percent of all expenditures by international NGOs has been made in Asia. This reflects not only the need that exists among the people of that continent but also the plethora of effective non-governmental organizations that exist and operate there. A relatively small share of that NGO involvement is American, however, and there is presently no public conduit for U.S. assistance to grassroots endeavors in Asia. A regional foundation initiative for the continent is overdue, but those who take that initiative have now a rich stock of experience upon which to draw.

As has been discussed in this chapter, there are a lot of "dos" and "don'ts" when it comes to establishing a new regional foundation. Those involved in the founding and operating of the IAF and ADF have learned what these are, often the hard way, and are important sources of support that can be tapped; the creation of the ADF certainly would have taken a lot more wrong turns had it not been for the advice provided by those involved with the IAF. Nor should any attempt be made to create a foundation for Asia without the direct involvement of people who have an understanding, from first-hand experience, of local-level Asian development processes. To the extent possible, Asian organizations working at that level should also be consulted, as should U.S. and other Northern NGOs working there. Finally, an initiative to create a new institution should not be undertaken unless there are people involved who are willing and able to work intensively over the long haul, not only to ensure its creation but also to protect the integrity of the concept, the legislation, and the foundation itself.

As discussed earlier, there is no way to ensure, except through the Senate confirmation process, that a capable and professional board of directors of a new Asia institution, or APDF, would be named by the White House. The involvement of insiders with these same qualities, such as those with the NSC at the time of the IAF's creation, is critically important. The President may make seven political appointments and thus put the foundation in jeopardy at the start. Any long-term damage can be minimized, however, by limiting the number of government officials on the board. The irony is that the public-sector board members have not created the major problems for the IAF and ADF. Their virtually automatic turnover, however, when Administrations change, allows a President to name a much higher percentage of board members than the drafters of the IAF legislation had apparently envisaged.

The ADF legislation, framed with the benefit of reflection on the tested strengths and weaknesses of its IAF counterpart, appears to have served the Foundation well through its early history. It should, therefore, serve as a model and provide a framework for the drafting of similar legislation for the APDF. Their general purposes, objectives, and functions should be the same, as should the restriction of funding and project-related decisionmaking to organizations of the poor. The specifics of the bill should be determined, however, by the development needs and capacities of Asia.

At first glance, there is no reason to believe that a decentralized internal decisionmaking structure would not serve an APDF well. The length of travel time to Asia may necessitate the stationing of U.S. field staff there, as the ADF has also considered. Care must be taken, however, to ensure that these personnel do not become part of any clique in-country, a fear that formed the basis of the IAF's long-time operating style. The APDF should also be careful to not overfund projects, a criticism sometimes directed at the Inter-American Foundation during its history. As it gains experience in the field, the new foundation might want to consider providing more institutional support than project funding. While such support is not a feature of IAF and ADF funding, some NGOs in Europe have found this "partnership" relationship with local organizations they have come to know well in the South to be effective and better suited to their grantees' needs.

The three regional foundations should form the basis of a new aid structure. (A fourth foundation, for the Middle East, might be necessary, if it is determined that the APDF could not effectively cover all of Asia without becoming a small bureaucracy.) By fostering the growth of indigenous representative or facilitator institutions, regional foundations help groups at the local level to gain access to appropriate assistance. As discussed earlier, these intermediary organizations may develop the capacity to operate loan funds perhaps capitalized by the foundations, and some, in fact, can evolve into sophisticated institutions with efficient mechanisms for the delivery of credits and other assistance to the local level.

Far closer communication between these foundations on the one hand, and AID, as well as the multilateral development banks, on the other, would enable the latter to provide larger-scale appropriate funding to those organizations that the foundations would help bring to their attention. At the same time, a regional foundation would be in a position to cover at least part of the pre-investment costs of important promotional, educational, or organizational efforts, which some large donors find difficult to cover through normal cost-recovery procedures. Furthermore, the foundations would be in a position to improve large-donor access to a variety of local sources of information and development knowledge that can significantly upgrade aid and development planning. Such a consultative relationship would be a boon to the large donors and, ultimately and most importantly, to the organizations of the poor in need of access to appropriate levels and forms of aid.

## RECOMMENDATIONS

1. The Inter-American and African Development Foundations should seek to improve upon their effectiveness and relationships with grantees by continuing to decentralize decisionmaking to staff closest to the field. They should also continue to build democratic internal structures to match those they expect in the organizations

they fund.

2. The IAF and ADF should take steps to maintain or achieve low-overhead, low-profile, field-focused operations that will maximize their impact overseas and generate increased congressional support.

3. The two regional foundations should refrain from defining and focusing funding on any particular sector or type of development activity. They should be fully responsive to the creativity and self-help initiatives of the poor.

4. The boards of directors of the two foundations should protect the institutions' independence and integrity and maintain a hands-off posture vis-à-vis internal decisionmaking.

5. A new Asian and Pacific Development Foundation should be established to serve as a counterpart to the IAF and ADF. The APDF would fill a gap that currently exists in the official U.S. aid structure by providing a vehicle for the transfer of public funds to participatory local-level initiatives in Asia. The Middle East could be the responsibility of the APDF or be covered by a fourth foundation.

6. An initiative to create a new institution requires a long-term, intensive involvement and constant vigilance to ensure that the integrity of the concept, the legislation, and the foundation is preserved. Such an initiative should be informed by the experience of those involved in the founding and operation of the IAF and ADF, people with direct involvement at the local level in Asia, representatives of Northern NGOs, and, foremost, Asian organizations engaged in grassroots development work.

7. The ADF legislative mandate should serve as a model for similar legislation for a new APDF. The legislation should reserve all project funding for Asian organizations that are engaged in or promote participatory development activity. The specifics of the bill should be shaped to correspond to the needs and realities of Asian societies. Funds should ideally be made available on a "no-year" basis.

8. The APDF legislation should establish a time frame for the nomination of a board of directors by the President. It should also minimize the number of public-sector representatives on the board, so as to prevent a large-scale turnover in seats with the change in Administrations.

9. Supporters of the APDF in Congress and in the executive branch should press the White House to name people of experience and integrity to the board. They should thereafter assist the board in providing the Foundation with the protective shield that it may require.

10. The board should establish the policy framework of the APDF and hire, with external, independent, professional assistance, a president experienced in the field of Asian grassroots development.

11. The president should hire a staff with a similar field background and establish a decentralized decisionmaking structure featuring regional teams to facilitate creative interaction and well informed project reviews. The APDF might want to consider the costs and benefits of placing staff in the field and/or contracting Asians to assist staff on a regional basis.

12. The APDF should support the change process in the region by being responsive to the perceived needs and development activities of the poor and their organizations. It should provide funding to organized groups so as to help engender a dynamic and an institutional base for constructive, non-violent, self-sustaining change.

13. The Foundation should take risks and should learn from any mistakes made. It should facilitate the transfer of learning among grantees, and its own learning should be based on lessons thus gained about the processes and vehicles of development and social change. It should experiment more than the IAF and ADF have done with the provision of institutional support. It should also take care not to damage organizations through overfunding.

14. The APDF, as well as the IAF and ADF, should invite representatives of grantee organizations to serve on its advisory council in order to receive important perspectives and well informed guidance on funding policy.

15. The work of the three regional foundations to identify and strengthen local institutions should be built upon by AID and other large aid organizations. The IAF, ADF, and APDF could also identify sources of input that would significantly upgrade aid planning and programming. This would require improved communication and increased interest within AID and the multilateral aid institutions in collaborating with effective non-governmental institutions.

# SIX

# Enhancement of the PVO Role

Private and voluntary organizations (PVOs) in the United States, like their non-governmental counterparts in Europe and Canada and the U.S. regional development foundations, have an important role to play in building bases for social change in the Third World. They are also well placed, as a result of their work at the grassroots level overseas, to inform the U.S. public, program officials, and policy-makers of the realities of life at that level and the impact, positive and negative, of official assistance programs. Hence, they are potentially important actors in a development assistance program designed to serve the interests of the poor rather than those of the more privileged sectors of society in both the United States and the Third World.

## THE PVO RECORD

Over the past decade, Northern voluntary organizations have played an increasingly important role in the development assistance process. In 1984, some 2,200 Northern NGOs utilized approximately $4 billion in assisting an estimated 100 million people in the Third World. This represents more than a threefold increase in expenditures since the mid-1970s. The NGO resource contribution to the total assistance effort now surpasses 10 percent of the combined annual bilateral and multilateral foreign aid budgets of the

OECD countries and nearly 20 percent of that total when the services contributed by voluntary agencies are included (van der Heijden, *Development Impact*, pp. 1–4; Smith, "U.S. and Canadian PVOs," p. 115).

Of equal note is the fact that governments and official multi-lateral sources have increased their support to the voluntary agencies tenfold over the same period. These contributions, which today constitute about one-third of NGO budgets on average, account for 4 to 5 percent of total Official Development Assistance (van der Heijden, p. 2). There are many reasons for this increase in official interest in the non-governmental sector. Failures in the development process across the Third World and on the part of donors to get a handle on the problem of poverty, as well as the need of the latter for an aid constituency in the North, certainly explain much of the interest. On the positive side, there has been a recognition that voluntary agencies can reach and assist poor populations more effectively and efficiently than can the larger, more bureaucratic aid institutions.

Able to work directly at the community level, which the larger assistance agencies can reach only indirectly, these organizations are in a position to ascertain local needs and priorities, base programs on local input, transfer technical know-how appropriate to a given setting, and organize or strengthen local institutions. At their best they are responsive, familiar with local populations, supportive of the truly poor, builders of self-reliance, flexible and innovative, participatory throughout the project cycle, and as interested in the long-term process of change as in immediate impact.

In reality, the PVO record is uneven. While an official Finnish evaluation, for example, concluded that aid channeled to and through NGOs generally reaches those in need (van der Heijden, p. 14), a look at U.S. PVO projects indicates that many do not include or benefit the poorest 40 percent of the population (Tendler, *Turning Private Voluntary Organizations*, p. iv). Other reviews reveal that the efforts of numerous organizations are not participatory (particularly in the identification and planning processes), do not sufficiently help organize and mobilize communities, are not innovative, and may unintentionally favor relatively well-to-do people by further skewing income distribution in project areas. On the other hand, administrative and managerial expenses are generally kept low, and the misuse of funds by recipient groups appears to be rare (van der Heijden, pp. 15–17; Smith, pp. 149–151). A detailed breakdown by NGO type and country of origin would make such assessments more meaningful.


## THE U.S. PVO COMMUNITY

Within the U.S. PVO community, there are many differences in style and objectives, as well as in performance. Aid analyst, Brian Smith, in his examination of North American NGOs, categorizes U.S. organizations as traditional disaster-aid agencies, technical-assistance PVOs, and institution and network builders. Several of the larger and older PVOs fall into the first category, as they address the effects of poverty with traditional tools, such as food aid; some of these, however, have been moving into other forms of development cooperation as well. A second group encompasses a new generation of smaller, mainly secular PVOs that emerged during the 1960s and 1970s and focus almost exclusively on the transfer of technical resources and skills. The third category incorporates those that build and strengthen private development institutions, as well as community organizations and networks, while responding to the needs and projects of the poor as the poor themselves define them (Smith, pp. 117, 133).

While this shift in emphasis from relief to development has taken place among PVOs in the United States since the post-war period, in important respects the style and attitudes of these organizations have not changed significantly. Only the third group of PVOs has come to view development as an essentially indigenous process of self-definition. A number of church development agencies and a few secular PVOs have maintained a consistent record of support for locally organized initiatives. A measure of support for community development and for individual capacity building is provided by members of the other two categories, but, by and large, their approach remains one of defining the local problem and solution (e.g., food aid, small-business assistance) and then involving the institution intimately in program operations.

Through the 1980s, many U.S. PVOs have continued to operate their own programs in the Third World, even in areas where considerable development capacity exists. In this respect, they differ fundamentally from most of their European counterparts. Increased U.S. government funding of their projects has further stiffened resistance to a change in this posture, as many U.S. groups rely upon these projects to generate the overhead needed to support their institutional expansion. Some have, indeed, played an important role in building indigenous non-governmental organizations, while others have responded to the demands of people locally to run their own show. But, if not as directive as they once were, there is still a tendency on the part of many in the PVO community to control the development decisionmaking process and to identify projects and needs in the sectors and in the areas in which they have expertise.

Whether these activities and needs are, in fact, the priorities of local populations, and whether the truly poor are actually benefiting from the application of their assistance, often appear to be of secondary concern to a lot of U.S. PVOS. Judith Tendler notes that many of them do not differentiate very well among the residents of poor communities, practicing as a result their own version of trickle-down development at the local level (Tendler, *Turning Private Voluntary Organizations*, p. vii). Another aid analyst, Warren van Wicklin, relates a similar view from his recent research in Central America, where he found projects of a number of U.S. PVOs, their rhetoric notwithstanding, to be controlled by local elites. When project decisionmaking is driven largely by financial concerns, there is little time or inclination for proper analysis within poor communities. Projects become too large and poorly designed, and partnerships with local organizations can become strained.

Smith reflects upon the growing uneasiness among Third World NGOs about what they see as a lack of true collaboration with North American counterparts who speak of partnership but continue to make all the key decisions themselves. He quotes Tim Brodhead of the North–South Institute in Canada, who, as former director of Inter-Pares, the Canadian Council for International Cooperation, and EuroAction-ACORD, brings an historical and in-depth perspective to this evolving issue:

> I believe NGOs in the North Atlantic region are in the twilight of their historical era. They began in the post–World War II era to bring money and resources overseas, and they encountered little resistance or critical challenge in foreign countries. Now, however, the Third World is coming of age. They have their own NGOs—and these nonprofit organizations are especially well developed in Latin America. They want to be treated as more equal partners . . . (Smith, p. 48).

On all three continents of the South, NGOs have been articulating the outlines of such partnerships. Their challenge to the North is that it relinquish control of the development process and support locally defined processes of change. This may well mean the shifting of Northern NGO resources from atomized projects to longer-term institution building, networking, analysis, and coordinated social action. In some quarters an improved flow of information between North and South is seen as necessary for relevant local NGO development programming. Northern NGOs that can respond positively to these priorities and that are willing to take risks to help achieve common goals based on common values will be considered true partners. Brodhead, as well as many people in the Third World, believe that such partnerships must include the assumption of greater responsibility by PVOs for changing public attitudes and the policies of governments and corporations in their own countries. These themes will be discussed later in this chapter.

Meanwhile, Southern NGOs are putting increasing emphasis on South–South NGO cooperation, both within a given region and across the Third World. Visits by staff, exchanges of personnel, and the transfer of technical expertise within the South are becoming Third World priorities. The flow of information among these organizations must also be facilitated. Those Northern organizations that support these and other efforts to build links within the South will be making a major contribution to their Southern partners.

## PROBLEMS IN THE AID–PVO RELATIONSHIP

As has been implied, it has been the availability of large amounts of public monies, the mechanisms and means through which they must be accessed, and the dependencies that they create that have been at the root of an evolving problem. The provision of Operational Program Grants, Development Program Grants, Matching Grants, and other public funds in the 1970s not only made many U.S. PVOs increasingly reliant on AID, but also tended to cut some off from their natural and original constituencies and broad-based support in the United States and made many of them less responsive and less accountable to the poor.

The erosion of PVO independence in the 1980s has been the inevitable result of the significant expansion of PVO relationships with AID during the 1970s and the subsequent rapid growth in PVO budgets, staff, and operations. In recent years this independence has been further compromised as a result of decisions by PVOs to package projects specifically for AID. (GAO, *AID and Voluntary Agencies,* p. 43). AID's interest in having PVOs carry out programs on its behalf also increased, particularly in countries in which the Agency had no missions or in some way felt limited in its actions. AID began to see U.S. PVOs as natural agents or extensions of its own programming rather than as independent institutions.

The U.S. Congress has recognized this threat to PVO independence. As part of Section 123, added to the Foreign Assistance Act in 1978, Congress stressed the importance of PVOs and cooperatives and warned against their compromising their "private and independent nature." Three years later, the Senate, in committee report language, noted the tendency of AID to view PVOs ". . . purely and simply as extensions of AID itself, not as development agencies with their own distinctive traditions, relationships, and styles" (GAO, *AID and Voluntary Agencies,* p.3). In its 1982 report on the AID–PVO relationship, the General Accounting Office observed that "[f]inancial dependency has led some PVOs to focus on what AID wants rather than independently identifying and responding to needs through their own networks" (GAO, *AID and Voluntary Agencies,* p.iii).

In short, by the early 1980s there was a very real fear and danger that PVOs would identify and address local development problems with a declining reliance on input from Third World NGOs and community groups. The pressure to do so has increased in the ensuing years. The AID Policy Paper on PVOs published in 1982 makes clear that all AID-financed programs must address the priorities of Third World governments, priorities which in many cases are, in fact, developed in conjunction with multilateral aid institutions and bilateral donors, including AID. Hence, in order to maintain access to AID funding, PVOs increasingly have to design projects that are consistent with the AID development model rather than objectively assess needs and realities (Schmidt, et al., *Religious Private Voluntary Organizations*).

Few PVOs protested, at least publicly, when AID officials made it clear at a meeting in the spring of 1981 that, in return for its funds, it expected political support for its budget in Congress and a responsiveness to its needs as they arose in particular countries. Today it is not uncommon for AID to request that PVOs include a specific component in their project proposals (for example, in an area to which Congress has given priority) in order to ensure funding, even if the organization has had no previous experience in that field. The fact of government intervention was confirmed by twenty of the twenty-four PVO representatives interviewed by Brian Smith for his study; they indicated that the freedom of action of their organizations was impaired as a result of their acceptance of government support. Thirteen of the twenty said that AID had pressured them on decisions regarding specific projects, and several believed that political objectives of the State Department were the cause of this pressure (Smith, p. 138).

Increasing government influence upon the operations of some PVOs is not the only problem created by dependencies on public resources. AID's overfunding of a number of groups has taxed their management capabilities, changed their institutional style, and made them more bureaucratic and unresponsive to the expressed needs of the poor overseas. According to a study prepared by the Center of Concern in 1981:

> Their energies are channeled into home office improvement—the acquisition of larger, more comfortable office space, more sophisticated management procedures, and the further accumulation of money. As these PVOs become more like AID in size and structure, they acquire the characteristics of profes-sionalism—high salaries, high overhead, and complicated technical projects that may not be applicable in the field. They lose the "voluntary" flavor and simple life style that made their work on the grassroots level so effective—and sought after by AID. The PVOs begin to design proposals for projects that will absorb money . . .

In the process, the study concludes, PVOs often have "lost touch with Third World realities" (Schmidt et al., pp. 68–69).

Such an institutional style tends to breed a change in staff perspectives and has often yielded shifts to new leadership that has little understanding of these realities. According to Smith, there is great danger in the ". . . almost unperceived attitude of deference for and even anticipation of, government wishes that has seeped into the mentality of some PVO executives and staffs, especially in the United States" (Smith, p. 157). These leaders talk of the need to pursue AID money in order to survive, but institutional survival takes on a rather odd meaning when it includes the need to protect high salaries and to maintain what have become worldwide opera-tions. Risk taking is the essence of change and development among the poor, whether it takes the form of organizing for social advance-ment or experimenting with new technologies, and it also is a critical element in the extension of Northern assistance to such en-deavors. High salaries, prestige positions, and fancy accommo-dations discourage risk taking. Slowly but surely institutional integrity and responsiveness erode and the steady process of increasing compromise unfolds.

The Development GAP's close association with PVOs over the years—through assessments of their work overseas, collaboration on projects, and the chairing of two PVO consortia committees—has brought it in contact with many dedicated professionals and institutions. It has also made it possible to witness the growing problems in some segments of the community. In 1982, The Development GAP made some of its concerns known to a congressional subcommittee that was exploring the issue of the role and financing of voluntary agencies:

> The expanded availability of AID money to U.S. PVOs in recent years has contributed significant changes in much of the PVO community. Many of these organizations have drawn on various AID funds, enabling them to grow rapidly, both in terms of the number of programs they have overseas and the size of program and support staffs. Similarly, many PVOs seek to move into new projects or new countries, not necessarily in response to the priorities of local communities, but rather out of their own institutional needs to have projects to carry out and to utilize the particular expertise they have developed. We need to know if the genesis of a project to be funded is legitimate, if the poor who will be affected see the approach taken as being consistent with their own goals and lifestyles, and if the intended beneficiaries are themselves to control the project. PVOs can get down to this level to determine these matters. If they do not, they are giving up one of their major advantages over the larger, more distant aid agencies.
>
> [T]o the extent that an expanded role for U.S. PVOs in our bilateral aid program is supported without careful consideration of the conditions of that involvement, a great disservice will be rendered to the PVO community both here and in the developing world. At this stage of our changing relationship with the peoples of the Third World, we do not need the further politicization of our aid program nor the propagation of more programs that are imposed from above or designed in accordance with the objectives of outsiders. Our goal must be to help develop, strengthen, and assist non-governmental organizations overseas that represent or respond to the needs of the poor, who often are neglected or manipulated by public-sector entities. By agreeing to help carry out AID, World Bank, and foreign government programs as a condition of major funding, U.S. PVOs would be trading off independence of action for their own financial growth and

stability. In the long term, this would be in nobody's best interest (D. Hellinger, testimony before the House [Appropriations] Subcommittee on Foreign Operations, 13 May 1981).

The Center of Concern summarized the principal problems in the PVO community in its 1981 study. It listed five major criticisms of U.S. PVOs:

- Many will work in any country, no matter the conditions, transferring a ready-made technical project
- PVOs go where the money is, leading to bad projects and often a negative impact on local populations
- Few ask if the project was initiated by the recipient community;
- There is a growing lack of accountability to taxpayers, Northern constituents, and the Third World poor
- PVOs are not challenging one another or self-criticizing (Schmidt et al.)

The Center's first criticism relates to a phenomenon found far more commonly in the United States than in other Northern countries. While there are numerous examples of U.S. PVOs, particularly in the church community, that seek, as their primary institutional goals, to support the emergence and expansion of indigenous organizations and to respond to the self-determined priorities of beneficiary groups, there are a steadily growing number of PVOs that concentrate their efforts in sectoral areas that are the conceptual creations of the aid community. "Functionally specific organizations," says Jorgen Lissner in his 1977 book on voluntary agencies, "are so absorbed by their particular objectives that they lose sight of the wider social context in which they exist; by singling out one particular set of problems for treatment, they promote an unfortunate compartmentalization of reality." According to Lissner, they ". . . offer 'one-dimensional' cures for highly complex ills . . ." (Lissner, *The Politics of Altruism*, p. 284).

This lack of commitment to the local definition of problems and solutions on the part of a broad segment of the U.S. PVO community represents a significant obstacle to the establishment of a truly effective development aid program. PVOs are not only best placed among all U.S. assistance organizations to build local development support institutions where there are none in the Third World and to provide appropriate technical assistance where requested, but they are also in a position to transmit their grassroots knowledge about the development and aid processes in the countries in which they work to other assistance agencies and the general public in the North. In order to have the major impact on the development process that many PVOs say they are seeking, these institutions need to strengthen local organizational structures overseas, educate the large donors about alternative aid channels, and advise program officers, policymakers, and the U.S. public about the effectiveness or counterproductiveness of the programs and policies supported by these donors.

Without fundamental changes in the U.S. foreign assistance structure, in the manner in which PVOs are supported, and in the criteria upon which that support is provided, there is little chance that this responsibility will be taken on by many groups. Commenting on the growing threat to the autonomy of many Northern NGOs, Jan Pronk, then deputy secretary general of UNCTAD and former head of the Dutch bilateral aid program, declared at a UN/NGO conference in December 1982 that

> the corruption of NGOs will be the political game in the years ahead—and it is already being played today. . . . NGOs have created a huge bureaucracy, employment is at stake, and contacts in developing countries are at stake. It will become impossible for them to criticize governments for decreasing the quality of the overall aid programme. NGOs will lose in the years ahead . . . they will be corrupted in the process, because they will receive enough money for their own projects but the rest of the aid programme will suffer (Pronk, "Opening Address").

Efforts to deal with these problems have been consistently insufficient. The 20 percent rule, for example, which dictates that PVOs must receive at least one-fifth of their funds from non-U.S. government sources, is a step in the right direction, but it does not go nearly far enough. Not only can AID exempt from the calculations those contributions it makes to PVOs for activities that it has initiated for its own purposes, but it is quite clear that it is difficult for any organization to follow an independent path when considerably more than half of its budget is financed from one source. This is particularly so when that source is a U.S. government agency linked to the State Department.

## CHARTING A NEW COURSE

Despite these shortcomings in the U.S. PVO community, some U.S. PVO and other Northern voluntary agencies can take pride in the contribution they have made to the growth of the non-governmental sector throughout the Third World. These organizations work with 10,000 to 20,000 Southern NGOs and, in good part through them, assist some 60 million people in Asia, 25 million in Latin America, and 12 million in Africa (van der Heijden, p. 2). Some observers have noted the significant impact Northern NGOs are beginning to have in such countries as Burkina Faso and Bangladesh, where collectively they are important donors in quantitative terms. Economist Albert Hirschman, who visited projects supported in Latin America by the Inter-American Foundation and PVOs, was struck by the existence of "an impressive, loosely integrated network of national and international (voluntary) organizations which, at the level of any single Latin American country, performs important functions of education, public health, housing improvement, agricultural extension, development promotion of handicraft and small business . . ." (Hirschman, *Getting Ahead Collectively*, pp. 92–93).

Still, many PVOs are seeking ways to "scale up" their activities and/or in other ways to have a broader impact overseas. Some point to the need for PVOs to become more professional—to improve their project planning, lessen their concentration on discrete projects, work more in consortia as a way of providing more comprehensive services, improve dissemination of their learning and replicability of their projects, and, of course, strengthen local NGOs—in order to have a "macro-impact" (van der Heijden, pp. 10–16). Many of these agencies, in working in partnership with Third World counterparts, have never seen grassroots projects as ends in and of themselves. Rather, they have viewed and utilized them as a means of supporting the development of community awareness, cohesiveness, organizations, capacity, and dynamism to stimulate self-sustaining change. Relatively recently, a number have begun to tackle the problem of "projectitis" by establishing long-term funding relationships with local institutions, in which the latter have greater freedom to support various activities within a broader program after a mutual confidence has been established.

In more cases than not, however, the development situation on the ground is exacerbated by government policies and donor-supported programs that overwhelm and often destroy the positive effects of local initiatives.   In a number of Third World countries, national and local governments are (perhaps imperfectly and with some difficulty) trying to respond to the aspirations of all their people or are at least open to constructive input.   In the vast majority of cases, however, governments and the less privileged of their citizens are at odds with each other, the former being under the control of local elites and/or the influence of foreign interests.   The larger assistance agencies become part of the problem when they ally themselves with these latter two groups.

In an effort to make a greater difference in the development equation, U.S. PVOs relate to these circumstances and sets of relationships in two very different ways.   There are many that have chosen to coordinate further their activities with the programs of these governments and donors, not just in isolated instances, but as a matter of policy in order to raise their involvement to a different level in these countries.   It is disturbing that so many in the PVO community have been calling for such arrangements without sufficient analysis of the terms of the relationships or their repercussions.   Hendrick van der Heijden, in an otherwise thoughtful piece on NGOs, calls for "enhancing complementarity with recipient government programmes" and closer collaboration among the parties, as "[t]his will help in enlarging the macro impact of NGO operations, and lead towards an overall increase in the effectiveness of development assistance" (van der Heijden, pp. 13, 20).

Such thinking, which is unfortunately becoming more prevalent in this country, is dangerous for the independence and long-term survival of NGO operations.   As others in the community contend, what is in question is not whether one relates to government and donor agencies—that in many instances is now almost unavoidable for PVOs and partner organizations—but, rather, the terms and the forms of the relationships that are established.   Coordination with government-controlled and -defined programs, in which PVOs can make only marginal modifications (generally limited to technical areas), will usually result in the further entrenchment of the status quo.   Government adoption and expansion of PVO programs without the integral involvement of local groups in policy setting and control will have a similar result.   There are unfortunately numerous instances of such an outcome.

A good example of the limitations and dangers of this type of coordination can be found in an AID evaluation of a rural road-building scheme in Sierra Leone.   A large U.S. PVO received an AID grant to participate in the program along with that nation's government, the World Bank, and two other external agencies. The impact of the PVO's specific contribution, which included the involvement of villagers in road construction and maintenance, was seen to be positive: improved educational and health facilities, greater access to agricultural inputs and markets, and less political siting of the road projects. On the other hand, the new roads ". . . encouraged a major shift from rice production for consumption within Sierra Leone to the production of cocoa, oil palm, peanuts, and livestock for export. Villages served by [the] roads experienced more severe rice shortages than did other villages" (Minear, "Reflections," p. 26).

A positive reference by van der Heijden to a government of Togo NGO support/liaison unit is particularly instructive. Although on the surface an apparently constructive mechanism to provide NGOs working in rural areas with support from technical ministries (van der Heijden, p. 20), this unit in fact posed a real threat to the independence of in-country NGO activities. And when the World Bank moved to establish an NGO coordinating body to facilitate an experimental program of donor financing in Togo, the government attempted to seize on the opportunity to control *all* external funding directed to NGOs in the country.

The alternative approach, pursued by many of the more responsive voluntary agencies in Europe, Canada, and the United States, has been to help local organizations leverage changes in their countries related to the programs, policies, and issues that affect their constituencies. This is usually reflected in support for the related long-term processes of institution building and empowerment. Leverage could be gained in the shorter term, however, were the larger assistance agencies, through their support and direct involvement, to legitimize the role of these local organizations in development planning. The misguided programs and policies of governments and large donors can no longer be left unaddressed by NGOs. The latter cannot afford to confine their attention to grassroots projects while the bilateral lenders and the multilateral development banks (MDBs) infuse their values, interests, and perspectives—uninformed by grassroots knowledge—into policy and program planning with government.

It is more realistic to expect that U.S. PVOs would have greater success and would expose their local counterparts to less risk if the immediate targets of their interventions were AID and those MDBs receiving U.S. government support rather than Third World governments. In most cases, this approach will be effective, as these external agencies are currently using their influence upon government programming, selection of implementing institutions, and policy formulation to shape many Third World economies. A reversal of roles is long overdue. PVOs have a responsibility to direct these aid institutions, as the latter seek more effective implementors of development projects and more relevant input for policy formulation, to indigenous organizations representing the interests of marginalized peoples. A joint PVO–AID initiative could do much to facilitate a measure of popular participation in national and local-level planning.

This is not to say that local-level and national governments overseas cannot be lobbied directly by international and local NGOs to make important changes in programming and policies. In a recent paper, Thomas Dichter, a PVO project analyst, contends that, with a professional approach and hard data, U.S. PVOs can successfully engage in policy dialogue with government. He demonstrates through case studies that it is clearly preferable and more effective that PVOs work in partnership with local organizations to develop the information and contacts required for a successful lobbying effort (Dichter, *Demystifying 'Policy Dialogue',* pp. 5–7).

While the cases cited by Dichter relate to fairly narrow, though important, changes in import, tax, and agricultural policy, PVOs must also stand ready to support their counterparts when the latter find it necessary to address the critical structural issues that constrain the advancement of their constituencies. PVOs have the responsibility, particularly now that policy dialogue is in fashion, to promote the viewpoints and interests that emerge from the local level rather than only those that are consistent with U.S. official policy or those limited primarily to their own institutional concerns. The risks PVOs must take in this regard in relationship to AID and future funding are no greater than those being assumed by project beneficiaries every day.

U.S. PVOs can play an important role in constructing the mechanisms discussed in Chapters 4 and 7 that would link AID and other agencies to effective and representative NGOs in the Third World. The efforts they have contributed to date to the maturation process of these local organizations will have greater significance if they can steer donor support away from unresponsive and ineffective agencies and, with considerable care and sensitivity, toward these more participatory and, hence, more relevant institutions. Similar mechanisms can be used for channeling local perspectives in a systematic fashion into donor programming and policy formulation decisions. In this regard, a prominent feature of legislation on development assistance to Africa that was passed by the House of Representatives in late 1987 is the requirement that AID set up such a mechanism with the help of PVOs, the African Development Foundation, and other intermediaries in every country in which AID funds on that continent.

The proposition in the AID 1982 Policy Paper on private and voluntary organizations (*A.I.D. Partnership,* p. 3) that U.S. PVOs participate in and contribute to AID's country programming process (through their involvement in the preparation of the Country Development Strategy Statements) has both great potential and real limitations. The emphasis in the plan is misplaced in two respects. First, while U.S. groups should, indeed, be involved in making their views known, their primary responsibility is to involve their Third World counterparts in the process to the maximum extent practicable. Second, while AID feels that it will profit from PVO advice, it unfortunately places greater emphasis on the advantages to be gained by PVOs from learning of the principal programming parameters in the country in which they are located and adjusting their use of AID funds accordingly. AID was also concerned at first that some PVOs would refuse to participate for fear of a loss of their own credibility, while another potential problem, noted by the GAO, was that of sectorally specific organizations distorting the assessment of local needs in the pursuit of self-interest (GAO, *AID and Voluntary Agencies,* p. 28). In the end, AID missions have not made these links a priority, and there have been, according to AID, only a few reported incidents of participation on the part of PVOs. The enactment and enforcement of legislation is clearly required in order to move AID to draw on the knowledge of local groups with the help of U.S. organizations.

It is clear that a new, public structure is required that would allow and encourage those PVOs that are interested in government support for their activities to operate independently from AID, to play an appropriate support role in the Third World, and to provide a more enlightened basis upon which our policymakers and the larger donors can design assistance programs. While PVOs must be free from political interference in the receipt and use of their public (and private) funds, there is also a pressing need to establish a sound set of operational and project criteria for those utilizing these monies. This has been made critically important by the steady erosion of standards in a broad segment of the PVO community.

Greater independence among government-supported PVOs

would also lengthen the rather short list of field-oriented organizations in this country willing to contribute constructive critiques of the U.S. foreign aid program. PVO staff operating in particular countries should be in a position to make known their own and local views of the overall AID program in those countries to the local AID missions, while their home office should be able to articulate a broader perspective, based on its more comprehensive field knowledge, in programmatic and policy circles in Washington.

To date, the quality of our aid has suffered for lack of ongoing independent appraisals of AID (and MDB) country programs. Larry Minear, a prominent church agency representative in Washington, reflecting upon the Sierra Leone road-building case, writes that responsible advocacy on the part of the participating PVO would have called into question the AID and Bank development strategy involved. Even NGOs not operationally incorporated into a project ". . . should be concerned about an export-cropping scheme which under the guise of development exposed small farmers . . . to the fluctuations of international commodity prices" (Minear, "Reflections," p. 31). There are far too few U.S. PVOs, however, that attempt to analyze and address the critical domestic and international obstacles to meaningful change.

Aid program officials, Congress, and the U.S. public would best be served by different types of information. If PVOs were to receive government support from an independent public institution, separate from the U.S. official bilateral aid program, perspectives and information on problems relating to host-country policies or U.S. aid could be taken to AID for consideration without fear of repercussions. The benefit of extending this advocacy role to the halls of Congress or to other public forums would have to be weighed, as a handful of U.S. PVOs do today, against the potential risks to the PVOs' status and relationships in host countries overseas.

## A FOUNDATION FOR PRIVATE AND VOLUNTARY COOPERATION

A PVO foundation, established along the lines of the Inter-American and African Development Foundations, would be an appropriate institutional mechanism for the underwriting of the costs of all these activities. In structure and operation it should also draw strongly upon the Dutch and Norwegian models of government–NGO relations. Two decades ago, the Dutch government incorporated four NGO mechanisms in a system to coordinate and publicly finance the efforts of Protestant, Catholic, secular and, later, humanist groups in Holland working in development overseas. Although these institutions now also (in fact, primarily) fund Third World organizations directly, they were initially utilized as independent intermediaries, funding up to 75 percent of project costs of Dutch groups meeting established criteria. A U.S. Foundation for Private and Voluntary Cooperation should operate as a single-unit version of the original Dutch concept, as the regional foundations could handle referrals of proposals that come directly from Third World organizations.

Combined financing of both PVO and local counterpart costs in joint activities should be an important element of the funding program, however, to encourage an assistance, rather than management, mode on the part of the participating U.S. organization. Decreased PVO involvement in project activities would be expected over time. To encourage local institution building and the phase-out of PVO involvement, program grants should be extended to those agencies that have demonstrated effectiveness in these areas. More flexible, longer-term funding would allow these PVOs to respond to requests for non-project assistance and to concentrate their activities in high-risk geographical areas that have little institutional infrastructure, as they would no longer have to rely heavily on individual project grants to finance their organizations.

Particular features of the Norwegian system should also be applied, in some form, to both project and program funding. As much as 100 percent of PVO and counterpart costs for project-related feasibility studies, local planning, local staff training, and evaluations might be covered by the foundation. A relatively modest contribution to home-office administration should be made to keep institutional style modest, as well; the preference here is for the payments to be made on a fixed, per-project, rather than percentage, basis to discourage unnecessarily large projects. Once effectiveness and commitment to local control have been established by a PVO over a sustained period of time and the organization qualifies for program aid, long-term support should be extended to cover operational costs, including approved staff positions for overseas work.

The foundation should be staffed by people with extensive work experience at the local level in the Third World and who are able to undertake comprehensive analyses of the societies in which they work as a basis for their programming. Like their regional foundation counterparts, they would travel to the field to assess projects following the submission of proposals and as part of an ongoing monitoring and evaluation process. Alternatively, regional representatives could be located overseas to facilitate direct field contacts by PVO staff and the review of projects. In addition, they would also take the opportunity to consult with indigenous NGOs in order to keep informed about local development needs. They would complement that learning with regular exchanges with regional foundation staff.

Such broad field exposure would also enable staff to play a constructive role as an intermediary among PVOs and between them and local organizations. They should assume the potentially important role, for instance, of recommending particular U.S. PVO assistance to local organizations seeking help. The adoption of such a process as foundation policy might help diminish the incidence of PVOs creating project opportunities more out of their own need than that of poor populations. At the same time, foundation staff could encourage PVO collaboration to help overcome local developmental obstacles that face indigenous NGOs but that cannot be tackled by any one organization. Such action could include the sharing of diverse institutional expertise, the bringing together of atomized local groups, the building of local institutional and small-scale physical infrastructure, and the enhancement of local NGO access and capacity to influence government program and policy planning and implementation. PVOs working in the same country or region might also be encouraged to integrate some of their project review, training, and evaluation functions for the purposes of learning and greater field effectiveness. The Ecumenical Working Group on Africa, established in 1985 by six U.S. religious PVOs, has been exploring such relationships and support for some such activities.

The institution would make grants and loans to U.S. PVOs and local counterparts in accordance with strict criteria that stress the local initiation of projects, the building of institutions, and the devolution of management to local control. Without appropriate funding criteria, established in the authorizing legislation, there is no assurance that PVO independence from AID would improve PVO accountability. Political manipulation of the board, which has been attempted in the cases of the regional foundations, or a growing influence of the PVO community over the governing body, which is not unlikely over time, could serve to soften funding criteria considerably. This has been the experience of the PVO funding consortium, Private Agencies Collaborating Together (PACT), whose U.S. member PVOs are potential grantees and also dominate its board. Neither the staff nor a project selection committee has had firm enough funding criteria with which to combat growing PVO self-interest and the eventual encroachment of AID, which, as PACT's virtually sole funder, has controlled the purse strings.

Hence, a minimum set of fixed project criteria, with strong operational implications, must be established. The following are suggested as a start:

1. All project ideas should originate from local base groups or from indigenous representative or support organizations that work directly with poor communities.

2. In those cases in which there are no such groups or institutions in a particular area or in cases in which U.S. PVOs have limited, sector-specific skills to offer, soliciting PVOs should demonstrate that they have spent extensive time in consultation with poor communities determining true needs before establishing their own programs and should demonstrate commitment to building the local institutions that can assume their role over time.

3. Projects should be designed to provide benefits directly to those with the least access to resources in the area in which the projects are being implemented and should be equally responsive to the needs, aspirations, and activities of all sub-groups in the beneficiary population, particularly women.

4. Project support should be oriented to the strengthening of local organizational capacity and community or group cohesiveness; to the enhancement of beneficiary involvement in decisionmaking; to increasing the leverage of local beneficiary groups to expand their access to, and control over, resources critical to their advancement; and to helping these groups to restructure their economic and social relationships with other groups in the population.

5. No less than 25 percent of project costs should be covered by soliciting PVOs with funds from non-governmental sources, and project financing should not increase the foundation's total contribution to a PVO's annual program budget to over 50 percent of that budget.

6. Soliciting agencies should submit to the foundation a general plan for the devolution of project management to local partner organizations or staff where and when capacity exists and for the

phasing out of their own project involvement.

7. Salaries and working conditions of staff and management of agencies soliciting funds should be consistent with the nature of the anti-poverty work of the PVO community, the principle of narrowing the economic gap between the rich and the poor, and the need to establish equitable relationships with partner agencies.

These criteria are recommended with the knowledge that many U.S. PVOs would have difficulty qualifying at first for project support without undergoing substantial internal reform. Indeed, the purpose of the criteria would be precisely to promote that reform, and the foundation should have the tools with which to assist those seeking federal funds to make the necessary modifications over time. It is anticipated that a fair application of these or similar criteria would bring about a meaningful and smooth transformation in the PVO community over the long term toward greater responsiveness and a more supportive posture vis-à-vis local organizations.

As part of this process, the foundation should provide a forum for in-depth discussions about important development issues and PVO operations in particular countries. Foundation staff would be in a position to stimulate the PVOs to analyze their own and one another's respective programming. This would be a major contribution on the part of the foundation, as today there is little questioning of PVO approaches and performance within the community. Another contribution would be the use of such a forum for an interchange of views between U.S. and Third World NGOs.

A final function of a PVO foundation should be the encouragement and financing of development education work by the organizations whose field projects it funds. The focus of these educational campaigns should be the development process overseas and not the need for greater levels of aid. In fact, from the forum discussions on development issues would ideally emerge an awareness among the PVOs that their public treatment of the aid issue must educate Americans about the need for quality development assistance. The U.S. public has rarely been treated to a critical analysis of the bilateral and multilateral aid programs by the very organizations that work closest to the ground overseas. According to Minear, "[g]lobal education . . . involves a strong critique of current economic and political arrangements, institutions, and systems, both here and abroad" (Minear, "Reflections," pp. 30–31).

John Sommer, in his 1977 book on PVOs, stresses the responsibility that field-based organizations have to educate the U.S. public:

It is because development *is* politics, both at home and abroad, that the need for citizen awareness is so urgent. And it is because the U.S. voluntary organizations are as familiar as any American groups with the grass-roots realities of the Third World that their role is critical. Just as the past tendency to ignore political considerations led to the failure of trickle-down approaches to ameliorate Third World poverty, so too will the failure to realistically present development issues to the American constituency perpetuate this sense of unreality and undermine, in the long run, the agencies' credibility in development. To the extent the simplistic sad child image is promoted, the more likely is the U.S. public to wonder why billions of dollars in past aid commitments have not served to stem the tears. Rather, the public must be honestly told the very long-term nature of the problem, the real impediments to change, and the modest—yet still potentially rewarding—progress that has been and can be observed in many areas.

He concluded with regret that PVOs were not more willing ". . . to stand up and be counted on their principles, especially where public education is crucial," and that "the American people are sufficiently sophisticated to appreciate honesty when the facts are properly put before them" (Sommer, *Beyond Charity*, pp. 138–139).

More than a decade later, little has changed. Brian Smith contrasts the difference today between Canadian and U.S. development education efforts among field-based groups:

Another major difference between Canadian and U.S. PVOs is how they define their missions to their respective home populations. Canadian PVOs, much more so than their U.S. counterparts, since 1968 have considered a large part of their work to be educating the Canadian public about the causes of underdevelopment abroad and encouraging Canadians to support activities with peoples in the Third World, including the establishment of networks of communication, intercultural exchanges, and pressure on governments. From 2 to 20 percent of the total budget of Canadian PVOs supporting programs overseas is now allocated to this education/advocacy function at home. . . . Moreover, the Canadian International Development Agency (CIDA)—the foreign aid arm of the Canadian government—through its Public

Participation Program (initiated in 1971) now allocates nearly $6 million annually for development education by PVOs (as compared to $1 million by AID) . . . (Smith, pp. 130–131).

Smith notes that only two of the fifteen U.S. groups he interviewed in his survey had given attention to the type of development education emphasized in Canada and in much of Europe. While the greater open-mindedness of the official Canadian and European aid agencies is a factor here, much of the blame for the poor showing in this area must rest with U.S. PVOs themselves. A new foundation, in developing criteria for the funding of development education activities, should consider making some project financing contingent on the execution of responsible educational work.

To achieve the purposes laid out here for a PVO foundation, the institution must have a strong and capable board of private- and public-sector Americans (appointed by the President) and a mechanism for receiving Third World grassroots input and incorporating it in decisionmaking. As U.S. law prohibits non-U.S. citizens from serving on the governing board of a public institution, it is strongly recommended that an advisory council composed of representatives of Third World NGOs be established. The board of directors could and should also include Third World representation, preferably in the form of a former leader of a Third World NGO, who has since become a U.S. citizen. Four other positions should be filled by representatives of the new bilateral aid administration and the three regional foundations to ensure the transfer of learning. A representative from the PVO community and an independent citizen knowledgeable about development would complete a seven-person board.

Alternatives to this model might include the establishment of a PVO funding mechanism as a unit of a new, autonomous Administration for International Development. A shortcoming of such a structure would be that, while the new AID would be less wont to politicize PVO financing than is AID today, some PVOs might still feel compromised in their development policy and education work by their dependency on AID for funding. A private foundation with public funds constitutes another option. In all probability, however, such a foundation would experience the same problems as has PACT, which was established on a similar basis. Left to PVOs to establish, the foundation's board would likely reflect the interests of the organizations seeking funds and thus compromise the organization's objectivity.

**RECOMMENDATIONS**

1. U.S. PVOs should support the emergence of indigenous organizations and the priorities determined by beneficiary groups, strengthen local organizational structures, educate the large donors about alternative aid channels, and advise program officers, policymakers, and the public in the United States of the effectiveness or counterproductiveness of the programs and policies supported by these donors.

2. PVOs should help steer large donor support away from unresponsive and ineffective agencies and toward effective local organizations representing the interests of marginalized people.

3. PVOs should help establish mechanisms in Third World countries for the purpose of channeling local perspectives in a systematic fashion into the planning and policy formulation of AID and other donor agencies. PVOs have a responsibility to help local NGOs leverage changes in programs and policies that affect the latter's constituencies in their respective countries. A joint PVO–AID initiative is required to facilitate popular participation in national and local-level planning.

4. There should be established a formal structure through which PVOs would be encouraged to channel, to AID, field-based information, perspectives, and concerns related to host-country policies and U.S. assistance for purposes of monitoring and improving the quality of the bilateral program.

5. There should be established a new Foundation for Private and Voluntary Cooperation that would enable and encourage those PVOs that are interested in receiving government support for their activities to operate independently of AID. The foundation should be an independent government corporation, directed by a board consisting of the presidents of the new bilateral aid administration and the three regional foundations; a former head of a Third World NGO who is now a U.S. citizen; a representative of the U.S. PVO community; and an independent citizen knowledgeable about development. Additional Third World input would be ensured through the establishment of an advisory council composed of representatives of Third World NGOs.

6. The foundation would make grants and loans for the projects of U.S. PVOs and give priority in its financing to the joint activities of PVOs and local counterpart organizations. An assistance rather than management posture on the part of U.S. groups would thus be encouraged. Proposals arriving directly from Third World

organizations would be referred to the regional development foundations, except in special circumstances.

7. The foundation should support only those PVO projects that develop from the ideas of local organizations that assist poor communities or, in cases in which such organizations do not exist, from direct PVO consultations with poor communities. Soliciting agencies should submit to the foundation a general plan for the devolution of project control to their local staff or to local partner organizations.

8. To receive support from the foundation, projects should provide benefits directly to those with the least access to resources, enhance the control of the poor over their own development, and strengthen the capacity of their organizations.

9. At least 25 percent of the costs of any submitted project should be covered by contributions from private sources, and the foundation should provide not more than 50 percent of the PVOs' annual program budget. The salaries and operating styles of the PVOs receiving foundation support should be modest.

10. The foundation should assist PVOs seeking its funds to make the necessary modifications over time so that they can satisfy the proposed conditions more consistently and should help the PVO community to adopt a more responsive and supportive posture vis-à-vis local organizations.

11. To encourage local institution building and PVO phase-out, program grants should be extended to those agencies that have demonstrated effectiveness in these areas. More flexible, longer-term funding would allow these PVOs to respond to requests for non-project assistance and to focus their efforts on high-risk areas that have little institutional infrastructure.

12. The foundation should cover as much as 100 percent of PVO and counterpart costs for project-related feasibility studies, local planning, local staff training, and evaluations.

13. The foundation should be staffed by people with extensive experience working at the local level in the Third World. They should travel to the field regularly to assess projects or be located overseas to facilitate direct field contacts by PVO staff.

14. The foundation should play an intermediary role in recommending particular U.S. PVO assistance to Third World organizations seeking help and in encouraging PVO collaboration for the purpose of addressing locally defined development constraints beyond the capacity of individual PVO action. PVOs working in the same country or region might also be encouraged to

integrate some of their project review, training, and evaluation functions.

15. A forum should be established at the foundation for PVO discussions of development issues and for PVO analyses of their respective programming and operations. Meetings among U.S. and Third World NGOs should also be arranged.

16. Development education efforts that address development processes overseas, the quality of development assistance, and the role of the United States in the Third World should be encouraged and supported. Some project funding might be made contingent on the establishment of such a program.

# SEVEN

# Transforming
# the World Bank

As the World Bank headed into the 1980s, it prided itself on being the enlightened leader of the development assistance community. Its "poverty focus" was applauded in the mainstream media, where it was assumed that the Bank's pronouncements about the participation of the "poorest of the poor" were reflected in its assistance programming. As the decade approaches its close, however, it is becoming clear not only that the Bank is more than ever a bankers' bank, but that its record as an anti-poverty funder has been greatly exaggerated.

In truth, the Bank has shown itself throughout its history to be ill-equipped in orientation, structure, and operations to support the types of projects, programs, policies, and organizations that truly involve and benefit the poor. The International Bank for Reconstruction and Development (IBRD), the original institution of what is now the World Bank Group, was established in 1945, two decades before the three regional development banks for Latin America, Asia, and Africa were born. Its primary purpose was to facilitate the flow of private capital to Europe and Third World nations. Although it has acted more as a lender than as the guarantor that was originally envisaged, its goal has always been to make countries "safe" for foreign direct investment and "creditworthy" so as to attract commercial bank lending. Forty years later, Third World foreign debt totals approximately one trillion dollars, new bank lending has slowed to a trickle, and standards of living among the poor and working classes have plummeted.

The basic assumptions about the development process which underlie this failure have, contrary to common belief, changed little since the Bank moved from a reconstruction to development emphasis in the 1950s. During that decade, the development of the physical infrastructure necessary to increasingly tie Third World borrowers to the world economy was emphasized. In addition, the International Finance Corporation was established so that private corporations could borrow from the World Bank Group without government scrutiny.

After he assumed the presidency of the Bank in 1968, Robert McNamara perpetuated and expanded this role for the institution, using the Bank as a conduit for the transfer of large amounts of private capital to developing countries. Moving money appeared all too often to be more important than reaching the poor. Unlike his predecessors, McNamara reacted to the persistent shortage of "good" projects by first borrowing large amounts of funds and then instructing his staff to find ways to spend them (van de Laar, *The World Bank and the Poor,* p. 225). Lending targets were set for each country and region, and projects were sought to meet these targets.

While McNamara did significantly increase funding in a number of "social" sectors, such as agriculture, rural and urban development, health, and education, traditional investments in infrastructure development also increased sharply under his management, as part of a 13-fold increase (fivefold in real terms) in Bank financing between 1968 and 1981. As much as two-thirds of the lending of the IBRD and of its sister institution, the International Development Association (IDA), remained of a traditional nature (Ayres, *Banking on the Poor,* p. 215). As late as 1977 only 23 percent of the commitments of the Bank and  IDA were financing projects the majority of whose benefits were intended to help  poor populations (Congressional Research Service, *Towards an Assessment,* p. 90).

Furthermore, at a time in history at which popular organizations were emerging across the Third World, the Bank was woefully out of touch with the people it was charged to assist. Mahbub ul Haq, then director of Policy Planning and Program Review, candidly acknowledged in the late 1970s that "[w]e all have yet to discover how alternative delivery systems can be devised to reach the poor people and obtain their willing and enthusiastic cooperation" (Hayter, *The Creation of World Poverty,* p. 91).

The Bank's primary commitment to the international financial community, the pressure upon it to loan money, and its lack of contact with, and methodologies to reach and involve, local populations in good part explain why its actions and record have fallen far short of the public image it has sought to project. Smaller-scale, participatory projects that truly respond to local needs and that can leave a foundation for ongoing development efforts have stood little chance of gaining Bank support when the alternative has been to spend tens of millions of dollars through large public and private institutions. Despite the many references to popular participation and grassroots development and the funding of so-called "new style" projects in the 1970s, the Bank continued to work through the same type of institutional channels in borrowing countries: government agencies, development banks, and special project units. It seemed to matter little that most recipients of Bank financing proved unable, or unwilling, to reach the poor segments of the population and to gain their confidence. Nor did the fact that a large number of projects implemented with Bank money were either slow to develop or developed into large-scale disasters fundamentally alter the Bank's institutional selection. This major problem in Bank operations continues to undercut its relevance to meaningful development.

By the same token, local participation has also been missing in Bank project planning and design. The pressure to make loans and the demands of the project cycle, as currently constituted, effectively preclude the elicitation of local input in these stages of project development. Without the views and priorities of "target" populations incorporated in decisionmaking, Bank policies and programming have always run the danger of being irrelevant, and indeed counterproductive, to their interests.

While "new style" projects were showcased in the 1970s, the real action was taking place in the area in which the Bank has always been most effective: the molding of national development strategies and policies. This was accomplished through the Bank's use of its own capital and, perhaps more importantly in recent years, through its role in certifying a country's creditworthiness to potential lenders in the private financial community. It may be that during the McNamara era, when it lent on a more narrow project basis than it does today, it was more difficult for the Bank to leverage major macroeconomic changes, but the institution has, in fact, wielded its power to shape national economies throughout its history.

Whether the emphasis is on ports or agriculture, on the public or private sector, or on project or balance-of-payments lending, the Bank's economic orthodoxy and its place in the financial community have consistently tied it to the same strategy: an export-led modernization that moves countries further into the international economy. Such an approach has historically strengthened export and import enclaves in Third World countries, rewarded those interests with connections to the international business community, and used scarce resources (e.g., land) and cheap labor to produce for overseas markets. It has also forced the poor across much of the Third World to create survival mechanisms to cope with their increasing marginalization wrought by this process. Finally, this strategy, given the high level of dependency on Northern markets that it creates and the gross misjudgments of Bank and other traditional economists regarding the terms of international trade at the end of the 1970s, was a key factor in the creation of the current international debt crisis.

By the end of his tenure, McNamara had begun to move the Bank to deal more directly with the emerging problems connected with this debt. In 1980, as the debt began to reach ominous proportions, the first structural adjustment loans (SALs), totaling over $500 million and representing about 5 percent of total loan commitments of the Bank and IDA, were made to five countries. These loans were designed both to leverage major changes in national macroeconomic policy and to provide governments with the foreign exchange needed to pay off their Northern creditors. Under McNamara's successor, A. W. Clausen, non-project lending increased well beyond the level envisaged by the Bank's founders, who specifically put a limit on balance-of-payments and program loans in order to curtail irresponsible borrowing. And while new President Barber Conable commented privately, upon assuming leadership of the Bank in 1986, that he did not see the institution's major responsibility as that of a central actor in the international debt crisis, plans are underway to virtually double Bank lending during the second half of this decade. Much of that—an estimated 35 to 50 percent of the total—will be non-project, policy-based lending, either in the form of SALs or broad sector credits.

## THE FAILURES OF INAPPROPRIATE ASSISTANCE

In a book sympathetic to the McNamara presidency, Robert Ayres raises the question of who really benefited from the implementation of Bank rural development projects, a mainstay of that era. He cites

Bank project officers who acknowledge that IBRD-supported projects in northeast Brazil and all those carried out by the Bank of Brazil throughout that country primarily assisted farmers with relatively large holdings, as well as such special interests as the textile industry, at the expense of the poor. A similar concern was expressed by project officers about the first large-scale PIDER project in Mexico. The Ingavi project in Bolivia also was plagued by a number of major problems, including the deflection of benefits away from the poor (Ayres, pp. 134–37).

Critics of the Bank's work in the Philippines offer similar examples of distorted rural development projects supported in that country. Internal Bank reports reveal that a number of projects primarily benefited large landlords, medium-sized and large commercial farmers, and foreign agribusiness. Agricultural credits, channeled through national agricultural and development banks serving the country's elite, wound up primarily in the hands of large landholders. The Development Bank of the Philippines, for instance, was acting as an agent of large landed interests, according to a Bank supervision report, at the same time that it was being used as a Bank implementing agency for a project that was intended for, but in the end did not assist, small landholders (Bello, et al., *Development Debacle*, pp. 45, 89).

Environmental organizations have been equally critical of Bank-supported projects in Latin America, Asia, and Africa. The Polonoroeste project in the Amazon area of Brazil and the Transmigration project in Indonesia have been characterized as ecological disasters that have badly hurt indigenous populations. In reference to the Brazil project and similar projects supported in Latin America by the World Bank and the Inter-American Development Bank, Bruce Rich of the Environmental Defense Fund writes that "[r]egrettably, the banks have done little to investigate, preserve, and utilize the knowledge of . . . native peoples. Instead, ill-conceived agricultural projects have accelerated the destruction of sound agricultural methods" (Rich, "The Multilateral Banks," pp. 692–693).

A Bank consultant on the Polonoroeste project, David Price, testified in Congress that his experience at the Bank led him to ". . . question the sincerity of that institution's commitment to safeguard the welfare of people affected by the projects it supports." He went on to denounce the Bank for funding the project, because he felt that the agencies that were to implement it clearly had not demonstrated competence. He accused the Bank of systematically distorting his findings and omitting from its report his allegation that one of the top officials of a key implementing agency had been positively identified as a former political torturer (Rich, pp. 725–26).

Environmentalists have also pointed critically to other types of Bank rural lending. They cite large-scale cattle projects in Latin America that have accelerated deforestation, displaced small-scale farmers, and contributed to a further concentration of land ownership. Tobacco projects were also a major focus of the Bank between 1974 and 1982. Attractive to governments as a dependable source of revenue and export earnings, this cash crop has depleted soil fertility, decreased food production, demanded expensive imported fertilizers, and accelerated deforestation. "In Africa," writes Rich, "regional deforestation for tobacco curing has accelerated the desertification on the entire continent" (Rich, pp. 690–700).

Unfortunately, history—and the Bank—appears ready to repeat itself. For that reason, it is worth quoting Rich at length about the future of agriculture, the environment, and multilateral development bank lending in Africa:

> Evidence of ecological and economic collapse in Africa and elsewhere underscores the urgency of this need to reevaluate the model of the development that the banks promote. The agriculture sector offers a compelling example of the need for change. Most large-scale ecological deterioration in the developing countries is linked to the wide diffusion of capital-intensive, export-oriented Green Revolution agricultural systems. These systems, promoted by the banks, have caused the dissolution of small-farmer subsistence agriculture and the concentration of land in the hands of fewer owners. As a consequence, farming of ecologically marginal lands, such as tropical forests and fragile, semi-desert areas, has increased. Simultaneously, the productivity of the lands where poorer small farmers remain steadily declines, as "increasing numbers of families try to extract a livelihood from land that is diminishing in area and deteriorating in quality because of the over-use and improper husbandry they are obliged to practice for immediate survival" (see Susan George, *Ill Fares the Land*, p. 51).
>
> In its latest public report on Sub-Saharan Africa, the World Bank identifies the "proliferation of non-viable projects" funded by aid agencies as one of the roots of the region's current crisis. . . . The report is silent on agricultural projects funded by the Bank and other lenders, although agriculture has been the most important sector for Bank lending in the region over the past decade. The report emphasizes that future development assistance in Sub-Saharan Africa must promote greatly increased agricultural

exports and the policy reforms to facilitate these exports. It fails to discuss, however, the possible connections among export-oriented agricultural development, ecological deterioration, and decreasing per-capita food production (Rich, pp. 739–40).

The support of inappropriate development policies, programs, and institutions has not been limited to the rural sector. The Bank's problems in urban projects in such places as Indonesia and the Philippines are also indicative of the basic failings of the Bank approach. Municipal authorities in the Indonesian cities of Jakarta and Surabaya followed a basically top-down methodology in Bank-supported slum upgrading projects, and the lack of local input and participation resulted in poorly formulated physical plans, inadequate maintenance of upgraded facilities, and problems for uprooted residents in receiving compensation for the houses they lost (Ayres, p. 188). In Manila, also in the mid-1970s, the Bank helped create the National Housing Authority from existing government housing agencies. The Authority proceeded to carry out an urban-upgrading effort in the large Tondo slum area without the participation of the residents. The relocation of some 4,500 squatter families to make room for international port facilities for foreign firms, the revision of pre-martial law to require remaining residents to pay substantially higher rents for their sites, and the overall authoritarian processes of project planning and implementation led the residents and their community groups to focus worldwide attention on the fiasco and thus slow down, though not stop, the project process (Bello, pp. 110–117). According to a Bank consultant, most of the residents simply wanted to know what was being planned for their community.

Working within the Bank between 1976 and 1980, The Development GAP learned firsthand about the conventional institutional relationships that the Bank normally formed in the housing, urban-upgrading, and income-generation sectors in Latin America and, to a lesser extent, Africa. Project officers, even in the then relatively progressive Urban Projects Department, typically developed projects in conjunction with agencies that had neither their roots in nor the trust of the communities in which these projects would be implemented. Except for the occasional socio-economic survey of said communities, the Bank's mission teams seldom drew their information and perspectives for project identification and design from the local populations that would ultimately be affected. Whether it be in urban development or other sectors, the Bank's country economic and sectoral analyses—the bases upon which lending programs are developed and financial allocations to specific sectors and projects are made—are rarely informed by local-level reality, certainly not by the perspectives and priorities of the marginalized populations of the borrower countries.

## INSTITUTIONAL WEAKNESSES

There are a number of factors that explain this critical institutional weakness of the Bank, one which severely limits its relevance to the lives of the world's poor. At one level, the Bank's primary commitment to international financial interests places it in a very different world than the one in which the poor live. Likewise, the conventional economic analysis it employs has little room for the type of information and perspectives gathered in urban slums and rural villages. Bank staff, with relatively few exceptions, have had limited, if any, village-level experience anywhere in the Third World. They relate more comfortably to those countries' elites and bureaucrats, with whom they generally establish professional relationships, often at the expense of relevant development programming at local levels.

Those at the Bank who understand and care about working more closely with local populations face formidable obstacles. Aart van de Laar, an employee in the 1970s, notes that the Bank's increased lending volume, bureaucratization, and need for external accountability and internal efficiency have induced widespread risk avoidance within the institution (van de Laar, p. 252). Pressured to put together substantial loan packages with as few delays as possible and caught between the Bank's internal hierarchy and the inklings of reality they inevitably confront when overseas, project officers usually shy away from innovation and deeper inquiry in the field. According to a paper prepared for the Bank and based on staff interviews, "[f]ield reality gets left behind as 'packages' are put together that will 'fly' at the Bank. The reporting process becomes an exercise in packaging and selling. . . . One outcome of the sanitizing process is that the Bank loses information about the field and about practice in the field" (Mattingly, "Urban Practice in the Bank," p. 11).

The same paper points out that the ". . . Bank has not done particularly well in trying to understand the broader impacts of development projects. The tendency is to evaluate projects in their own terms." More to the point, the paper contends that the institution ". . . has not developed in its practice a really satisfactory way of engaging the views of the locals" (Mattingly, p. 19). Others at the Bank take this issue a step further:

> To plan for the future one must understand the strength and pace of the evolution of the historical cultural forces at work. . . . An understanding of these forces leads to an identification of the major constraints and opportunities that will affect the choice and design of a rural development project. No foreign team, even with several missions and the ablest of program staff, can adequately accomplish this task. Nor can the vested interests of government departments be totally relied upon to give an adequate perspective of the constraints and opportunities for a rural development program. Perhaps wider participation by the relevant sections of the community likely to be affected by rural development or able to contribute to it should be attempted at this stage. (Smith, Lethem, and Thoolen, *The Design of Organizations*, p. 34).

The strengthening of Bank control over the project development process is seen by van de Laar as impeding ". . . creative and timely reaction to the dynamics of grassroots organizations representing the target groups which the Bank tries to reach" (van de Laar, p. 252). Not surprisingly, risk taking is generally not rewarded when it comes to identifying more direct channels to poor communities. It has been in fact discouraged in recent years through the reduction in the length of the identification phase of the project cycle. Hence, in order to avoid delays and the risk of failures that can be laid specifically at their feet, most project officers play it safe and return to the same implementing institutions that had been utilized previously. According to van de Laar, ". . . the phenomenon that 'one loan leads to another' through contacts that build up during appraisal and negotiation and lead to the extension of others, proves to be a major method by which the Bank builds its project pipelines" (van de Laar, p. 236).

It is clear from visits to Bank-financed projects that inappropriate organizations are generally chosen to implement anti-poverty projects. Projects meant to serve poor artisans and women's income-generation groups might be carried out, for example, by a corrupt government housing bank or a development finance company that had previously served only large and medium-sized businesses. Due to inadequate outreach, institutional inefficiency and corruption, and the tendency to "rachet up" both the size of credits and the income level of the borrowers, such organizations are rarely successful in extending loans to the poor. Often, in fact, very few, if any, loans are made during extended periods, backing up Bank disbursements and increasing supervision costs. Ironically, an additional reason why large, often inappropriate institutions are sought as implementors by the Bank is that project officers are pressured to commit large amounts of money according to a rigid timetable.

Through the years, the Bank itself has recognized the short-comings of the institutions that it has financed to carry out "poverty-oriented" projects. Christopher Willoughby, the first director of the Bank's Operations Evaluation Department, acknowledged in 1977 ". . . that among the Bank's relative weaknesses, one might mention its frequent difficulties in participating effectively at the level of borrower's institutional arrangements, training, and staffing issues." Yet, these issues, according to a former Bank staff member, "are often at the core of the success (or lack of success) of development projects. They formed the main problem area for agricultural projects old-style, and are recognized as a major problem for rural development projects 'new-style' . . ." (van de Laar, p.201).

Poor management, high staff turnover, cautious staff, political interests, and poor interaction with project beneficiaries are cited as common difficulties. Ayres, in his 1983 book on the Bank, pointed to cozy relationships between Bank project officers and local implementing officers as part of the problem (Ayres, p. 164). Warren Baum, when he was vice-president of the Bank's Projects Staff, wrote in 1978 that "[e]xperience indicates that insufficient attention to the institutional aspects of a project leads to problems during its implementation and operation." He went on to say that the ". . . Bank has come to recognize the need for a continuing re-examination of institutional arrangements, an openness to new ideas . . ." (Baum, "The Project Cycle," p. 6). This need has continued to exist, however, to this day.

Bank insiders, examining the issue of institutional selection in 1980, expressed the view that the key failure in this regard was still the attempt to move too rapidly to the choice of an executing institution. They concluded that "[n]ot enough time is spent in exploring and weighing alternatives and having those who will have a role in implementing the final choice themselves suggest alternatives" (Smith, Lethem, and Thoolen, p. 38). Emerging organization design concepts, they note, ". . . stress the need for people to become involved in and committed to what they undertake in the community. . . . Organization design that stresses human resources and community capability finds ways to increase the control of all participants over their environments and gives them greater choice of action consistent with their own motivations, perceptions, and skills. Knowledge rather than resources becomes the key to development" (Smith, Lethem, and Thoolen, p. 67).

The search for good projects and institutions to implement them led the Bank for a number of years to create new entities, or project units, in various countries. The use of these semi-autonomous government agencies may have given the Bank greater control over project execution, but it did little to influence or reform the line agencies in the public bureaucracy and even less to increase public participation in decisionmaking. It has been argued, in fact, that the accountability of such units primarily to the Bank itself weakened the accountability of governments to their people, undermining democratic forces and processes. Curiously, efficiency gains were also unimpressive; project implementation often proceeded even more slowly than under the national bureaucracy (van de Laar, pp. 35, 145). The Bank has largely disbanded this approach, but its experience does underscore the institution's long-standing frustration with the performance of organizations that implement Bank-supported projects.

## AN ALTERNATIVE APPROACH

A logical alternative to these ineffective project implementors are the numerous organizations around the Third World, usually of a non-governmental nature, that work directly with the poor in their own communities in a responsive manner. Many such institutions have been supported and strengthened through the years by smaller donors and PVOs, as well as by some bilateral donors, and are in a position to utilize harder credits and other forms of funding effectively to assist their respective constituencies. The Bank, for instance, building on the efforts of a local priest and the early support provided by the Inter-American Foundation and other small funders, made two sequential loans in the mid-1970s to a housing foundation in El Salvador supporting mutual-help housing among the poor. These were subsequently cited as highly successful projects, as they actually reached, involved, and aided the poor populations that needed assistance.

Over a period of four years, The Development GAP worked

frequently on a contractual basis with the Urban Projects Department of the Bank for the purpose of further demonstrating how institutions that work responsively, directly, and intensively with the poor in their own communities can be identified and supported in the design and implementation of projects. With the responsibility for the income-generation components of urban projects in both Latin America and Africa, The Development GAP selected the most appropriate institutions—governmental and non-governmental—to plan and execute the programs that addressed the needs of the most disadvantaged segments of the population.

One of the cases in which The Development GAP identified an NGO for these tasks was Nicaragua. In 1977 it chose a private non-profit foundation to develop and execute the income-generation component. The Somoza government subsequently refused to allow the foundation's participation and financing. The loan for the entire project was thus withheld, and it still had not been made in late 1978 when open warfare commenced in Nicaragua.

When the war ended and the Sandinista government assumed power in July 1979, virtually all of Nicaragua's major cities and towns were devastated. The government approached the Bank for assistance in the reconstruction of its urban areas. The Development GAP was given the responsibility for the small-scale enterprise rehabilitation program, one of three components in the new urban project. It worked in Nicaragua with representatives of the nationalized banking system and its special development fund, the Ministry of Industry and Commerce, municipal government *juntas*, and community organizations in the design of a decentralized program that involved all of them actively in its implementation. This project component, which was based on a successful model provided by a Nicaraguan NGO, was a principal element in what a subsequent Bank Project Completion Report called ". . . probably one of the most effective urban projects supported by the Bank" (World Bank, "Nicaragua Urban"). The significance of the entire loan program lies in the positive correlation that is demonstrated between project success and a constructive relationship between government agencies and local-level organizations.

In Guatemala, where such relationships did not exist in 1979, The Development GAP consulted with a handful of urban-based Guatemalan NGOs and cultivated Bank mission interest in supporting a coalition of these groups in carrying out major aspects of a full urban program of housing, community upgrading, and income generation. Although the coalition did eventually develop into a formal NGO consortium, the project itself did not get off the ground due to a diversion of energies toward saving a previous Bank-financed project poorly implemented by an ineffectual government bank. The Development GAP subsequently concentrated its efforts on re-routing the loan funds for that project's income-generation component to a private cooperative federation. The Bank's Project Completion Report in 1984 praised the federation as ". . . well organized, efficient, and dedicated to the development of its member cooperatives, and through them, to its members, most of whom appear to be from the lower income group. . . . [The component] demonstrated the feasibility of using dedicated non-profit organizations . . . to help implement social and economic programs" (World Bank, "Guatemala Urban Reconstruction").

This experimentation with non-governmental and other appropriate institutions was supported by the Urban Projects Department because of the problems encountered elsewhere in highly volatile urban areas. There was at least tacit recognition that the financing of inappropriate institutions (in all sectors of Bank work) had been at the root of the lack of meaningful popular participation, the poor project management (and sometimes official corruption), and the economic and physical dislocations (land speculation, relocation of populations, etc.) that often characterized Bank-financed projects. The Development GAP was specifically asked to enter two major urban slum areas in Cameroon, to look outward, and to find ways and institutional mechanisms to deliver credit and other assistance to those who had theretofore been left out of Bank-supported projects. Outright opposition within the Bank and a subsequent lack of significant follow-through limited the implementation of The Development GAP's recommendations in the Cameroon case, and the overall support for this approach proved to be fleeting when the top management of the Urban Projects Department changed in 1980. Attempts to take the issue to policy levels at the Bank also subsequently failed.

## PUBLIC RELATIONS OR AN INTEREST IN CHANGE?

For reasons discussed earlier, the Bank, as a bureaucratic institution with various agenda, will not seek the participation of marginalized populations without pressure being exerted from the outside and mechanisms being created that facilitate that involvement. Only the victims of Bank-supported projects, like those in the Manila slums, and organized Northern lobbying groups, such as a coalition of environmental organizations in the United States, have been able to exert that pressure. In response, the Bank has improved its rhetoric, but, as the environmentalists have found, talk and even the establishment of internal guidelines mean little if the primary intent is public relations (Rich, p. 712).

When the Bank launched a formal dialogue with Northern NGOs in 1981, ostensibly to promote cooperation among the parties, there was some expectation that this forum would stimulate the incorporation of local participation in Bank-supported projects. Bank officials subsequently acknowledged privately, however, that the original intent of their institution's initiative was to develop a lobbying constituency for IDA replenishments. Unfortunately, until late 1987 the Bank continued to use the dialogue, which had been joined by Southern NGOs, primarily for public relations purposes. The Northern NGO members of the dialogue committee allowed the Bank to set the agenda, and a number of the more skeptical non-governmental groups, including a major Third World NGO, left the committee out of frustration. No attempt was made to build on the successes and learning experiences of the 1970s. As a result, the committee has not had the respect of the broader NGO community (particularly outside the United States) and it has not been taken seriously by Bank operations staff—if, in fact, they have even heard of it. The fact that the International Relations office rather than the Operations office managed the Bank's participation in the dialogue until the institution's 1987 reorganization made the discussions of the committee largely irrelevant to the mainstream activities of that institution.

In 1986, a Bank official who was involved in the dialogue commented that:

> by and large, actual efforts for increasing collaboration with philanthropic and self-help NGOs, as part of project preparation and implementation, are still not systematic. A major reason for this is the understandable tendency for hard-pressed project staff to follow the beaten track and during a busy project preparation or preappraisal mission not have the needed time for consultation with borrowers and NGOs in having useful NGO involvement in the project cycle. Another reason is government resistance to NGO participation in projects. NGO involvement is also seen as something difficult . . .
> Taking this line of least resistance at the beginning of the project cycle often results in serious problems  of project design

and lack of community participation which arise during project implementation and require time to resolve—often more time than what would have been invested during project preparation. . . . NGOs are a functional, low-cost alternative that in some instances may facilitate the design and implementation of people-related development projects. They sometimes uniquely represent the viewpoint of the project beneficiaries, have close-to-the-ground delivery systems, have involvements that are sustained over time, and are deeply committed to poverty elimination.

I suggest that the time has come to make appropriate changes to the OMS [Operational Manual Statement] on project preparation to factor the NGO element into the project cycle. Specifically, we should make it a requirement for the preparation of "people targeted" type projects to include consideration of NGO collaboration in project preparation and implementation up to the time of issues/decision stage. A determination could be made at the time of the preappraisal departure meeting, based upon the available data gathered during project preparation, as to whether NGO involvement should be appraised and, if agreed, a final decision taken at the issues/decision meeting . . .

It is estimated that the additional time needed for this activity would be on an average of one day each during project preparation (two missions), preappraisal and appraisal—a total of an extra four days. This time would be more than offset by the lower supervision requirements relative to mobilizing community participation . . . (Churchill, "Involvement of NGOs," pp. 1–2).

At the November 1987 meeting of the Bank–NGO committee, the NGOs for the first time put forward a comprehensive agenda for action, challenging a new team of Bank representatives to commit its institution to a structured relationship with Third World NGOs at regional and national levels. Southern NGOs stated their intent to organize forums in their respective regions, to which they plan to invite IBRD resident representatives and Bank officials from Washington to discuss grassroots project and policy priorities. The Bank will participate in these forums, and its representatives agreed in principle that Bank mission teams and resident representatives would consult regularly and systematically with NGOs in its economic and sector work and in its project, program, and policy planning through NGO-established in-country mechanisms. It was also agreed that NGOs on the committee would assist the Bank in making changes in the OMS that would ensure the injection of NGO input throughout the project cycle and in policy dialogue with government. In addition, the Bank will explore other internal changes necessary to foster greater NGO involvement in Bank-supported programs, and it will indicate to governments the value that it attaches to information and expertise drawn from NGOs and other grassroots sources.

The Bank and NGOs will demonstrate their interest in implementing these arrangements through their actions in the months ahead. For NGOs, including members of the broader community not directly involved in the dialogue, it is a question of whether the work and risks involved in organizing themselves and collaborating with the Bank are outweighed by the opportunity to alter Bank programming and policy positions, and those of their own governments. For the Bank, it will be a matter of how much leverage its representatives on the NGO committee have within an institution primarily committed to the imposition of economic adjustment policies, which hit the poor particularly hard, in borrower countries.

## A REORIENTATION OF OPERATIONS

NGOs can provide the Bank with critically important resources. They can be the Bank's window to cultures that it does not know and, through current relationships, cannot reach in a meaningful way. The Bank needs to expand its knowledge base and diversify its lending. It needs to build on what is emerging on the ground rather than impose its own development orthodoxy through large-scale entities and programs that do not incorporate the poor. Northern NGOs can guide the Bank to local alternatives. Southern NGOs can help provide those alternatives and, just as importantly, inform Bank representatives about local conditions and problems. They can also participate in program and policy planning to ensure the relevance of that planning to their respective constituencies.

As a first step in this direction, the World Bank (and the regional development banks) needs to become more a people's bank and less a government or bankers' institution. It will have to pluralize its lending by reaching down and responding to local organizations (public and non-governmental) that have bankable projects. Strict development criteria should be applied to *all* projects; foremost among these criteria must be the requirement that the project beneficiaries be the country's poor and that they participate actively in project identification, design, and implementation. Other criteria would emphasize environmental soundness, institution building, self-sustainment through local control and management of longer-term activities, non-discrimination in beneficiary involvement, a broad distribution of benefits, technical feasibility, and appropriate technological choice.

If these criteria were applied, much of the Bank's lending would probably still be provided to government entities, particularly to those at the provincial and municipal levels. The difference would be that these public entities would be competing with more grassroots-oriented organizations for funds, and they would thus be forced to improve their outreach, decisionmaking processes, management, and overall effectiveness. At the moment, governments have little motivation to reform their institutions, and in many countries these agencies will agree to almost any Bank conditions, without honest intentions of execution, in order to secure funds and the spoils that go with them.

This desire on the part of governments to maximize their access to and control of Bank funds is largely responsible for the reluctance to provide loan guarantees required for the Bank to lend to non-governmental organizations. In order to expand further the opportunities for NGO involvement, the Bank's board of governors should amend both the IBRD and IDA statutes to permit the guarantee of loans by official regional and private financial institutions.

The Bank can be an important actor in a new assistance paradigm because it is in a position to build upon the aid of bilateral donors and PVOs and provide significant funds on relatively hard terms to organizations that can effectively utilize and manage them. It can in this way help build the capacity of Southern NGOs that work with broad segments of the population and, in so doing, enhance their legitimacy vis-à-vis government. Just as important, it can provide more enlightened leadership in structural adjustment and other policy-based lending by involving the poor in the Bank's policy analysis and then ensuring that national and sectoral policies serve the interests of these populations.

The Bank's recent reorganization affords it an opportunity to make these significant contributions to the promotion of equitable development. While the reorganization was designed in part to cut staff levels and to shift senior vice presidents in order to please the U.S. Congress and the Reagan Administration, and in part to allow the Regional vice presidents to select their own staff for their respective Country and Technical Departments, the Bank's internal restructuring has effectively decentralized power and authority for operational decisions to these Regional offices. This decentralization can be used to increase the amount of local input into decisions about both project and policy lending.

The principal reason, however, that the Bank was reorganized was to improve its efficiency as it heads into an era of major structural adjustment and sector lending. Personnel levels can be reduced, as policy-based lending is less staff-intensive than project work. Decentralization will enable the Bank to apply economic adjustment measures more effectively, and it is likely that the suffering of the poor will intensify as a result of the more efficient application of these measures.

The Bank's experience, however, with adjustment lending is already proving to be far less satisfactory than was initially claimed. Not only are the attendant policy measures increasing the hardships endured by the poor, but the economic performance of the borrower countries is falling considerably short of the Bank's expectations. As a result, some at the Bank have begun a search for alternative approaches. To date, these alternatives have been reformist in nature. They include the organization of compensatory programs of food and social services for the poor and the modification of austerity measures so that the burden of adjustment is shared more fairly within Third World societies. Options incorporating more fundamental changes in Bank policy and operations are clearly required.

The Bank must recognize that the decentralization of its decisionmaking processes provides it and its project officers with the opportunity to be more responsive and innovative in their field work. Project officers must be seen as the point people, bringing back to Washington relevant project proposals and local perspectives that are then used as the bases for program and policy planning, as well as for determining country and sector lending levels. Rewards to personnel should be based upon their demonstrated success in promoting popular involvement in projects and on the projects' performance and long-term sustainability (lower supervision costs is one indicator), rather than on their demonstrated ability to allocate large amounts of money rapidly as part of a central plan.

While the project cycle itself should remain as compact as possible, the Bank's identification and preparation missions should be lengthened to permit more comprehensive contact with local organizations, initiatives, and ideas. Shorter and less frequent supervision trips would be one of the beneficial results. With time, the absorptive capacity of good implementing institutions will grow.

For now, the pressure to spend current funds, much less the increase that is envisaged through 1990, is destructive to a meaningful assistance program.

At the same time, the Bank, like most other large official assistance agencies, needs to establish and/or utilize mechanisms for relating to non-governmental and other appropriate organizations in the Third World. While dealings with NGOs are currently coordinated in a unit within the Bank's Policy, Planning, and Research (PPR) office under knowledgeable and committed leadership, real action will only take place in this area when NGO relations are also institutionalized within the Operations and Regional offices and reflected in the project cycle.

Women's issues require the same serious operational treatment. In the mid-1980's, after ten years of research, review, and "experimentation," the Women in Development policy office was still speaking of turning study into action. Environmental concerns have been accorded greater attention due to the effective advocacy campaign waged by U.S. and Third World environmental organizations. Time will tell if the Bank keeps its pledge to create some fifty environmental positions in Operations and PPR offices and fills them with qualified people. The Bank, in order to be responsive to these concerns and promote more relevant and sustainable development, should establish units within each Region that would have the responsibility for ensuring that (1) projects and program planning are based upon local input and the capacity of responsive institutions; (2) equal support is provided to the activities in which women are involved; and (3) projects are environmentally sound and regenerative. Upgrading of Bank staff, particularly at the level of project officer, would be required for the achievement of these goals.

Under the auspices of the Bank–NGO committee, regional consultations will be held between the Bank and a broad range of indigenous NGOs to establish mechanisms for ongoing consultations within each country. These mechanisms could be complemented by a relatively small, inexpensive NGO unit in Washington with which Bank project officers would confer on a regular basis. While professional responsibility would preclude Northern NGOs from providing lists of their partners in the South (as is often requested), the unit could, upon a serious request from a project officer, identify through the NGO network those effective and legitimate groups in a particular country and sector that could participate in the design and implementation of a Bank-supported project. (This would be particularly useful in the cases of those countries in which no local consultative mechanisms were established.) The appropriate contacts would be made before the arrival of the Bank team in order to determine the local NGOs' interest and to establish a level of trust among the parties. The Bank officials, on their part, would have to consult seriously with these organizations, give them careful consideration as executing agencies, and report back to the NGO unit on the outcome of their trips.

As mentioned earlier, work of the nature that The Development GAP carried out for Urban Projects in the late 1970s is not without its difficulties and challenges. These range from providing the necessary assurances to local groups to helping them organize themselves and follow Bank guidelines; from dealing tactfully with local government to working within the pressures of the Bank project cycle; from dealing with structural constraints on overseas missions to facing opposition from other Bank offices upon return. Yet, it is possible to work successfully in such an environment. The Development GAP's learning about successful methodologies in this area—i.e., how to involve Third World NGOs in Bank-supported projects—is presented in Appendix B. If such work were to become a matter of approved Bank policy—and ideally a priority within the institution—and appropriate NGO consultative mechanisms were established, most of the obstacles facing a project officer would be removed.

Constructive and structured relationships with NGOs would allow the Bank the advantage of learning firsthand about the milieu in which the poor live and enable it to receive feedback on the projects and programs that it is funding. Staff could be rewarded for visiting local communities, projects, and organizations in order to bring fresh perspectives and options into the institution. Northern NGOs could facilitate this contact. Conversely, if the Bank is seriously concerned about popular participation and the impact of its work on the poor, it should provide institutional support, in conjunction with other funders, to local NGOs to monitor Bank-supported projects in their respective countries. This would constitute a highly relevant and relatively inexpensive vehicle for project oversight and would significantly assist the Bank in the future selection of implementing agencies. Involvement in the monitoring of Bank-supported projects would also enhance the analytical abilities and hence the quality and relevance of the programming of the participating NGOs, while a diversified funding base for these activities would reduce the risk of co-optation.

The half-dozen recommendations discussed above, if implemented, would place the Bank for the first time in a position to execute a lending program that is both relevant and beneficial to the poor. Project officers would be guided by NGOs and other aid institutions, including some bilateral agencies, to the most representative and effective organizations that have matured—or, in the case of some public-sector organizations, reoriented or reformed themselves—to the point of being able to effectively absorb and utilize Bank credit. Large-scale programs carried out by capable public entities would benefit from the involvement of popular organizations throughout the project cycle, from project identification and planning to monitoring and evaluation.

## A REDIRECTION OF IDA RESOURCES

The problem still remains, however, that the terms of IBRD lending often preclude the involvement of the truly poor in project activities. When the International Development Administration was established in 1960, some argued that its highly subsidized and long-term credits should be used for non-revenue-producing projects in a wide spectrum of countries. In fact, a report at the time by the Bank's executive directors called for the funding of high-priority activities even if they were not directly productive. Furthermore, there was no absolute bar in the Articles of Agreement against lending to higher-income countries (World Bank, *IDA in Retrospect*, pp. 4, 7). If such a course had been followed, the world's poor and their activities would have been more frequent beneficiaries of IDA financing than they have been to date.

In practice, however, IDA from the beginning has lent to the poorest countries—not necessarily to the world's poorest people. Through 1982, half of IDA's lending had gone into basic infrastructure (energy, transportation, communications, etc.), industry, and non-project activity. The great bulk of the other half has been directed to the agricultural and rural development sectors (*IDA*, p. 30), with the benefits, as we have seen, not necessarily accruing to the poor.

The reason for the original decision to direct IDA credits to poor countries, without regard to the income level of the actual beneficiaries, was a financial one. At the time of IDA's founding, the IBRD, with only close-to-commercial rates to offer its borrowers, needed a subsidy arm to allow it to continue to lend to a growing number of low-income, "problem" countries, according to Robert

Asher and Edward Mason, semi-official Bank historians. More specifically, IDA was created and folded into the World Bank's operations because the loss of creditworthiness of two such countries, India and Pakistan, was threatening the relevance of the IBRD in the international financial community (Payer, *The World Bank: A Critical Analysis*, p. 32).

In the 1980s, the problems of debt repayment and country creditworthiness have spread across the Third World, and the poor have taken the full brunt of the adjustments. Under the circumstances, it is difficult to accept the allocation of scarce IDA resources—essentially non-interest bearing, long-term money raised directly from Northern taxpayers—to projects that have a higher economic rate of return than do audited IBRD projects. As of 1982, the average quantified rate of return on 183 completed IDA projects was approximately 20 percent (*IDA*, p. 61).

IDA funds would best be utilized to maintain and improve important education, health, and other services that reach the poor and, just as importantly, to support the poor's own social-sector activities and to involve these populations in the productive activities of their country. They could be used to cover the costs of preparing people (by way of education, training, organization, and social promotion) for involvement in economically viable projects, to finance highly integrated projects with both social and economic components, and, if blended with IBRD credits, to reduce the cost of housing, small-business, and agricultural loans so that the truly poor can participate in Bank-supported projects.

While political problems continue to plague IDA replenishments, IDA's financial resources are not insignificant relative to the harder credits made available by the IBRD. Perhaps greater citizen and congressional support could be generated in the United States if it were demonstrated that poor people were actually the direct beneficiaries of these funds. This could be accomplished were the funds applied only to poor people's initiatives and concerns, with priority perhaps given to sub-Saharan Africa. Safeguards would have to be placed on IDA lending to a number of highly indebted countries, particularly in Latin America, to ensure that it is being used to assist the millions of victims of economic recession and austerity and not to pay back commercial creditors. (As it is, an increasing percentage of IDA resources are being used for policy or balance-of-payments lending despite the stipulation in its Articles that lending shall be for specific projects except in special circumstances.)

## POLICY LEVERAGE AND THE POOR

While the Bank has always been involved in the shaping of national economies through the leverage of its project loans and its relationships to private commercial institutions, it has moved into the domain of the International Monetary Fund with its new emphasis on structural adjustment lending. Often described by critics as indirect bailouts of imprudent commercial creditors, SALs are designed explicitly to leverage national-level policy changes that project lending could not elicit.

Such balance-of-payments or commodity-import lending (the most common forms of SALs) was frowned upon by the Bank's founders and subsequent leadership. The Articles of Agreement, like those of IDA, specify that the institution's lending shall be for specific projects except in special circumstances. A generation after the fact, the founders still were mindful of the "problem" balance-of-payment loans made during the 1920s. Broad program lending fell into further disfavor much later when IDA industrial import credits with weak links to specific projects were extended to India and Pakistan in the 1960s and encountered difficulties. Program lending, composed mainly of sector financing, fluctuated between 2 percent and 9 percent of IBRD/IDA commitments during the next decade, with 10 percent interpreted as the legal ceiling (van de Laar, pp. 47–48).

In 1980, the first SALs were made, with specific "macro-conditionality" attached. Such lending reached the level of 9 percent of the Bank portfolio in 1983 and totaled $4.5 billion through 1985. By 1987, non-project lending, including sector loans, had risen to approximately 23 percent of Bank financing, and it was rumored in some quarters that the Bank task force studying the institution's restructuring that year was considering a future level as high as 50 percent. This rapid expansion in policy-based lending is consistent with the broad outlines of the Baker Plan, hastily composed by U.S. Treasury Secretary, James Baker, in 1985—a time when additional commercial bank lending to the Third World was drying up and Latin American countries were discussing a debtors' cartel. The plan pushed the Bank—which was encouraged to foster longer-term growth than had the IMF through the promotion of exports and attendant policy changes—into the center of the arena of debt crisis management and created the illusion that its lending would leverage major influxes of new private capital into the Third World (see Hellinger and Soles, "The Debt Crisis," p.7).

In keeping with the position of the IMF, the Bank has pre-scribed policy changes that place the burden of adjustment on the South's poorest populations, who had nothing to do with incurring their countries' debts of the 1970s. Policies that promote exports shift domestic resources from production for local needs. Increases in agricultural prices may help some farmers in Third World countries, but they severely hurt the growing numbers of urban poor and rural landless, particularly when coupled with the removal of food subsidies. Furthermore, it is not altogether clear that most small farmers do in fact gain from such increases when they relate mainly to export crops, or if they are not accompanied by national investments in the infrastructure and support services needed by farmers to effectively access improved markets.

The typical package of imposed austerity measures—including cuts in wages, jobs, social services, and subsidies on essential goods and services—has devastated the poor from Argentina to Zambia. With governments increasingly unable or unwilling to continue retrenchment in the face of popular unrest without additional outside assistance (Zambia and Ghana were two such cases in 1987), the Bank has made minor modifications in the adjustment package and, as was mentioned earlier, has initiated compensatory programs of food and other assistance targeted at affected populations. It has solicited the involvement of NGOs in these programs as service deliverers, but not as organizers and educators within poor communities. Hence, many NGOs are reluctant to participate. The director of an official European aid agency that has joined the Bank in imposing and financing adjustment programs has, with reference to compensatory programs, privately expressed his opposition to his agency serving as a "firefighter" for the Bank.

A fundamental problem has always been the manner in which the Bank has formulated the policy recommendations that it has taken to governments. Not unlike the typical process of project development, Bank policy formulation seldom, if ever, has involved the very people who are supposed to be the beneficiaries of national policy changes. Rather, Bank economists give macro-economic policy advice in the "neoclassical mode" and, even during the McNamara era, have dealt with poverty alleviation "in a largely subsidiary fashion" (Ayres, p. 235). This explains in good part why structural, distributional, and social issues and policies that most concern the poor—those relating to agrarian reform and land tenancy, for example—receive little emphasis at the Bank.

Instead, the focus has been on agricultural pricing, industrial policy, exchange rates, trade liberalization, export promotion, budgetary policy, cuts in public-sector investment, public-service user charges, and financial and debt management. A study sponsored by the Asian Development Bank summarizes the general package of policy prescriptions recommended by the multilateral development banks, including the World Bank, to Third World borrowers:

> Countries must move away from inefficient import substitution policies and free the economy of import controls, foreign exchange controls, and price controls. The Green Revolution must be promoted as a 'genuine dynamic force' of economic development. . . . [A]gribusiness should be invited to cooperate in a country's drive towards self-sufficiency. Resource allocations must shift from domestic production to export crops for the world market. Local support, generous tax incentives, [and] profit registrations should be provided for foreign investors and legislations must be enacted to create a 'climate of stability' for foreign investment (Rupesinghe, "Export-oriented Industrialization," p. 247).

These are policies that serve other interests than those of the poor. They derive from the analysis of so-called experts far away from the problem.

A knowledgeable U.S. environmentalist criticizes all the multilateral banks for promoting capital-intensive and export-oriented agricultural policies and programs that help push large numbers of poor farmers from suitable land to marginal areas, increasing ecological deterioration and undermining the long-term productive bases of their respective countries. He quotes a Brazilian agronomist, who testified at a special congressional hearing in 1984 that for thirty years such policies had deliberately been shaped to deny the interests of the peasants in his country (Rich, pp. 689, 743).

As the Bank emerges from the trauma of its reorganization, it is being forced to confront the failures of the economic policies it has supported and imposed in the Third World. Current adjustment policies, as a package, add up to little more than the same prescription it has handed out for four decades. If the institution is to escape from the narrow analytical confines defined by its economists and by its commitment to the interests of the international financial community, it will have to draw on the knowledge and perspectives of local populations and their organizations.

**THE U.S. AND THE MDBs**

The myth of the apolitical nature of the World Bank, as well as that of the other multilateral development banks (MDBs), has gradually been put to rest. According to a Bank observer:

> [T]he separation of economics and politics was never achieved or even approximated in the MDBs. But for more than two decades the fiction of separation was possible because the clublike atmosphere of the World Bank permitted the most powerful member to express its political preferences silently and effectively. . . . By the late 1960s, it was not always possible for the United States to work quietly behind the scenes. . . . Stripped of its camouflage, the U.S. position revealed a consistent, inevitable blending of politics and economics (Schoultz, "Politics, Economics, and U.S. Participation," p. 539).

The rather close, informal relationships between Bank and U.S. government officials have always permitted the latter to influence loan proposals, particularly and most importantly early in the preparation process (Schoultz, p. 543).

A 1982 Treasury Department report on the banks is clear on the subject of the use of U.S. influence within these institutions. According to the report, the United States has been instrumental in shaping the structure and mission of the World Bank, in particular, along Western, market-oriented lines. The Treasury notes that those involved in various ways with MDB operations ". . . know from past experience that we are capable and willing to pursue important policy objectives in the banks by exercising the . . . leverage at our disposal" (Department of Treasury, *United States Participation*, p. 47). The report proceeds to document the extensive success of the United States in changing bank policy, practice, and procedure during the 1970s. The 1980s have witnessed a further increase in U.S. pressure.

Unfortunately but predictably, the Treasury, which plays the pre-eminent role within the U.S. Working Group on Multilateral Assistance, and which maintains an exclusive relationship with the U.S. executive directors to the MDBs, has not used its influence within the banks to serve the interests of the poor. Accordingly, it should be the policy of the next U.S. Administration to appoint the head of its principal bilateral aid program as the official link to these directors, a change seriously contemplated at the time of the creation of IDCA in the 1970s. Protected to a degree by the increased autonomy of a restructured AID, the AID leadership and the U.S. executive directors would be able to utilize their influence and cast their votes within the banks primarily on a developmental basis. In lieu of executive branch action in this area, Congress should legislate such a change in U.S. representation in the MDBs.

But Congress must go further than this. It has to exercise more actively its oversight responsibility toward these institutions and utilize the power of the purse—that is, its appropriations function—to pressure for changes in the operations of the World Bank and the other banks. To exercise its oversight function effectively it needs better access to information. While U.S. legislators cannot require the MDBs to furnish them with appropriate documents, they should be able to obtain bank materials from the Administration, which does have access to information on MDB internal operations and policies. But the executive branch—and the Treasury Department, in particular—has always refused to work in partnership with Congress in this area and has kept it in the dark about the most basic MDB policies (Sanford and Goodman, "Congressional Oversight," p. 1064).

In the late 1970s, Rep. Clarence Long (D–MD) fought a battle for greater disclosure of the activities of the MDBs from his position as chair of the House (Appropriations) Subcommittee on Foreign Operations. He opposed the expansion of the banks on the grounds that their assistance was

> not responsive to Congress in the same way our direct foreign aid is. It has not gone to help the really poor people. It has been done in the *name* of the poor, but when you look over the projects, there's very little evidence that it's ever really gone to help the poor. . . . There's no openness. You can't get an audit in the same way that American institutions like AID can be audited.

He praised the Congress for trying

> to make foreign aid helpful to the really poor people of the world. I don't mean just the poor countries, since some of the richest people are in the poor countries. I mean poor *people.* . . . It's pretty clear why help doesn't go to the poor people. Poor people don't have a voice. . . . What happens in a country where they have no vote at all? Of *course* they're not getting anything (*Euromoney,* April 1978).

The appropriations committees of Congress do have the power to hold the MDBs more accountable to the people who underwrite their operations by delaying or limiting appropriations until there is greater disclosure from the Administration and basic changes are made in the banks' operations. But as part of their oversight responsibilities, the Senate Foreign Relations Committee and House Banking Committee should demand comprehensive reports on MDB projects and programming from the banks and apply development rather than financial criteria in monitoring the banks' operations. Particularly now, when the MDBs are being used to help Third World governments repay their countries' foreign commercial creditors at the expense of the poor, it is critical that members of these congressional committees fulfill their responsibility to ensure that the interests of the poor are protected and promoted. The House Foreign Affairs Committee should also participate in the oversight process by providing the Banking Committee with the analysis required for a thorough monitoring on development grounds.

The accountability of the MDBs to the people of both the North and South would be further enhanced if these institutions were required to make their records publicly accessible, to make information on their project and policy planning available to grassroots groups, and, as discussed earlier in this chapter, to involve NGOs in the monitoring of the projects they support. Grassroots organizations and other NGOs in the North and South would then be in a position to provide real information and analysis to their respective governments and to the banks. Congressional committees would be able to determine whether the banks were promoting the interests of the poor in accordance with a set of development criteria and more accurately establish appropriations levels for IBRD recapitalizations and IDA and other MDB replenishments.

These criteria should emphasize at a minimum that:

1. All bank-supported projects, programs, and policies be developed in consultation with indigenous non-governmental organizations whose constituencies are affected by bank activities
2. All potential implementing organizations, including local NGOs, be considered by the lender as project executors and that they be judged on the basis of their respective effectiveness and the strength of their relationships with the

affected local populations

3. The MDB under review support only those projects and policies that promote environmental sustainability and the interests of indigenous populations

4. The economic activities of women be supported on an equal basis with those of men

5. Project and policy support be focused on increasing a country's and/or region's level of economic self-sufficiency

6. The internationally recognized rights of workers and the human and civil rights of all citizens be respected in policy design and in the course of project implementation

7. All grants and soft-loan funds, including those of IDA, be utilized exclusively to support the activities of the marginal populations of all the countries receiving bank financing

A more complete and refined set of criteria should be developed in consultation with representative Third World grassroots organizations.

The congressional appropriations committees have, in fact, tried to use their leverage to hold the banks more accountable to the poor. The first major attempt to earmark U.S. contributions to an MDB for a particular purpose was made in 1975 by Senator Daniel Inouye (D–HI) of the Appropriations Committee, who sought to compel the Inter-American Development Bank to spend $50 million to assist cooperatives, credit unions, and savings-and-loan associations. In 1980 The Development GAP assisted Rep. Long's subcommittee in the drafting of report language that accompanied an appropriations bill and instructed both the U.S. executive director to the World Bank and the director of IDCA to explain and justify the selection of Third World implementing institutions by the Bank and AID. Attention to the application of this provision dissipated, however, in the transition from the Carter to the Reagan Administration.

More effective has been the work of the coalition of U.S. environmental groups referred to earlier. This coalition has helped Congress to develop and pass legislation that requires the Secretary of the Treasury to instruct the U.S. executive directors to the MDBs to promote change within these institutions related to local land use and the protection of Third World environmental resources. This amendment to the Foreign Assistance Act directs U.S. officials to promote within the MDBs a modification in project and country program preparation that ". . . will encourage staff and borrower countries to . . . actively and regularly use the resources of available nongovernmental conservation and indigenous peoples' organizations . . . in the preparation of environmentally sensitive projects and in Bank-supported country program planning and strategy sessions . . ." (U.S. Congress, *Congressional Record*, 16 December 1985). Whether MDB action—and not just their rhetoric—changes significantly in these areas in response to U.S. pressure remains to be seen.

More recently, action by the House Banking Committee has yielded an amendment to the International Financial Institutions Act by way of the final Continuing Resolution of 1987. By law, the Secretary of the Treasury must now instruct the U.S. executive director to the World Bank to facilitate discussions with the other directors of the IBRD and IDA and to propose the establishment of a Grassroots Collaboration Program ". . . to develop improved mechanisms for involving, directly and indirectly, non-governmental organizations in the design, implementation and monitoring of development projects financed by, and development policies established by, such institutions in order to alleviate poverty and promote environmental protection . . ." The legislation suggests that $50 million from the Bank's net income be set aside to facilitate liaison with NGOs as part of mainstream operations and requires a report from Treasury on steps the Administration has taken to promote action in this area and on the response and actions of other Bank executive directors related to this program.

In the end, the governments and people of the Northern industrialized countries must decide what type of institutions they want the World Bank and the other MDBs to be. The assumption by the Bank of part of the IMF's responsibility to apply economic adjustment measures that increasingly allocate borrower country resources to the payment of foreign creditors while imposing austerity measures on the poor has once and for all destroyed the myth that the institution is committed foremost to alleviating poverty in the Third World. Policymakers and public-interest groups do not serve the interests of marginalized populations when they support funding for the MDBs solely in the name of multilateralism, or because they believe that U.S. economic interests are necessarily consistent with those of the poor overseas. Instead, tougher, more critical analysis is required. This analysis should be followed by hard-nosed decisions that would reduce U.S. financing of the Bank and the other MDBs to the extent that they are not supporting sustainable, locally defined development that involves and benefits poor people. Congress and the executive branch should give serious consideration to terminating U.S. support for these institutions if they do not make significant progress in reorienting their operations in a reasonable period of time.

**RECOMMENDATIONS**

1. The World Bank and the other MDBs should shift the export focus of the projects, programs, and policies that they support, and which often damage the local environment and the interests of the poor, to an emphasis on greater regional, national, and local economic diversification and self-reliance. Policy-based lending should support such a reorientation of Third World economies rather than place the burden of economic adjustment on the poor.

2. The Bank should elicit the views of affected marginalized populations, in a systematic and comprehensive fashion through their own organizations, for infusion into its economic and sector work and in its project and program planning, as well as in the formulation of the positions it takes in policy dialogue with governments. Regional and national mechanisms for consultation that are established by local NGOs should be utilized by Bank officials on a regular and systematic basis in order to improve Bank programming.

3. In order to expand its knowledge base and to receive feedback on the projects and programs it supports, the Bank should arrange for local NGOs to help monitor the Bank's loan portfolio in each country.

4. The Bank should pluralize its lending by considering, selecting, and funding more effective, representative, and participatory local organizations as project implementors. It should call upon knowledgeable Northern NGOs and bilateral donor agencies for guidance in the identification of appropriate local non-governmental institutions and public agencies at the provincial and municipal levels that are in a position to utilize its financing effectively in assisting their constituencies. The Bank should require that national government institutions upgrade their outreach, decisionmaking processes, management, and overall effectiveness in order to continue to borrow at the same level.

5. A small NGO advisory unit should be established in Washington, with partial Bank support, to help the Bank gain access

to more appropriate Third World implementing institutions, particularly in countries in which no local NGO consultative mechanisms are in place. The unit should, upon a request from a project officer, identify through the NGO network those effective, locally relevant organizations in a particular country and sector that could participate in the execution of a Bank-supported project.

6. In order to expand further the opportunities for NGO involvement, the Bank's board of governors should amend both the IBRD and IDA statutes so that, in addition to governments, official regional and private financial institutions are permitted to guarantee Bank loans.

7. There should be a reduction in the level of project and program lending, as well as adjustment lending, until the absorptive capacity of relevant and effective institutions can be determined and expanded.

8. IDA funds should be redirected from the poorest countries to poor people, to their activities, and to the social services that facilitate their advancement within all the countries in which the Bank lends. The funds should be used to cover the costs of preparing poor people for their involvement in economically viable projects, to finance highly integrated projects with both social and economic components, and, if blended with IBRD credits, to reduce the cost of other loans so as to enable the truly poor to participate in Bank-supported projects.

9. The Bank should build on the strengths of its recent reorganization—i.e., the decentralization of authority to the Regional offices and to the Country and Technical Departments—by encouraging project officers to be more responsive and innovative through more extensive contact with local organizations in the field.

10. While the project cycle itself should remain as compact as possible, identification and preparation missions should be lengthened to permit more comprehensive contact with local organizations, initiatives, and ideas.

11. Rewards to personnel should be based upon success in promoting popular involvement in projects and upon the projects' performance and long-term sustainability, rather than on one's success in rapidly allocating large amounts of money as part of a central plan. Incentives should be provided to encourage visits to local communities, projects, and organizations in order to bring fresh perspectives and options into the institution.

12. Operational units should be established within each Regional office in the Bank and be given the responsibility for

ensuring that (a) projects and program planning are based upon local input and the capacity of responsive institutions, (b) equal support is provided to the activities in which women are involved, and (c) projects are environmentally sound and regenerative. The capabilities of Bank staff in these areas should be upgraded.

13. The next U.S. Administration should appoint the head of the new, autonomous AID as the official link with the U.S. executive directors to the World Bank and the other multilateral development banks, so that the United States can utilize its influence and cast its votes within the banks on a primarily developmental basis.

14. The World Bank and the other MDBs should be held accountable to Northern citizenry, who underwrite and directly fund their activities, and to the Third World poor, in whose name they undertake their assistance activities. To this end, the records and reports of these institutions should be accessible to the public in general and to the U.S. Congress in particular. The executive branch should be required to share MDB materials, including comprehensive reports on projects and programming, with the relevant congressional committees, so that the latter can knowledgeably carry out their oversight and appropriations functions.

15. The congressional appropriations committees should utilize their influence over the levels of U.S. contributions to IBRD recapitalizations and IDA replenishments to hold the World Bank accountable to its stated commitment to the poor. They should hold up, limit, and/or deny MDB appropriations until there is greater disclosure of bank documents from the Administration and the banks themselves and until basic changes are made in the latter's operations, including a redirection of IDA funding. The criteria by which to judge the banks' performance, which can be found in good part in existing congressional legislation and report language, should include at a minimum the extent to which they: involve Southern NGOs in project, program, and policy planning, and as project implementors; promote environmental sustainability, the activities of women and minority populations, and the rights of workers and other citizens within all bank-supported projects, programs, and policies; provide project and policy support to foster a country's or region's economic self-reliance; and promote a development process consistent with the skills, experience, and interests of local populations.

# EIGHT

# Constructing a New Aid System: Summary and Conclusions

Forty years after the launching of the first development assistance programs, most of the Third World is in desperate shape. Having pursued economic development strategies promoted by foreign aid agencies, these countries find themselves deeply in debt and apparently unable to extricate themselves from a deteriorating situation. Resources invested in production for foreign markets have been yielding diminishing returns, while many countries that were once self-sufficient in food now cannot feed themselves. The poor, who have seldom been more than bit players in scripts written in capital cities (in the North and South), have been further marginalized within their own societies. Not only has poverty not diminished, it has, in fact, spread and intensified throughout the Third World.

Yet, the creativity of the poor themselves and a new set of development organizations to serve their needs have emerged from the bankruptcy and poverty of these failed systems. Change and development are processes ongoing at the local level. Individuals, families, and communities continually plan, organize, and act to improve their lot or, as has characterized the present period, simply to survive in a hostile environment. Some of these grassroots initiatives have developed, at times with the support of small Northern donor institutions, into ongoing organized efforts. Tens of thousands of such entities have been identified across the Third World. Very site-specific, these community organizations, women's groups, church organizations, pre-cooperatives, peasant groups, and other popular entities serve as important vehicles for change for their members and constituencies.

Through the federation of some of these organizations and the emergence of a new generation of support institutions designed to assist and service a broad range of grassroots endeavors, a critically important institutional capacity has developed in the South. The best of these organizations promote a high level of beneficiary participation within development projects. Effective and meaningful participation begins with the articulation of needs by local populations and requires their ultimate control over the process of planning to meet these needs. Local commitment, perhaps the most essential factor in the fostering of self-sustaining development, is best achieved through meaningful participation of this kind. Furthermore, the most appropriate solutions to local problems will arise from, and be best implemented by, those most directly affected by local circumstances.

This approach calls not for the laying of Western-styled modernization upon traditional societies, but for the sensitive extension of development support to Third World populations as they attempt to build upon the strengths of their traditional social and economic systems. The diverse requirements of their activities signal the need for maximum flexibility in assistance programming. The successful implementation of such programs involves the decentralization of the delivery of that assistance in order to reach numerous self-development endeavors and institutions and to respond effectively to the expression of diverse human needs. Decentralization is further impelled by the fact that the needs of these local participatory development endeavors vary greatly according to region, culture, project type, relative level of sophistication, and physical environment.

Effective development assistance programs and organizations focus upon the promotion of programs and projects that clearly demonstrate central elements of beneficiary participation in, and direction of, development processes. They also approach the identification of projects in a responsive rather than initiatory manner wherever local institutional capacity exists, and they institutionalize direct contact by their field staff with those local-level and intermediary organizations to verify participatory mechanisms and directly assist in assessing needs. Except when consultation with local groups yields a request for direct involvement, these aid providers deliver assistance on a hands-off basis that appropriately complements ongoing or emerging self-development endeavors in the field. This assistance is channeled directly through democratic development institutions whose roots extend into the local community fabric or is used to build those organizations where they do not exist. Local groups are helped in attaining the resources and leverage necessary to control and manage their own development.

If there is to be a change in the mode of delivery of development aid, there must be sustained contact between aid officials and grassroots development organizations. This is the level at which genuine development takes place and these are the organizations that require support to make it happen. Awareness, understanding, and sensitivity are imperative on the part of aid personnel if these organizations are to receive the appropriate types and amounts of backing at the appropriate moments in their evolution to enable them to grow, thrive, and promote the interests of their members and constituencies with increasing effectiveness.

The Inter-American Foundation and, more recently, the African Development Foundation, were given such mandates by Congress and have effectively taken up the challenge of responding to the priorities and initiatives of the poor. Protected by institutional autonomy, they have been able to be risk takers in the identification and strengthening of local institutions that provide marginalized populations greater leverage in the stimulation of constructive, non-violent change within their respective societies.

Through its history, the IAF has taken a responsive, low-profile approach and has resisted current fashions in refusing to give preference to any particular sector or type of activity. Rather, its decentralized operations are driven by participatory proposals that enter the institution from below.   Likewise, the ADF, in supporting grassroots activity and institutional development in Africa, has in its early years relied upon Africans, rather than Northern "experts," to guide it. The efforts of these foundations represent to the people of Latin America and Africa a respectful recognition, on the part of the U.S. government, of their right, need, and capacity to define their own development and to forge the future of their societies.

Similarly, the more effective Northern non-governmental organizations, being in direct contact with local representative counterparts in the South, have been able to help build a dynamic process of change and self-reliance. Some have assisted communities to build organizations where none previously existed, while others have been able to transfer adapted technical know-how in a form and manner appropriate to the specific setting.

The record, particularly among U.S. PVOs, however, is very uneven. Relatively few U.S. groups as yet view development as an essentially indigenous process of self-definition. Many still operate their own programs overseas, defining development problems and solutions and maintaining a high degree of operational control. As the U.S. government has dramatically increased its funding of PVO activities over the past decade, too many have sacrificed their independence of action and, in certain instances, have become extensions of AID programming. Losing touch with local realities and the networks and relationships that should form their information base, U.S. PVOs, as a community, have not lived up to their potential as important links between the people and institutions of the United States and those of the developing world.

## FAILURE OF THE PRESENT SYSTEM

Of even more fundamental importance is the fact that the major aid programs operated or controlled by the United States and their assistance strategies have consistently failed to relate in any significant manner to these realities. Inherent in these strategies is the belief that poverty can be successfully addressed in the Third World through the work of outsiders lacking associations with, and understanding of, the poor and their communities. As a result, the major U.S. and multilateral aid agencies have helped to create a modern institutional infrastructure in the developing world that did not emanate from local reality and which has little relationship to it. They work through these structures because, being near-mirror images of their own institutions, they are easily identified and accessible and often share short-term Northern interests.

Billions of dollars are spent on Third World institutions that have no links to the poor and no capacity to incorporate or respond to them. Most Third World governments have relied on a limited, elite skill and institutional base to put to use the large amounts of financing arriving from the United States and other countries. As most of the benefits from aid accrue to those who control the resource flows, the relative standing of the poor has declined as a result of this approach. Thus dualistic economies and societies have often developed, leaving the majority of the population without the resources, capabilities, and opportunities to participate in, or contribute to, meaningful development and engendering social and political polarization and instability.

Export-led growth, free trade, and the expansion of foreign investment have been consistently promoted by the principal aid programs and the institutionalized aid lobby. Private companies have reaped the benefits of aid-funded infrastructural development, investment guarantees, export credits, and procurement contracts. Commercial banks, whose investments have been underwritten by international financial institutions, are today, amidst the deepening debt crisis, particularly supportive of World Bank and AID funding and policy leverage in the Third World. Land-grant universities, consulting firms, many PVOs, and other special interests linked legislatively and/or programmatically with our aid program have chosen to focus on their own more narrow concerns rather than challenge a development and aid paradigm that has failed to involve and support the poor in their self-defined development endeavors.

The New Directions legislation of the 1970s was designed to reverse the top-down assistance approach that grew out of U.S. strategic and economic interests following World War II. While the legislation addressed the objectives and functions of bilateral assistance, it did little to reorganize it or to make its directives operational. AID remained within the State Department and, lacking structural independence, continued to respond to the demands of U.S. short-term foreign policy, those of vested economic interests and, ultimately, those of its own bureaucracy. The direct participation and expressed interests of the poor, in spite of some good intentions in Congress and a great deal of new rhetoric from the aid community, remained, operationally, relatively low priorities.

Serving a variety of U.S. interests has, of necessity, meant for AID throughout its history the assumption of a directive, rather than responsive, posture vis-à-vis the Third World poor and their development interests. Along with the other large aid institutions, it has continued to define and direct the development process and to promote production and the distribution of its benefits as two separate functions. This has been facilitated by the centralization of development planning, programming, and resource control overseas in the hands of a public-sector and private-sector elite. The New Directions legislation, its participatory language notwithstanding, did little to alter the centralized decisionmaking processes of donors and host governments alike and hence has done little to foster self-sustaining development among the poor.

When conservatives assumed control of the White House in the 1980s, they also assumed control of an oversized, overly centralized, and inefficient aid bureaucracy that had channeled billions of dollars through public-sector counterpart institutions that it had helped to create throughout the Third World. The Reagan Administration, however, has misused development aid at least as extensively as had previous administrations. Its commitment to the private sector in development—manifested in AID's policy directives, its large-scale private-sector initiatives, and its Bureau for Private Enterprise—is particularly striking in its fundamental conflict with the language, intent, and spirit of the New Directions legislation and in the support that it has yielded for the already well-to-do. Furthermore, U.S. interests in the security and military spheres have received primary attention within the overall assistance program and budget.

U.S. aid has thus come full circle without, in any significant way, having addressed the fundamental causes of poverty or the profound inequities in wealth that exist in much of the Third World. To the contrary, there has been no period during the forty-year history of U.S. economic assistance when the vast majority of that aid has bypassed the privileged members of those societies. It is hardly surprising, therefore, that these funds have been used primarily to advance the economic and political interests of their relatively small elite, as well as counterpart interests in the United States.

The aid establishment travels in different circles and on different roads than do the poor. They, and the institutions with which they associate, rarely have much contact. As Third World non-governmental intermediary organizations that are representative of and responsive to the poor mature, they have become viable alternatives to the ineffective and autocratic public institutions often chosen by major aid to carry out development projects. Their expanding constituencies make increasing demands for credit and other services. In response, many of these institutions have developed, often with outside assistance from smaller aid organizations, strong administrative capabilities and the ability to manage increasingly more sophisticated credit mechanisms and programs and larger amounts of funds. At this point in their evolution, the resources available from the smaller foreign assistance organizations become insufficient. With funds from domestic institutions generally inaccessible, some of the Third World's most effective development organizations have looked to the larger international aid agencies for the scale of financing that their constituencies require.

To date, however, such support has rarely been forthcoming from AID, the World Bank, and other major providers of aid. It has remained consistently marginal rather than integral to their mainstream operations. Few have recognized popular organizations as the engines of development and relinquished to them control and direction of local economic activity. None, for sure, have included these representative organizations in planning and programming within their own agencies or with host governments, despite the fact that they are usually the only dependable sources of information about local-level needs, priorities, and capabilities. Consultations between aid donors and governments have, as a matter of course, excluded such representation of the poor, denying planners essential perspectives and input and virtually ensuring that other interests will be served. For this very reason, the effects of "policy dialogue," as presently designed, will likely continue to do more to undermine the position of the poor than to advance it.

**LIMITATIONS OF THE MAJOR AID INSTITUTIONS**

The deviation of AID from its development mandate has led Congress to demand stringent reporting on the part of the Agency. This is ironic, for many of the non-developmental interests that affect AID's performance have been promoted legislatively. Nonetheless, the effect has been the development of a cumbersome bureaucracy geared to respond to Congress rather than to the Third World poor. Despite recent changes, AID's procedures for program and project development and review remain enormously complicated and time-consuming. The demands and length of the project cycle hinder the ability of the field missions to be responsive and to support emerging endeavors at critical junctures in their evolution. Decisionmaking is still highly centralized, and the demands of headquarters drown the field missions in paperwork. Consultants are hired to do most of the missions' project-related work. AID mission staff have become largely removed from the local realities, and the disincentives to risk taking have, in fact, driven them to try to define and control the local project environment.

Severe, self-imposed limitations on the range of institutional choice is one of the principal outgrowths of AID's internal systems. The nature of the project cycle, the heavy paperwork, the lack of incentives to take risks in optimizing project quality, and, in some countries, the pressure to move money generally lead project officers to select large projects operated by established institutions rather than smaller participatory endeavors run by organizations outside AID's normal sphere of contacts.

Finally, as the Agency moves increasingly toward policy and program lending, even the potential for links to local organizations and populations through the project development process is being lost. This leaves all of AID's work, including its policy dialogues with government, increasingly ill-informed by local reality. The recent move to further decentralize staff overseas will have little effect on the quality and relevance of the development that AID promotes if the Agency remains systematically divorced from the poor and their daily circumstances.

Similarly, there exists a variety of factors that limit the World Bank's ability to respond to the new generation of participatory institutions in the Third World. Although the Bank shifted toward a poverty focus last decade, its relationships in the field, its internal reward system, and, indeed, its basic purpose as an institution remained essentially unchanged. As a facilitator of private capital flows, the Bank has been driven by the need to move money, build necessary infrastructure, and shape open economic systems within borrower countries. This, in turn, leads officials to establish and maintain funding relationships with government ministries and development banks that can theoretically absorb (if not effectively use) large sums of money for projects under centralized control. Under these circumstances and the pressure of the project cycle, project officers are not rewarded for engaging in grassroots consultations, for risk taking, or for innovation in the field.

Not surprisingly, a good number of Bank-supported projects have failed, even when judged by the Bank's own standards. While it is recognized by many within the Bank that a lack of local participation and commitment and the poor selection of implementing institutions have been at the heart of these failures, little has been done to rectify the situation. The Bank continues to provide financing to institutions that have proven unable, or unwilling, to reach the poor segments of the population and gain their confidence, and has not promoted local participation in planning and project design. Limited, but successful, experimentation in the late 1970s to involve more appropriate, primarily nongovernmental, institutions as project executors has stimulated little follow-up action. It remains to be seen if the recent progress made within the context of the ongoing Bank-NGO dialogue toward establishing consultative relationships between the Bank and Southern NGOs will lead, in fact, to the inclusion of the latter in the identification, design, implementation, and monitoring of Bank-supported projects.

The interests of the poor will likely continue to be lost in the Bank's rush to loan even more money during the next five years. Smaller-scale, participatory projects that truly address local needs stand little chance when the alternative is to spend tens of millions of dollars through large public and private institutions. These problems will intensify with the growing use of structural and sector adjustment lending to leverage policy changes and underwrite commercial bank loans in borrower countries. The Bank, as well as the other MDBs, has encouraged government policies that have, for example, promoted capital-intensive, export-oriented agriculture. This type of production has, in turn, harmed both the environment and small farmers. Until local populations are consulted through their organizations in Bank policy formulation, the local impact of many government policies will be decidedly negative and the burden of economic adjustment will continue to fall on the poor.

**PROPOSALS FOR CHANGE**

For U.S. and multilateral assistance to help build the bases for democratic change and development overseas, the aid programs must themselves be transformed. Specific recommendations for achieving this end conclude Chapters 4 through 7. These proposals are summarized below and, on the basis of these reforms, a new decentralized development assistance structure is suggested that would enable aid institutions to support, in a logical and consistent manner, the growth and development of participatory institutions throughout the Third World.

The regional development foundation model, which has worked successfully in the cases of the IAF and ADF, should be applied to Asia, to the public funding of PVOs, and, most significantly, in the restructuring of our principal bilateral aid program. In all cases, board members and presidents should be named who understand the realities of local-level development and who will protect their institution's independence from political interference.

To fill a current gap in the official U.S. aid system, a new Asian and Pacific Development Foundation should be established as a vehicle for the transfer of public funds to local-level initiatives in Asia. The ADF legislative mandate should serve as a model for similar legislation for the new foundation, though the specifics of the bill should be shaped to correspond to the needs, capabilities, and realities of Asian societies. All project funding should be reserved for Asian organizations that are engaged in, or promote, participatory development activity, with the goal of building a basis for self-sustaining change.

The three foundations should refrain from defining and focusing their funding on any particular sector or type of development activity. Such a posture, if accompanied by decentralized decision-making structures and experienced field staff, should enable the institutions to be fully responsive to a broad range of truly local initiatives.

For similar purposes, there should be established a new Foundation for Private and Voluntary Cooperation that would channel public funds to PVOs adhering to relatively strict operational standards and project criteria. As an independent government corporation, it would serve to shield PVOs from the current pressures to operate as extensions of AID. Project funding should be directed toward the building and strengthening of local organizational capacity and the enhancement of beneficiary participation in decisionmaking. To encourage local institution building and the phasing out of PVO involvement, program grants should be extended to those agencies that have demonstrated effectiveness in these areas.

The Foundation would assist PVOs in making necessary changes in their field operations and in their internal administration as part of its mandate to help the PVO community to adopt a more responsive posture vis-à-vis local populations and organizations. It should encourage collaboration among U.S. and indigenous NGOs to address locally defined institutional and development constraints, giving priority in its financing to those activities undertaken jointly by PVOs and their local counterparts. Finally, forums and assistance should be provided for the discussion of development and programmatic issues among voluntary agencies, with program officials and policymakers, and with the U.S. public.

In order to increase the independence and relevance of the principal U.S. bilateral aid program, Congress should authorize, through a Development Assistance Act, the creation of the Administration for International Development, as a government corporation with a board of directors, to replace the present AID and the moribund International Development Cooperation Administration (IDCA). It should provide the new institution with a clear development mandate and thereafter restrict its own involvement to the exercise of its appropriations and oversight functions; its oversight capabilities should meanwhile be upgraded so as to enable it to hold AID more accountable to the poor. Aid for political and security purposes should be designated as such and kept legislatively and administratively separate from development assistance. The State Department should control and manage those Economic Support Fund resources designated for non-developmental purposes and should be prohibited from utilizing those funds to influence development policy.

AID should be streamlined, with most functions and responsibilities decentralized to the field. The staff of country missions should be based largely in provincial centers, from where they can better identify and assess the performance and legitimacy of development organizations and provide support for region-wide endeavors. They and knowledgeable representatives of popular organizations should participate in the mission's program and policy planning sessions. AID's principal programmatic responsibilities, as well as most of its technical expertise, should be centered, however, in sub-regional "cluster" offices, which would group countries by their proximity and their ecological and ethnological similarities. Final determinations regarding policy, programming, and individual project funding should be made at this level, if they cannot be made satisfactorily at the country level. Regional offices should be small and provide administrative and logistical support to the "cluster" and country offices.

The new aid administration should formulate country assistance plans and budgets based upon local input and projections of the needs and absorptive capacity of effective development institutions. This should allow for smaller AID budgets in the short to medium term. So as to enable AID to be truly responsive to evolving needs and opportunities, Congress should permit unutilized funds to be carried forward at year's end and, once AID is structurally independent, eliminate functional accounts. The new AID should provide program assistance to those governments that have exhibited a commitment to equitable development and whose agencies have demonstrated a capacity to promote it. Other countries should receive aid on an institution-by-institution basis, with assistance being reserved for those organizations in the public and non-governmental sectors that have a demonstrated capability in the promotion of participatory development and in the management of funds.

It is critical that the World Bank also implement a number of reforms that enhance local participation in Bank-supported projects and in Bank decisionmaking. Adjustments should be made in the

Bank's project cycle, reward system, and internal decisionmaking structure to encourage project officers to expand their search for effective projects and implementing organizations so as to include NGOs and other institutions working directly with the poor. Lending levels should be reduced and then parallel the growth of the absorptive capacity of such institutions. The systematic use by the Bank of consultative mechanisms established by Southern NGOs on both a regional and national basis would provide the former with the field contacts and grassroots perspectives necessary to form a new basis for program and policy planning, project identification, and funding allocations.

Under its new, decentralized structure, The Bank should ensure that priority is given to grassroots concerns by coordinating its decisionmaking and actions related to environmental issues, women's activities, and NGOs within operational units in each of its Regional offices in Washington.

At the same time, it should encourage the establishment in Washington of a new independent advisory unit by non-governmental organizations to facilitate access by its project officers to effective Third World NGOs that have often been supported in their expansion by groups in the North. To further enable the funding of endeavors that truly incorporate and benefit the poor, as well as to cover the costs of important social services presently threatened with budget cuts, IDA resources should be directed to the needs and activities of marginalized populations in all the countries in which the IBRD funds. In the policy realm, the Bank must systematically draw upon grassroots views, as expressed through local organizations, in its structural and sector adjustment lending to ensure its relevance.

The U.S. government should appoint the head of the new bilateral aid administration as the official link to the U.S. executive directors to the Bank and the other MDBs in order to ensure that decisions and votes are taken on a primarily development basis. The Congress should direct the executive branch to pressure these banks to make necessary reforms, including those the former has mandated in recent legislation and report language. The congressional oversight committees should receive all relevant MDB documents from the executive branch so that they can exercise their responsibilities in an informed manner based on a set of development criteria that emphasize, in very specific terms, the principles of equity, participation, sustainability, and self-reliance. Congressional appropriations to the MDBs should be reduced or eliminated if these institutions do not reorient their operations within a reasonable period of time.

## STRUCTURING A MORE RESPONSIVE AID SYSTEM

The current aid structure must be turned on its head if it is to hold any significance for the majority of the people of the Third World. The large assistance agencies must support non-governmental intermediary organizations and public-sector institutions that represent the aspirations of the poor and help foster constructive change. They should not be expected to provide support directly to organizations in villages and urban slums; this is the job of the regional development foundations (RDFs), PVOs, and other Northern NGOS. They must, however, be in contact with these local realities and the organizations that work in them if they are to be relevant to the processes of change in any society.

A host of small aid organizations in the North, including the RDFs and a number of U.S. PVOs, have effectively cultivated and supported the growth of Third World popular organizations. They have important roles to play in the provision of the educational, technical, managerial, and financial support that these organizations require as they emerge and evolve into more sophisticated institutions. While the RDFs should be expected to help establish this institutional base for change, the work of individual PVOs is, indeed, private and voluntary. As a result, their contributions to an official aid effort cannot—or at least should not—be programmed. Some PVOs may choose, however, to provide technical or managerial support to local NGOs referred to them by the RDFs, and funding would be made available from the new PVO foundation for this purpose. Conversely, the RDFs would consider for grant funding those project proposals from the Third World groups referred to them by the PVO foundation.

An important result of the work of these smaller aid organizations has been the emergence and growth of larger representative and intermediary NGO structures that respond to the needs of local groups and populations. While logic would call for the major donors to build on these efforts and provide the support these Third World institutions need to meet the growing demand of their constituencies, these donors continue to invest the vast majority of their funds in conventional institutions that have an abysmal record in the management of resources and in the application of those resources to successful development endeavors. This dualistic aid approach clearly makes no sense. Millions of dollars are spent to develop an effective, broad-based institutional capacity, which is subsequently ignored by funders who place billions in institutions that have far more often been the problem rather than the solution. The result is the creation and perpetuation of dualistic social structures that parallel the present aid paradigm.

Structural autonomy and a decentralized internal structure would enable AID to participate in a revitalized aid program reoriented to assist the poor through more appropriate institutions. These changes would put AID in a position to recognize the development capacity of these institutions and to respond to it appropriately. It could provide large-scale grant support or financing on soft terms (depending on the nature of the development activity and the strength of the organization) to federated structures, service organizations, and other intermediary and facilitator institutions, as well as to the more responsive public-sector agencies, particularly those at the municipal and provincial levels. It could provide the long-term support that institution-building activities, for instance, require. It could also help these organizations convert simple revolving loan funds into more sophisticated financial mechanisms, upgrade their administrative discipline, and enhance their leverage with national government agencies and access to their decisionmaking, resources, and services.

When their internal administrative and financial systems are in place, these intermediary and service organizations become prime candidates for financing by the World Bank, as well as the Inter-American, African, and Asian Development Banks. Building on the longer- and harder-term lending of AID and other bilateral aid institutions, the banks would provide larger amounts of credit at somewhat less than prevailing international interest rates. With credit generally unavailable from domestic public and private sources for non-governmental development activity and with local-level government often lacking in resources, Bank financing can be a critically important injection of capital for local endeavors.

If IDA funds were available for poor people rather than poor countries, they could be used alone or mixed with IBRD funds to reduce the cost of borrowing and support a broader range of development programs. They might also be used in much the same manner as are the low-interest loans of the Program for the Financing of Small Projects of the Inter-American Development Bank (IDB), which provides financing of up to $500,000 to indigenous NGOs. While the IDB program serves a useful purpose, it has done little to influence the institution's mainstream operations, which continue, for the most part, to bypass Latin America's most effective development organizations. It would be logical for the recipients of support from the Small Projects unit eventually to become candidates for normal Bank financing, and for the unit to be an advocate within the IDB for a major project implementing role for these organizations. The IDB and the World Bank, as well as the other MDBs, might also fund these NGOs to help monitor the environmental and development impact of the projects that the banks finance.

While formal coordination among the various aid institutions can endanger the independence and responsiveness of the smaller funders, communication among them, both in Washington and in the field, is essential. Interaction in Washington should be limited to the sharing of learning, which would constitute a significant contribution by the RDFs and PVOs to the larger aid organizations. This transfer of learning would be facilitated by the recommended participation of the presidents of the RDFs and the PVO foundation on the board of the new bilateral aid administration.

Communication on program-related matters should be restricted to the field. There, the discourse would ideally be more structured. AID should elicit the assistance of local NGOs in each country, in accordance with Africa aid legislation under consideration in Congress, to help it establish consultative mechanisms through which knowledgeable NGO representatives could, on a regular basis, advise AID on matters ranging from institutional choice and project "find" to programming and policy formulation. The contacts with NGOs and the informal advisory sessions could be arranged by representatives of the RDFs, U.S. PVOs, and other Northern NGOs, who might also participate in these meetings. Quarterly or semi-annual meetings might be held for the specific purpose of injecting local-level input into the preparation of Action Plans, Country Development Strategy Statements, and positions for policy dialogue.

It must be made clear, however, that, while AID might propose the establishment of the consultative mechanisms, control of the consultative process itself would have to be in the hands of the participating NGOs. It is they who have the more extensive contact with local-level realities and who understand the context and pertinence of the information and perspectives they would be sharing with AID. If AID were permitted to direct the consultations and elicit the information it needed to fit into its own preconceived plans, little progress will have been made and the position of local popular organizations could be jeopardized. Until AID has gained greater autonomy and far more experience with, understanding of, and sensitivity to such organizations, there are many small aid organizations that will refrain from playing an intermediary role.

Most Northern NGOs would probably take the same position vis-à-vis the World Bank and the other MDBs and international aid organizations. Regional forums and national mechanisms for consultation must be organized by Southern NGOs (with Northern NGO assistance where requested) to ensure that they are structured to promote local development objectives. For their part, most Northern NGOs would also be wary of participating in the establishment of a World Bank advisory unit unless the Bank demonstrated a sincere interest in responsibly supporting the independent efforts of their Southern counterparts. Once trust had been established, the unit would assist World Bank project officers preparing to travel to the field to identify potential implementing institutions; it would facilitate field contacts and prepare Third World institutions for Bank staff visits. Should relationships develop in the field, Northern counterpart NGOs might play a useful advisory and supportive role during project development. The debriefing of project officers by the unit upon their return would help to build an important knowledge base about a relatively new set of aid relationships.

## LINKAGES ON THE PERIPHERY

A major question is where within the U.S. government structure responsibility should lie for multilateral bank policy. When IDCA was established in 1979, Treasury prevented the usurping of its authority in this area by the IDCA director. Many have continued to urge that the head of our bilateral aid program become the U.S. representative to these banks in order to bring a developmental perspective to bear on them. In some European governments, such is already the arrangement (but it is difficult to assess the impact that it has had). In the current context of U.S. foreign aid, it is difficult to see what, if any, difference such a change would make. Were AID to be transformed into an independent administration, however, its control over MDB policy would indeed be significant. If control were not wrested from Treasury, the new aid administration should be given the responsibility to monitor MDB-supported projects in the field and to report to Congress, suggesting ameliorative actions. The aid administration should not go so far as to establish structured relationships, or participate on coordinating committees with other government institutions, such as the State and Treasury Departments, whose purposes are other than developmental. There is little evidence that such formal interactions have moved the latter to become more "anti-poverty" in nature, while these structured contacts can have unfortunate reverse effects on development assistance organizations, as history has shown.

An independent and restructured AID could play a constructive role, however, vis-à-vis the Overseas Private Investment Corporation (OPIC). In 1977, The Development GAP assisted the House Subcommittee on International Economic Policy and Trade in drafting a development mandate for OPIC that was subsequently included in the congressional report accompanying the OPIC Amendments Act of that year. Eleven criteria, by which OPIC-assisted projects were to be judged, were laid out. OPIC's development office has made a good-faith effort to comply with several of them, particularly those relating to the generation of employment and to forward and backward linkages to local enterprises. Yet, it has been unable, because of its small size, to assess, for example, the effects of investments on *net* local employment, the supply and distribution of basic foodstuffs, and the degree of concentration of the ownership of land and other productive resources.

A fundamental problem facing OPIC is that it is, by its nature, not capable of complying with this mandate. Although authorized under the Foreign Assistance Act, the Corporation is not a development assistance institution and thus should not be included in a new development assistance structure. Its principal mandate is to assist U.S. companies through the provision of investment guarantees or financing. Hence, its resources are not provided directly to the poor and the benefits they generate trickle down, if they are enjoyed by the poor at all.

Wherever OPIC is located in the government, there is a need nonetheless to ensure to the maximum extent possible that its efforts have a positive impact on development overseas. Its development mandate has been somewhat helpful in this regard, and it appears that recent legislation backed by environmentalists is being taken at least as seriously by OPIC. Both environmental and aid institutions could and should channel to OPIC and Congress the local-level input they need to monitor effectively the impact of investments at that level.

The objectives of the Peace Corps, on the other hand, are consistent with those of the regional development foundations and many of the PVOs, as well as with AID's congressional mandate. It can—and already does to a limited extent—play a constructive role at the local level by informing AID and the RDFs of promising participatory development initiatives. This role, and the Peace Corps' overall effectiveness, would be enhanced if it were to program greater volunteer involvement with organizations that work directly and in a participatory fashion in poor communities.

The Peace Corps would also become more relevant if it did not prescribe development strategies. It has jumped on the small-enterprise bandwagon, for example, and is expanding its program in this area, emphasizing small-business development in its discussions with host-country governments. Such initiatives, which compromise the responsiveness of the organization, are, in good part, the outgrowth of a large bureaucracy in Washington. The Peace Corps would be far better off if it were to reduce the size of its Washington staff dramatically, and encourage all programming to be handled in the field. Its recent success in depoliticizing the selection of country directors should greatly improve the quality of local programming.

The emphasis on small business also reflects the political pressures the Peace Corps has faced, especially over the past several years. It has effectively resisted many of these, but expansion of its program in Central America and the Caribbean on the heels of the Kissinger Commission report and the Reagan Administration's Caribbean Basin Initiative raises serious doubts about its true independence. Like the regional development foundations and the proposed aid administration, the Peace Corps could exercise greater independence of action if it were to be reconstituted as a government corporation and provided with an independent board of directors, as has been proposed in congressional legislation.

Whatever the strengths and weaknesses of the Peace Corps, it provides an invaluable experience to its volunteers. They constitute an important resource that AID and other aid organizations should bring in-house to an even greater extent than they do today.

## DOING MORE WITH LESS

While field-experienced staff can do much to improve the quality of development aid, the importance of its quantity can be, and has been, overemphasized. It is becoming increasingly evident that increases in aid have not been paralleled by improvements in the lot of the Third World poor. It is equally clear that the institutions that gobble up large amounts of our assistance have far less to show for it than do smaller initiatives requiring relatively little support.

This raises a number of fundamental issues. First, the question of *who* receives aid is far more important than the amount transferred. Second, as aid by itself cannot resolve the poverty problem in the Third World—where at least three-quarters of most countries' populations are poor—aid must be able to help stimulate a development dynamic that can call forth the enormous amount of human, physical, and technological resources that are found at the local level. The recipients of our aid should therefore be chosen on the basis of their ability to generate and support local processes of participatory development. Third, aid should be provided to these organizations in amounts commensurate with their absorptive capacity, and not on the basis of country budgets predetermined by assistance agencies and their desire to move money.

A decade ago, Robert Mashek of the Inter-American Foundation reached similar conclusions after reviewing ten projects financed by AID, the World Bank, and the IDB in Latin America. In a subsequent memorandum to the International Division of the Office of Management and Budget, he criticized the top-down approach taken by the three institutions and suggested that they support ". . . those programs and projects that people and organizations plan and support with their own resources, be they money, manpower, or political will." He concluded that "global increases in foreign assistance budgets should be postponed until major changes are instituted. . . . Absorptive capacity cannot be determined until there is some sense for the initiatives that the developing people will take" (Mashek, *Memorandum*, pp. 3–4).

This and similar advice from others has gone unheeded for years, but now the U.S. deficit crisis is forcing a curtailment of the expansion of aid programs and budgets. Selective cuts could be made that would preserve the institutions and programs that have been effective in promoting equitable development, while eliminating investments in counterproductive programs and those expenditures that do little to enhance programmatic effectiveness. Congress would be able to make significant cuts in development assistance if the institutions that dispense it were limited in their project and program funding to providing support to those organizations with successful track records *only*, in amounts that match their absorptive capacity. Additional savings could be achieved though a sizeable reduction in both AID's Washington-based staff and in its dependence on consultants to handle project-related work in the field. Of course, substantial cuts could be made in ESF and military assistance without any adverse effects on the efforts of the poor.

Aid appropriations could be further reduced if Congress were to reject requests for increases in the IBRD's capitalization and IDA replenishments linked to the massive expansion planned for World Bank lending. A significant portion of these credits will be made available for structural and sector adjustment purposes in an attempt to help commercial banks recover their problem loans and to turn government policies further in a direction that has been disastrous for the Third World poor over the past forty years. The use of taxpayers' money to bail out these banks would be an irresponsible act on the part of taxpayers' representatives. Similarly, Congress should limit its appropriations to the other MDBs until they reorient their lending and demonstrate that they are supporting institutions and programs that incorporate and benefit the poor and their activities.

Meanwhile, the growing demands and dependencies of the PVO community on government funds could be effectively and responsibly reduced by restricting the government contribution to PVO budgets to 50 percent of their respective incomes. In determining the budget of the new PVO foundation, Congress could project the prospective demands on the foundation by calculating the current level of PVO fundraising among their constituencies and in the private sector in general.

The regional development foundations, on the other hand, should receive modest and steady increases in their budgets. The Inter-American and African Development Foundations have demonstrated their abilities to respond to the self-help efforts of popular organizations, to restrict their funding to this clientele, and to follow faithfully their congressional mandates. The increases should be modest, to enable the two foundations (as well as a new Asia counterpart) to learn from their grant-making, avoid over-funding, and resist bureaucratic impulses. Overhead, in the meantime, should be kept low.

It is not enough, however, that the more responsive aid institutions satisfy themselves with effective small-scale funding. At one time, the building of a broad base for change would have been sufficient. It is still critically important, but not enough in and of itself. Over the past several years, the impact of aid and of the development strategies it has fashioned has been dramatic, as the circumstances of the poor have deteriorated rapidly. Increasing numbers have slipped into survival modes. No amount of local-level funding can check this tide as long as Northern governments promote national policies and programs overseas that are antithetical to the well-being of the poor and the processes of social change. Those Americans who work at the local level in the Third World and who understand this reality have a responsibility to convey this perspective in the public arena.

Anger and resentment linger just under the surface in much of the developing world. Those in this country who do not recognize this—who do not discern the rapid marginalization of much of its population—are seriously out of touch with Third World realities. One has simply to view these societies from within their urban slums and rural villages to understand that the system is continually working against rather than for the poor. From those vantage points it is not difficult to see the absurdity of people thousands of miles away continually shaping new solutions to problems they have never experienced, for societies they do not understand, for the purpose of assisting people whom they have never consulted. It is as much this arrogance as the impact of our policies that angers so many in the South.

We are at a crossroads. The profound problems that the trillion-dollar Third World debt both reveals and creates will not go away. We have a choice. We can continue to define development for the people of the Third World, wrapping it in the rhetoric of whatever fad or cliché follows "basic human needs" or "private-sector initiative," or we can let go and allow the poor to define their own needs and support them as they take their own initiatives. We need to change the paradigm, turn it upside down, and build respectfully from below. If we listen to the voices of the poor, recognize and underwrite their institutions as engines of social change, and withdraw support from those structures that are now impeding that change, we can play a role in the engendering of equitable, broad-based, self-sustaining development and new democratic structures.

For many decisionmakers in the United States and in the aid world, letting go and leaving room for the intended beneficiaries of our assistance to define their development courses is a risky proposition. It provides no assurances that the routes chosen will be familiar or that they will lead in directions that appear compatible with short-term U.S. interests, however they may be defined. Yet, from a national-interest perspective, this is the very strength of a foreign aid approach that is responsive to the needs and efforts of the people of the Third World.  It represents to those populations a recognition on the part of the United States of their right and ability to determine their own future.  This recognition is the basis for sustained economic and social stability and holds the promise of lasting relationships of mutual appreciation and respect.  It is in the building of this stability and such relationships that true, long-term U.S. interests lie.

The paradigm we have presented holds this promise.  We recognize its limitations and some of the difficulties it would create were it not to be implemented appropriately.  It is not designed to allow us to solve the Third World's problems, nor to provide a quick fix, nor to manage the development process.  Its strength is in its responsiveness, in the trust it implicitly places in the Third World poor and their own organized efforts, and in its recognition of the creativity and resiliency that exists at the grass roots throughout the Third World.

Those who would question an investment of so much faith in popular organizations need only reflect upon the folly of channeling billions of dollars through unresponsive, ineffective bureaucracies of often corrupt and repressive governments or through private structures controlled by these countries' small, wealthy elites in the hope of helping the poor and generating a process of self-sustaining development.  It is bad enough that we have poured so much money down this drain.  What is worse is that it has been used to further concentrate power and wealth, and that its effect has been the perpetuation and exacerbation of poverty.  Certainly, there is no developmental basis for a continuation of our assistance through the major aid institutions unless they become vastly more effective and accountable to the poor populations that they claim they are serving.

The only truly successful aid programs have been those that have responded to the requests of poor people's organizations and helped to build a support system from below.  The foundations of such a system already exist in the public and non-governmental sectors.  The need now is to build the right structure upon it.

# A Strategy for Popular Involvement in Regional Development Planning

While the use of conventional data has afforded regional planners the capability to generate technically feasible plans, problems can arise in implementation due to the planner's lack of understanding of the dynamics at play at local levels. A valid understanding of local and regional dynamics can only come about through communication between the planner and public. Beyond this, there has been increasing recognition of the need to involve local populations, especially the poor, in determining the nature of projects and programs from which they are to benefit.

In order to accommodate public input, successful participatory planning has usually involved a decentralization of the planning process in which local plans are aggregated to form a regional strategy. While the logic in favor of such decentralization is strong, most existing regional planning entities are in fact centralized, and it is unrealistic to presume that they can be dramatically reoriented and restructured in the short term. It is far more practical to move toward decentralization gradually; that is, to pursue the initial opening-up of conventional planning to allow for meaningful public participation.

Adapted from *Public Participation in Regional Development Planning,* by The Development GAP, in conjunction with Avrom Bendavid-Val (1980), a synthesis and elaboration of two reports on the subject commissioned by the Urban Office of USAID's Development Support Bureau.

There are two major considerations which govern the initial attempt to elicit public participation at the regional level. First, meaningful participation will best result from ongoing dialogue between the planning entity and local populations, rather than from the elicitation of one-way, one-time public inputs. Second, to assure the effectiveness and utility of public participation to planners, public inputs must be made to conform, in form and content, to the different data needs of the various stages of the planning process.

There are various approaches to eliciting participation, and the utility of a particular approach in any given planning context must be assessed according to a few key criteria. These include: (1) the *dependability* of the information which would result from the use of a given approach; (2) the *practicality* of the approach with regard to cost and efficiency; (3) the approach's *integrability* with the regional planning process; and (4) the amount of *local support* for the plan which a particular approach may generate.

A summary and initial assessment of the categories of participatory approaches available to planning entities are as follows:

1. *"One on one" approaches*: all approaches employed to elicit local input on an "individualized" basis from the general local population. This general approach has two principal strengths. First, it provides a sound basis for eliciting a broad sampling of individually expressed needs. Second, it gives the planner a high degree of control over the precise form and content of the information injected into the planning process. On the negative side, the approach does not provide a reliable means for gaining a "depth of understanding" of felt needs. Furthermore, it engenders a "passive" posture on the part of respondents and therefore does not constitute a vehicle by which intensive local support for the implementation of the plan can be mustered.

2. *Communication with community leaders;* interaction with local leaders that are representative of their community, have some degree of authority, are sensitive to the development concerns of the community, and understand the broader planning context. This approach ranks high in terms of practicality and integrability since community leaders are usually visible, approachable, and often more knowledgable about development issues than the average citizen. They can also be valuable allies in the attempt to implement a plan. On the other hand, they may in fact not be highly representative of the local population—neither in terms of their status nor their perspectives—and can thus prove to be undepend-

able sources of needs information, as well as drawbacks to sustained program implementation. In addition, the costs of attempting reliably to determine leader "representativeness" can often outweigh the benefits to be derived from the use of this approach.

3. *Interaction through community meetings:* the convening of community meetings or public hearings to discuss important planning issues and receive helpful feedback regarding local needs. If carried out with consummate skill, this approach can render reliable, collectively expressed needs information, while providing the basis for the creation and growth of an authentic movement toward development at the community level. It is also practical, since it does not require the existence of institutional bases at that level; in fact, it might stimulate the creation of such institutions. Community meetings can be difficult to organize and control, however, and skill is required to elicit broad, democratic, and technically manageable responses. Accordingly, this approach necessitates the involvement of experienced community organizers.

4. *Interaction with representative community and multivillage organizations:* communication with established, representative local-level organizations which have a life of their own beyond functioning in response to the planner's request for input into the planning process. Although considerable time and effort are often required to identify and assess the representativeness of these organizations and their leaders, the expense can prove worthwhile. Representative, local-level institutions can provide an efficient and viable basis for both the reliable elicitation of expressed needs—either on a one-time or ongoing basis—and the generation of local support for the implementation of a plan. In order to assure the cooperation of these institutions, accommodation may be required in the planning process for delays caused by intraorganizational decisionmaking and for adjustments in response to organizational feedback.

5. *Interaction with representative, functional organizations:* communication with local-level organizations whose existence, structure, and operations are based upon a specific production-related function. The considerations here relate quite closely to those regarding representative community organizations. Again, considerable time and effort must be spent in determining representativeness, and some flexibility in the planning process must be demonstrated to insure ongoing cooperation. Functional organizations can be most useful in: (a) the elicitation of highly accurate information, and expertise, related to their respective service

specializations; and (b) the lending of experienced support to the implementation of a plan. As functional organizations may not represent to any significant degree the population as a whole, they do not provide reliable sources for the general elicitation of expressed needs.

6. *Interaction with representative, regional-level organizations:* communication with regional-level organizations composed of numerous local groups which may be both community and functionally oriented. A major consideration with regard to this approach is whether the considerable expenditure of time, effort, and other resources required to determine the degree of representativeness of regional organizations and their leaders is worth the potentially large payoff that they may produce. Dividends can include highly accurate and useful information, effective planning assistance, and region-wide support for the implementation of the plan. To the extent that these organizations are representative, their broad perspectives and experience in planning render them extremely valuable assets to the planner. This approach can call for the planner to surrender some control in order to better coordinate regional and local-level planning processes.

**CONSIDERATIONS**

While participatory approaches must be assessed in specific planning contexts, in most cases no single approach will sufficiently satisfy total informational needs, ensure adequate public representation, or conform to the specific process demands of planning. As previously discussed, sole reliance upon surveys can yield broadly representative data on specific issues but does little to promote active or continuous participation on the part of the public. Interaction with representative organizations, on the other hand, can generate information which effectively addresses aggregate concerns. However, not all regions in the Third World can boast of organizational structures broad enough in both popular and sectoral representation to be able to provide effective and comprehensive inputs throughout a regional planning process.

Therefore, there is a need, in all but the rarest of circumstances, to use various approaches to eliciting public input in a combination appropriate to the specific characteristics of both the region and the planning process. The design of such a participatory strategy must in all cases be based upon a few key considerations.

First, the data needs of the rational-process planning cycle are such that public input must correspond to the planning process. Specifically, the content of public input must proceed from being more general in nature to more specific. At the goal-setting stage of planning, there is little use in eliciting direct, individual expressions of needs, since the planning has not progressed to a level of specificity which can accommodate direct, individual input. Rather, the public input should provide a working definition of the social and economic concerns of the population as a whole. At this stage, the objective is to provide planners with insightful, aggregate information upon which the initial goals of regional planning can be at least partially based. As the planning cycle disaggregates geographically and sectorally and defines alternative strategies and projects, public participation and its information outputs should become, in turn, more direct and specific in addressing these alternatives.

Second, sound planning decisions relating to project implementation require public input of significant depth. The planner must have information that presents more than static, one-time development preferences from the local population if he or she is to effectively plan projects that complement local social and economic dynamics. To understand and interpret these dynamics within various groups in different communities, the planner must have some notion of the values that underlie the preferences adopted by different segments of the regional population. Valid, in-depth information will best result from a focused participation strategy that facilitates ongoing dialogue rather than the elicitation of one-time inputs (Burke, "Strategies").

Third, the formulation of a participatory strategy should be based upon specific regional and sub-regional characteristics which are relevant to the inhabitants' participation in planning. Given the diversity of regional settings within the Third World, a complete analysis of relevant local variables must be made on a case-by-case basis. There are, however, a few factors which should be assessed in all cases. They are the following:

1. *The existence of representative organizations:* Since such organizations can provide the cornerstone of a sound and efficient participatory strategy, it is essential to locate such entities and assess their representativeness in the strategy's preparation. To the degree to which such organizations can act as facilitators and conduits of representative local input, less reliance needs to be placed on more

individualized approaches, such as indirect or group surveys.

2. *The depth and current status of democratic traditions within the region:* An assessment of this factor will reveal the degree to which a participatory endeavor *per se* may represent political and social change. It will allow the planning entity to determine the level of intensity of participation that can intitally be pursued without creating undue tension within local governmental and planning establishments and jeopardizing the participatory process and consequent planning benefits (Fagence, *Participation*).

3. *The level of planning experience among the local population:* The public's capacity to participate in planning should be assessed to ensure that initial participatory mechanisms do not make unrealistic demands—a cause of public frustration cited in a number of case studies (Fagence, p. 366). To the extent that local populations have participated in planning exercises, their ability to contribute more quickly and more substantially to the planning process is enhanced. In cases where local experience is significant, participatory mecha-nisms such as local "charrettes," which are based upon "shared planning" concepts, may be utilized. In other cases, more basic methods—such as community meetings and interaction with local functional organizations—must be utilized as a means of providing initial experience to local communities. Overall, the greater the understanding the local population has of the external reality affecting it and of the relationship of local conditions to that reality, the more relevant and significant will be its contribution to regional planning.

The foregoing points suggest a few basic guidelines that should be followed in forming a participatory strategy. Most fundamentally, the final selection of public-input mechanisms to be used within a particular region or sub-region can only be made, in most cases, after instituting local contact. The appropriate selection of an approach, such as interaction with local development organizations, for example, can only be effected after some type of canvassing of such organizations has been conducted; this is necessary to find out if and where they exist and to what extent they represent the local population. Similarly, interaction through either community meetings or community leaders must be preceded by some analysis of local social structures, both formal and informal, in order to determine the quality of local communicative channels and capabilities. These measures are necessary not only to enable the planning entity to select appropriate participatory approaches at the regional level, but also to specify which mechanisms would best be used in different parts of the regions. In addition, this will allow for the identification of the results expected to be yielded by the participatory process within a given time frame.

Conversely, perhaps the most fundamental mistake that could be made would be to impose a participatory strategy constructed on a deductive basis solely to conform to the needs of the planning cycle. The major problem with strategies that do not evolve out of an analysis of local areas is that they may by-pass efficient and politically sensitive local institutions and/or pursue mechanisms of public input simply unsuited to local norms. An example of this would be the use of survey techniques within areas in which traditional village meetings are the normal means of commmunicating with outsiders.

It becomes obvious that the most effective type of public participation will evolve from a patient, flexible approach that "feels its way through" at local levels, using combinations of participatory mechanisms which correspond to both the specific characteristics of the areas or sub-areas in question and the ongoing needs of planners. The basic objective is to construct a participatory system based upon the social and organizational strengths that local populations inherently possess. To fully realize this, field analysis of local areas should be among the first steps in the design and implementation of a participatory strategy.

## A GENERIC STRATEGY

While it is obviously impossible to construct a specific participatory strategy for application throughout the Third World, it is possible to outline a generic approach which may serve as a guideline in designing strategies for particular areas. Accordingly, a two-phased generic strategy will be outlined which roughly satisfies the requirements of both the planning and participation systems. The two phases, or cycles, of the strategy correspond to the two most appropriate entry points for initial public input: *goal setting* and the comparative *assessment of options*. This approach assumes little or no previous experience in the elicitation of public participation on the part of a planning entity, and thus represents the first step in a transition toward participatory planning. Planning entities that have previously adopted, or are currently adopting, participatory techniques can modify this approach to meet their own needs.

The *first phase* of the participation strategy corresponds to the goal-setting stage of planning and has three primary purposes: (1) to introduce the planning exercise and its limitations (in terms of funding, technology, etc.) to local citizens and organizations and inform them of their opportunities to play a role in it; (2) to determine the most appropriate mechanisms of public participation for use in the second phase of the participatory process; and (3) to elicit the public's general development concerns for the planner's use in goal formulation. Because the needs of the planning cycle at this stage are wide ranging and exploratory in nature, public input should be as broad and inclusive as possible.

The basic methodology utilized during the first phase would best follow the lines of a loosely structured approach to participant observation. Field staff would initiate contact with local leaders, institutions, and private citizens to discuss the general purposes of the planning process and obtain their initial feedback on local development needs. This approach should remain informal rather than highly structured, as the object is to elicit broad opinion while gaining a basic understanding of the social, organizational, and economic systems in place at local levels. Field staff should also be encouraged to get to know local communities as well as possible through such means as attending public meetings (formal and informal) and spending time in local markets and even taverns. (This suggestion may not seem serious at first glance. However, in the U.K., the University of Nottingham's School of Planning elicits participation in urban planning by constructing portable scale models of communities and then having local residents actually lay out their community the way they would like it to be. One of the best enviornments they have discovered for doing this is in the pubs.)

Since no decisions that would have immediate impact on local areas are made at this planning stage, public input can be elicited through indirect as well as direct mechanisms. Thus, reviews of relevant literature and research and, where appropriate, structured surveys can be undertaken to complement the ongoing field work within the region.

The major output of this first stage should be a coordinated series of reports, composed on a sub-regional and sectoral basis, that attempts to define creatively the major development concerns of local populations. These concerns should be related both to the social and economic contexts at local levels and to the scope and limitations of the planning process. In addition, an analysis of local organizations and planning capabilities should be completed as a preliminary step in the planning of the second phase.

The initial reports on local development concerns should be synthesized to present common problems, concerns, and development ideas on both a region-wide and sub-regional basis. These syntheses, together with initial assessments of local-level development activities and capabilities, should be fed to planners for analysis in the setting of regional development goals.

Once alternatives are generated within the planning process and translated into local options, field staff would return to local communities in a *second participatory phase* for specific responses to these options. Responses would be sought here through some combination of direct public-input mechanisms, such as community meetings, individual and group interviews, and the canvassing of local organizations—the choice of a specific second-phase design having been made through an analysis of local social and organizational variables in the first phase. The direct-input data generated in this phase would then be processed in quantified form and disseminated, on an option-by-option basis, to the planning units charged with responsibility for the geographical area and/or planning sector relevant to each planning option.

Although flexibility should be maintained in the selection and implementation of mechanisms, this second phase must, by necessity, be more structured, direct, and specific than the first phase. As the planning process has now moved to a stage of specific strategy and project options, public feedback must now be direct, offering affirmative, negative or alternative replies to each option presented. While field staff should pursue broad public response to options through whatever mechanisms are appropriate, responses should be systematically recorded and later quantified for inclusion in the data analysis process.

This second phase should be viewed as ongoing and repetitive in nature, and should not be considered as a limited, one-time phenomenon. Since the planning process continues over time, and generates optional strategies and projects in an iterative fashion, public input should, correspondingly, continue along with it. Furthermore, through this extended process of local participation, there should evolve local-level participatory systems related to planning which would facilitate public involvement in subsequent project planning and implementation.

While other valid strategies can be developed to facilitate participation, their design should include some of the critical elements of the participatory approach presented here.  By deepening the level of specificity of public inputs over time, this approach closely parallels the planning process itself, providing appropriate data at appropriate stages.  At the same time, its "two-phased" cycle facilitates a process of iteration and dialogue at local levels which is crucial to eliciting valid public input.  Similarly, its emphasis on repeated contact would allow field staff to establish trusting relationships within the communities in which they work.  Lastly, its "open-ended" approach to the selection of participatory mechanisms provides a critical element of flexibility in determining an appropriate level of participation in the initial stages without compromising the validity of results.

## PLANNING ENTITY ROLES RESULTING FROM USE OF MODEL STRATEGY

The use of the basic strategy outlined will lead the planning entity toward a particular set of activities depending upon the participatory and organizational factors present in the region or sub-regions. While it is clear that such factors will be present in varying degrees within different regional contexts, it may be useful to examine the roles that the planning entity would adopt when such characteristics are exhibited in the extreme.  Toward one end of the spectrum, for example, one might well find regions that possess a strong democratic tradition of public involvement in local decisionmaking, a sound network of local and regional organizations, and a significant degree of local experience in planning of one form or another—characteristics which may often, in fact, be found together. In contrast, other regions may have little tradition of formal participation in either local decisionmaking or planning and few representative organizations.

In the latter case, in which the level of organizational develop-ment and local planning experience is low, the participatory system will be characterizerd by a reliance on more basic approaches such as participant observation, small group interviews, and interaction with traditional community leaders.  Correspondingly, there will be a direct and rather pervasive involvement by the planning entity (or its intermediary agent) in eliciting public input.  In these circum-stances, formal, more structured participation by local residents must be initiated to some degree within communities.

While valid public input can be generated through this process, such results will be achieved without the advantage of the time- and resource-saving shortcuts provided by local participatory structures that already exist. However, such a basic participatory approach can yield substantial gains in terms of local capacity building, organizational development, and local involvement in project implementation. Such capacity building is in itself developmental, and would be necessary to the future development of such a region in any case. Thus, resources allocated to this process should not be considered unimportant to either planning or project development.

In the opposite case of a region with a high level of participatory and organizational development, public involvement can be facilitated through local structures already in place, with more basic approaches being used in a more selective and complementary manner. The involvement of the planning entity in the elicitation of local inputs need not be as direct; instead, advantage can be taken of local organizational experience in facilitating public input. The focus in this case would necessarily shift toward the use of "shared planning" approaches, in which, after initial outreach efforts, the planning entity would assume both a planning and advisory role with local organizations and communities.

This shift toward shared planning would result in many cases from the expectation of local residents in such regions to participate not only in the assessment of project options presented to them, but also in the design of their own local projects. In such cases, the planning entity would still present its own project options for local response, but should also advise local groups on the technical feasibility of their own project ideas and on how well these fit within the regional strategies being developed. On the basis of such a dialogue, a complementarity of effort should evolve whereby both larger, centrally planned projects and local self-development endeavors would conform to a regional strategy and be mutually supportive.

## ORGANIZATIONAL FUNCTIONS AND REQUIREMENTS

The implementation of a participatory planning strategy, even a first-step strategy, will, in all cases, require some alterations and additions to the planning system. The exact type of changes or additions called for will, of course, vary widely according to particular regional and sub-regional characteristics. Our purpose here is to discuss the general *functions* and concomitant organizational *capabilities* and requirements that are essential in any attempt to engage in regional participatory planning. There are three sets of functions and related capabilities the planning entity must incorporate in order to implement a participatory program. These functions are external, internal, and intermediate to the planning process itself. (This breakdown of functions corresponds to three systems-theory dimensions of external, internal and intermediary [or interface] environments.)

The necessary functions *external* to the planning system, encompass:    (1) the contacting of local populations and organizations to inform them of the scope and general purpose of the planning; (2) an investigation of the general social and economic needs of the region's inhabitants for input into the goal-setting stage; (3) an assessment of local organizations and local planning capabilities; (4) the relaying of information on planning options and alternatives to local levels; (5) the elicitation of feedback on these alternatives (including information on locally developed plans); and (6) the feedback of the public-input information to the planning entity.

These external elicitation-feedback functions will require in all cases the employment of *field staff* with capabilities in social research, specifically in data collection and analysis. The personnel engaged in these elicitation tasks should have strong communication skills—including the interpersonal skills needed to form trusting relationships in diverse local situations—and at least some foreknowledge of, and familiarity with, the region itself. For this reason, staff charged with these functions should have prior experience in working with local populations and organizations within the region. In this regard, the advantage of utilizing indigenous personnel to represent the planning entity in eliciting local needs cannot be overestimated. Also, while prior familiarity with general development is necessary in carrying out these basic needs-elicitation functions, field staff need not have professional planning expertise.

However, in regions with enhanced planning capabilities within which independent local planning and project development activities may already be ongoing, a more technical orientation may be necessary. In such cases, the planning entity's external role must include the eliciting of information on such plans and the offering of advice on both their technical feasibility and their "fit" within the regional strategy. To the extent to which the adoption of a more technical planning and advisory role is necessitated by local activities, expertise in planning must be considered as a necessary external capability.

The necessary functions *internal* to the planning system encompass: (1) the reception of public input, both general and alternative-specific; (2) the dissemination of this data to appropriate planning sub-units at the appropriate stages of the planning process; (3) the monitoring of the analysis of public input within various sub-units; and (4) the elicitation and outward dissemination of planning alternatives/options as they arise within the planning sub-units.

These internal functions are essentially managerial in nature. They require that a sound management and communication system be established to coordinate both the diffusion of public inputs within the planning structure and the timely elicitation of project-option information from planners for public response. To assure coordination of internal functions, planning entities would be well advised to place responsibility for these functions within a specific staff unit or working committee. This unit or committee should be positioned at an organizational level high enough to assure continued access to all planning sub-units. Staff assigned to these tasks should be experienced in both management and intra-organizational communication.

The crucial *intermediary* function consists of the two-way *translating* of planning outputs and public inputs. This function relates to one of the major constraints to participatory planning; that is, the failure on the part of the lay public and the technical planner to communicate. On the one hand, planners have traditionally found that the public's articulations of planning problems do not form a clear consensus, are "too loose," and are not tied to the multiple alternatives and trade-offs which must be faced. In short, the planning system cannot "comprehend" raw, unordered public input. On the other hand, the public—even in the First World—simply cannot readily comprehend the technical jargon of planning. There is therefore a need for an "intermediary translator" function to render the technical outputs of the ongoing planning exercise meaningful to the lay public while systematizing public-input data for integration into the planning process.

Successful *outward* translation is in large part dependent on the abilities of field staff to render planning goals and options understandable to the lay public. While this basic ability can be upgraded through training, planning entities would be best advised to employ field staff from the outset who are sensitive to local language and custom and at the same time knowledgeable of the development process.

The *inward* translation of public input for use by planners presents the technical problem of incorporating differing responses from local residents and organizations on various planning options presented to them. For example, surveys produce multiple responses, while interaction with representative organizations may produce a single position paper, quantified consensus opinions from a membership meeting, or a single informal response from an organizational leader. To be usable within the planning process, these numerous responses must be ordered, quantified, and then stored in a manner that allows for continual recall, supplementation, and re-evaluation. This systematization is complicated by the fact that planners require recorded information on both individual and collective responses to each planning option presented locally. Information on each response should include: (1) the *position* taken with regard to any given option—including alternatives to the options presented; (2) the *reasons* given for the option or alternative selected; (3) the *method* used to obtain the input (e.g., direct or indirect interview, organizational meeting, etc.); and (4) the *source* of the response (e.g., farmer, local savings cooperative, etc.).

There is, therefore, a need to utilize some type of data-processing system that is simple, adaptable to numerous planning situations, and able to order numerous, unstructured inputs. The specific adaptation of such a system should be made by internal coordinat-ing staff in consultation with both planners and field staff.

## INITIATION OF A PARTICIPATORY PROGRAM

There are a few final considerations regarding general organizational structure and function that are relevant to the initiation of a participatory program. Foremost among these is the need to maintain *flexibility* with regard to the structure, staffing, and operations of such a program. To be consistent with the two-phased approach to participation outlined previously, the planning entity should "feel its way" in constructing a participatory program, making decisions on long-term structure and staffing requirements as it continually gains knowledge of the social and organizational characteristics of the region.

At the beginning stages of a participatory program, a relatively small unit composed of internal coordinators, planners, and field agents should be sufficient to design and implement the broad needs-elicitation process within the region, to generally assess participatory and organizational characteristics locally, and to design the more in-depth phases of participation that will follow. Further staffing and operational decisions can be made during or after this stage on the basis of greater familiarity with the region.

In carrying out initial outreach and canvassing efforts, planning entities in some cases may wish to acquire the services of an independent organization already engaged in social research and/or development within the region. In situations where the regional planning authority already enjoys relatively sound familiarity with local populations and organizations, such an option need not be exercised, and the agency can immediately move ahead to assemble its own field staff. In other cases, the authority may wish to engage a professional organization already well versed in local affairs and trusted within local communities to initiate outreach on its behalf, and advise it on the longer-term structuring of a participation program. Such agencies can also be utilized in the training of planning authority field staff and in the building of analytical capabilities among local populations.

When outside research and promotional agencies are used, however, care must be taken to ensure that their work is integrated with that of internal staff. As outside personnel enjoy familiarity with neither the staff nor the planning process, their work can quickly become extraneous to everyday affairs, and public inputs may remain isolated to ongoing planning efforts.

Finally, it should be recognized that any transition toward participatory planning must be paralleled by an openness on the part of the planning authority to accept some measure of innovation. While the strategies and approaches outlined herein do not call for any major revamping of normal planning procedure, firm policy support from planning officials for the inclusion of public input within decisionmaking processes must be forthcoming from the outset. Otherwise, the exercise may not be taken seriously by either the public or the planning staff, and meaningful public contributions to the design of appropriate strategies and projects will not result.

# Guidelines for Collaboration Between Major Donors and Third World NGOs

Over the past few years, as aid programmed through Third World government agencies and the private sector has shown the limitations of its effectiveness in assisting the poor, some of the major donors have begun to take an active interest in non-governmental organizations (NGOs) as vehicles for the pursuit of this objective. At the same time, increasingly tenuous support in European and North American legislatures for the budgets of these donors has led a number of the aid institutions to actively cultivate relationships with Northern NGOs, which they view as potentially effective allies.

Whatever the reason for this increased interest in NGOs, it is welcomed news as long as constructive relationships are subsequently established. Third World (or Southern) NGOs (TW NGOs) have for a long time experienced problems in securing financial support from their governments and their countries' commercial banking systems. Many have evolved and expanded in terms of their constituencies, their institutional structures, their capacities to manage credit and other resources, and their need for such resources. Most of the major aid institutions have until now either ignored this need and capacity or have marginalized their support for TW NGOs within their overall lending programs. Rarely have TW NGOs been given access to financing from these donors' mainstream operations, despite the fact that they are often the most effective development institutions in their countries and frequently possess an implementing capacity greater than that of the larger public-sector and private business organizations.

The potential for a more significant set of relationships exists, even if the rhetoric of the major donors still exceeds their willingness to forge these partnerships. The dangers in the establishment of such arrangements are numerous and serious, however, and current indications are that many of these will be realized unless the donors become more educated and responsible in their actions.

The problems that are likely to arise are related to the tendency on the part of the larger donors to view TW NGOs as agents which can effectively carry out programs designed by the donor and the government. TW NGOs, however, have generally had extensive experience working with the poor and are usually in a far better position than the government or the donor to conceptualize, design, and manage a development program that will have a constructive impact at the local level. The proclivity on the part of some of the major aid institutions and host governments to try to control the development process runs counter to the need to follow the lead of those local organizations working directly with the poor. If donors assume a directive rather than responsive posture toward TW NGOs, they will not only lose the greatest benefit that can be derived from working with NGOs, but they will also compromise the independence, the responsiveness, and ultimately the effectiveness of organizations upon which the achievement of meaningful development is in large part dependent.

An example of an effort by a donor to reshape the environment to fit its own needs is the creation and imposition of a structure to coordinate the work of TW NGOs. In light of the diversity among TW NGOs in any country in terms of objectives, methodologies, constituencies, and relationships with their government and with donors, such an action is, at very best, presumptuous. Temporary or long-lasting consortia can develop or, if they already exist, be strengthened through a series of independent decisions by TW NGOs as to whether to participate in the development of a project. A unilateral action by an outsider, however, or, worse yet, a bilateral action by the donor and government to link private development organizations with one another and with government will stimulate resentment and a range of problems with which the TW NGOs, but not necessarily the donor, will have to live.

Problems of this sort are more prone to arise when donors lack experience in local-level development and a sensitivity to the circumstances of the local populations and organizations engaged in it. Those large donors that wish to promote development that incorporates and benefits the poor must have on staff people who know how to identify, assess, work with, and upgrade local organizations that represent the poor and their interests. Without this knowledge, it is easy, for example, to select an inappropriate institution (e.g., a TW NGO created through foreign intervention and without roots in the local environment), to overfund and thus undermine an institution, and to consume the limited time and resources of a TW NGO without ultimately providing any benefit.

Having dealt extensively with both local-level and intermediary non-governmental organizations in the Third World, The Development GAP began to work with the World Bank in 1976 to demonstrate, through on-the-ground implementation, how institutions that work responsively, directly, and intensively with the poor can be identified and supported in the design and implementation of projects. During the ensuing four years, we worked in seven Latin American and African countries with the Urban Projects Department of the Bank with responsibility for the income-generation components of urban development programs. Through these efforts we demonstrated how institutional arrangements can be made to maximize the involvement of the poor in effective, relatively large-scale projects with a few million dollars in financing. These arrangements included: an NGO programming and on-lending funds from a government bank; a collaboration among four NGOs; a large NGO acting alone; municipal governments and community organizations collaborating with a government ministry and a national banking system; a private bank working in conjunction with an NGO and a government agency; and a collaboration among NGOs, community organizations, and credit unions.

As a result of these and other similar experiences with other donors and TW NGOs, we have learned a great deal about the pitfalls and potential that lie in the formation of relationships between major donors and non-governmental organizations. We have found that many project officers who recognize this potential have not pursued opportunities because of their unfamiliarity with the non-governmental sector. Others would be willing to venture forward if systems were in place within their organizations that reward the project officer for the deliberate selection of more appropriate implementing institutions and for the ultimate on-the-ground project effectiveness that it yields, rather than for the rapid disbursement of large sums of money through institutions that have never demonstrated such effectiveness.

Hence, we offer the following guidelines for incorporating Third World NGOs in major development programs to project officers who are interested in more promising institutional arrangements, to program directors who must provide a supportive environment and sanction this approach as part of mainstream operations if it is to be widely adopted at the project level, and to others who, like ourselves, want to see the organizations that are most experienced and effective in working with the poor become the principal counterparts of the major aid institutions.

1. *Research TW NGO possibilities through Northern NGO counterparts*. A great deal of knowledge about Southern NGOs in most every Third World country can be found among NGOs and other relatively small donors in Europe and North America. It would be rare to find a case in which there are not one or more Northern organizations that have funded or established another form of support relationship with a TW NGO that would have the capacity to be considered for major donor financing. Furthermore, some major aid organizations have special small-scale NGO-support programs, such as the Inter-American Development Bank's Small Projects unit, which help upgrade the capacity of TW NGOs and which are thus good sources of information about them.

Many Northern NGOs will not, understandably, share information about their Southern counterparts with major donors, however, without first establishing the seriousness of the latters' intentions and their commitment to protecting the integrity of the local organizations. Under no circumstances would a responsible NGO simply provide names of TW NGOs to major donor representatives unless a relationship of trust had previously been established. Although they may be accused of being paternalistic, small donors that have nurtured TW NGOs during their evolution are well aware of the damage that an abrupt expansion in funding, programming, organizational size, and institutional relationships can have, and they thus take seriously their responsibility to prevent this from happening.

Hence, once an NGO is convinced that the major donor will promote the interests of the TW NGOs, it will generally provide information of considerable value to all parties involved. This includes information pertaining to:

(a) TW NGO programmatic thrusts and experience

(b) TW NGO institutional capacity, including financial absorptive capacity and functional skills ranging from group organizing to financial management

(c) The TW NGOs most representative of local populations and their interests

(d) The environment in which TW NGOs must operate in that particular country

(e) The most beneficial contacts to make in-country, both within and outside TW NGOs

This information and these contacts will save project officers a great deal of time and many wrong turns once they are in-country and are indispensable unless the officers have spent considerable time already at the ground level in that country.

This process can be greatly facilitated by the establishment of a simple consultative mechanism by Northern NGOs, which would be particularly useful to larger funders in those countries in which indigenous non-governmental organizations are not organized to consult with outside agencies. The Development GAP and other NGOs first presented such a proposal to the World Bank in 1981, offering to gather TW NGO-related information from within the NGO community and to provide it through a small, structured facility to project officers about to undertake identification missions. Although the Bank did not demonstrate interest in such a service at that time, it may be incumbent upon the NGO community at this point to discuss the establishment of this mechanism (which can be accomplished quickly and at low cost) and to extend a challenge to the major donors to utilize it as a vehicle for upgrading the quality of their mainstream operations.

2. *Inform government of intention to assess the capacities of both public and private institutions as potential project implementors.* Ultimately all donors must account to government, whether it be to receive a government guarantee of a loan, to fulfill the terms of bilateral agreements, or simply to maintain permission to operate in-country. It makes no sense, therefore, to work clandestinely and run the risk of raising government suspicions and putting TW NGOs contacted in jeopardy. In most situations, an open relationship with government will be productive. Thus, upon entering the country, project officers should let the government know that they will be considering the inclusion of the best institutions in the project regardless of the sector in which it is found.

This is not to say, however, that officers must consult with government before they make each TW NGO contact. Officers must be able to operate freely and to engender a relationship of trust with

TW NGOs through open and frank discussions. If government constrains those discussions, any subsequent project with TW NGO involvement will likely be fraught with difficulties. It is incumbent upon the donor in such circumstances to lay out clearly its position of identifying and selecting the most capable institutions and to back this up with decisive action, if necessary. This is what the World Bank did, for example, in 1977–1978, when it withheld a loan to Nicaragua after The Development GAP, as Bank consultants, had selected an NGO and the Somoza government had subsequently refused to allow its funding and was unable to identify an equally capable government institution.

3. *Consult with TW NGOs in-country to determine interest and capabilities regarding project involvement and provide frank assessment of risks and advantages of involvement.* Most TW NGOs have never dealt with a major donor organization. The experience of those who have has generally been confined to the receipt of relatively modest sums of money through special grant facilities or, more recently, through interest-free loan programs. Participation in a multi-million dollar program, with or without subsidized interest rates, is, however, a very different proposition, one that requires a clear understanding on the part of all parties before it is pursued.

The project officer must determine the capacity of the TW NGO first-hand following consultations with third parties, including local NGOs that may be organized to deal collectively with foreign assistance institutions. Some experience or appropriate training is helpful here, for the structures, objectives, and operating styles of TW NGOs are usually different from those of government agencies. If the organization can play a constructive project role, the project officer must explain all aspects of the project cycle and the demands that will be made on the organization at each phase. The TW NGO must be aware of the administrative requirements, relationships with government, financial arrangements, and the many other features that a project encompasses so as to make an informed decision regarding its involvement and to prepare itself to handle these matters if it decides to go forth. The presence on project preparation missions of a representative of a Southern NGO with experience in this area would likely be helpful here. Nonetheless, it is not improbable that some organizations will conclude that the demands on staff time and the consequent effect on the program make participation in a sizeable loan program inadvisable.

4. *Select institutions on the basis of their involvement with, and credibility in, poor communities, as well as their capacity for*

*executing all or part of the project or project component.* TW NGOs are important forces in development only to the extent that they represent the poor and their interests and appropriately identify and address their needs. Some Third World organizations lack this involvement and it is critical that donor representatives recognize which ones they are. Such organizations, like many public agencies, lack the community-level credibility that is an indispensable element in project success.

The size of a TW NGO need not necessarily be a factor in institutional selection. As donor-supported projects are often composed of a number of components, a Southern NGO's role can be limited to one of them. Furthermore, within that project component a TW NGO can join forces with other organizations and confine its activities to specific neighborhoods or specific functions.

The choice of the appropriate institution(s) for the design and implementation of a project is clearly the most important decision that a project officer will make. It is therefore well worth the extra time and effort that may take at the identification stage in order to ensure that serious, time-consuming problems can be avoided later in the project cycle. A typology of TW NGOs and a more comprehensive set of criteria for their assessment should be developed to facilitate this effort.

5. *Support collaboration among TW NGOs for the purpose of complementing one another's areas of expertise, skills, and geographical foci.* As TW NGOs are consulted regarding the development and execution of a project, the bases for TW NGO collaboration will likely become apparent to both the TW NGOs and the donor. In some cases, one TW NGO will possess the capacity to handle an entire project component on its own. Frequently, however, no one NGO will have the breadth of community involvement, the multi-sectoral experience, or all the project skills required to achieve project objectives. (Of course, this is also true of many public agencies.) In this event, a TW NGO will probably either: suggest the involvement of other organizations, including national, regional, or local government agencies, whose capabilities complement its own; accept a donor suggestion that it and other TW NGOs collaborate in order to merge their various capabilities; or agree to project involvement with sole responsibility for design and implementation in particular communities.

Whatever configuration such collaboration takes, it is of utmost importance that whenever a consortium of organizations is required it be formed by the TW NGOs themselves. The donor or Northern

NGOs can serve successfully as catalysts, but a donor attempt to impose an arrangement among TW NGOs will create divisiveness among those organizations and resentment toward the donor. In light of the promise that a major donor loan holds for TW NGOs and their constituencies, the donor can usually count on these organizations to establish a constructive set of relationships so long as it provides the opportunity and environment for frank discussions.

6. *Provide guidance and support to TW NGOs in project proposal preparation and ensure priority consideration.* Most TW NGOs have staffs that have some experience in project planning and in the preparation of proposals to donors for funding. Few, however, have ever written proposals for major aid institutions, and they thus often need guidance. This can and should be provided by the donor's project officer, who generally has taken an active hand in the drafting of many proposals from government agencies.

The provision of such assistance to TW NGOs is also important because of the relative scarcity of their resources and the time-consuming nature of major proposal preparation. A project officer can make an additional contribution by helping the TW NGO to identify a source of funding for its project preparation work. Of greatest importance, however, is that the donor simply not mislead the TW NGO, causing it to expend precious resources on project and proposal development when the chances of donor support are not, in fact, high.

7. *Place project design and project policy determination in the hands of the implementing TW NGOs,* rather than leave Southern NGOs as implementors of a government-designed and controlled project. This is undoubtedly the most important consideration when one is arranging the involvement of TW NGOs in a project. TW NGOs' work in poor communities has given them not only an expertise in project execution but also an excellent knowledge of local needs, local capabilities, programming requirements, and an expertise in project planning and development. Their interest is to obtain resources from the major aid institutions to help expand programs that they have designed in conjunction with local populations or to enable them to design and initiate projects based on previous experience.

This, indeed, is the challenge for the donor. Donors have their own needs, their own institutional imperatives, as well as their relationships with government, and relinquishing control of the design of a project is difficult. It is essential that it be done, however, as project success depends on it. In the first place, chances are that the better TW NGOs in any country would not agree to an arrangement that has them implementing donor and government policy. They pride themselves on their independence and are not prone to give it up. Second, if government maintains control of a project, it is bound, by virtue of its relative distance and short-term political exigencies, to come into conflict at some point with the implementing TW NGO and the interests of the constituency which it represents. Finally, and most importantly, the top-down approach implicit in a government-controlled, TW NGO-implemented project will likely result, at best, in the satisfactory execution of a project that is of questionable relevance to the needs of the poor.

8. *Inform government of the selection of, and support for, TW NGOs as project designers and implementors,* and exercise this support throughout the life of the project. Major aid institutions have considerable leverage with most governments which they utilize in various ways. One constructive use of this leverage is in the selection of appropriate implementing organizations. Most governments, even those hostile to independent organizations, will accept donor determinations in this area, particularly if public agencies are not excluded from all the project's components and if considerable amounts of foreign exchange are involved. If, however, government refuses to permit TW NGO participation and is unable to recommend an equally capable public institution to take its place, the donor should be prepared to withhold project funding until a change in policy occurs.

It is important that the donor reiterate its support for the implementing institution as the project evolves, as it is not unlikely that the government will in time attempt to assume some measure of control. Usually this occurs through the manipulation of resource flows from the donor through a public financial institution. In such instances, the donor may have to play an active role to ensure that the implementing TW NGO receives its funds on the agreed-upon terms and on a timely basis.

9. *Allow TW NGOs to work out their relationships with government* regarding program latitude, cooperation with public agencies, financial arrangements, and the terms of programmatic and financial oversight. Virtually all of the TW NGOs with which a major donor will come into contact have dealt with government in some manner. Some may work closely with public agencies in the design and promotion of development programs. Others, operating

in less friendly environments, have frequently had to reach accommodations with public officials that enable them to continue their activities unimpeded. All, however, have formed informal relationships with officials at various levels of government, and it is such relationships, especially in most Third World contexts, that often enable seemingly difficult obstacles to be overcome.

It is generally the wish of a TW NGO to utilize these established relationships to reach an understanding with government regarding the project in question, and the donor should respect this desire. Constructive arrangements that will facilitate project implementation can be made far more easily in this manner than through formal negotiations at the highest ministerial levels. It is incumbent upon the donor, however, ultimately to translate these arrangements into formal agreements and to lend support to TW NGOs whenever intractable difficulties arise in their mid-level discussions.

10. *Maintain project flexibility so as to enable implementing TW NGOs to determine appropriate project scale and sectoral and geographical parameters in response to changing local needs.* During the life of a project, local conditions change, the potential and interest in replication in other communities often develop, and the capacity of the implementing institution evolves. TW NGOs are particularly accustomed to making project adaptations in midstream in response to community needs. If the donor can maintain a degree of flexibility in its sectoral and geographical delineations and allow for the expansion of project size if and when appropriate, it will have helped to foster constructive changes, in terms of institutional development, community initiative, and project replication, beyond the original, limited objectives of the project.

11. *Incorporate TW NGOs in future program and policy planning with government in order to give voice to local perspectives and needs on a structured and ongoing basis.* TW NGO participation in projects supported by major aid institutions will usually result—by virtue of the TW NGOs' continuous on-the-ground presence—in project design, development, and implementation that are directly relevant to the needs, interests, and capabilities of local populations. This project experience should demonstrate to donors and to government the significant contributions that TW NGOs can make to the process of program and policy planning. Not only have they developed an expertise that is pertinent to these activities, but they also constitute channels of communication between poor community groups and public officials. To the extent that donors successfully advocate the participation of TW NGOs in national-level

and regional planning and programming, the development results will be significant and far-reaching.

Underlying these guidelines is a fundamental principle, adherence to which is essential if relationships between major donors and Third World NGOs are to be productive. This principle, alluded to continually in these pages, is that the donors should respond to, promote, and build upon the interests and strengths of the TW NGOs. The latter are generally the most effective agents of constructive change, incorporating the participation of the poor in the determination of the development avenues that they take. As the shortcomings of conventional institutions in the public and private sectors become increasingly apparent, the importance of TW NGOs as major forces in development has also become clear. The large donor institutions have a responsibility to work actively and respectfully with these organizations.

We have prepared these guidelines in the hope that they will assist in the establishment of constructive donor/TW NGO relationships and out of a concern, shared by others who work in the Third World, that the major aid institutions will, even with the best intentions, unwittingly undermine Southern NGOs and their development efforts. Signs still exist that these donors view TW NGOs as vehicles for the accomplishment of donor-determined objectives. The distinction between this directiveness and the responsive posture that is required may appear subtle, but it is fundamental to Southern NGOs, Northern NGOs, and all those who seek to promote participatory development. It implies a need for the major donors to alter their operating methodologies in a manner that reflects a perception that the change agents are not the donors but the organizations of the poor themselves.

# Selection of Third World Projects for Funding: Suggested Criteria

1. *Genesis of the project:* Does the project concept either originate from the beneficiary group or evolve from an iterative process of discussion between that group and the funding or intermediary institution?

2. *Participation:* Is the beneficiary group involved in the planning, design, implementation, and evaluation of the project?

3. *Decentralization of control and responsibility:* Do outside participants disengage themselves from the project over time? Do indigenous institutions assume increasing responsibility? Is a structure in place for the progressive decentralization of project control to the local level? Is a process of democratic decision-making a present or planned element of the project?

4. *Institutional building:* Is an objective of the project the enhancement or development of an indigenous institutional capacity both to administer this and subsequent projects and to identify and undertake new initiatives that contribute significantly to social change? Will this capacity be developed to the point where it can obviate the need for substantial foreign inputs?

5. *Self-sustainment:* Is the project expected to stimulate a local development dynamic in which project participants, implementing organizations, and/or other local actors will contribute the energy, resources, and skills to carry out this and/or other activities beyond the project period?

6. *Scale and pace:* Is the size of the project appropriate to the

stage of development of the beneficiary group and the implementing institution? Will it be implemented at a speed that will allow effective participation and control by the project beneficiaries?

7. *Technical feasibility:* Has the technical viability of the project been assessed in basic terms and can the project reasonably be expected to achieve its stated goal with the level of technical skills and resources available to it?

8. *Technological choice:* Is the nature of the technical inputs to the project such that they can be effectively managed by the beneficiaries? Will prolonged outside expertise be required? To the extent that it is required, will that outside assistance represent a reasonably minor percentage of project costs?

9. *Environmental soundness:* Will the project, in its implementation, serve to maintain and restore the renewable natural resource base, thus providing the foundation for sustainable develop-ment in the area?

10. *Income group:* Will the direct and principal beneficiaries of the project belong to the poorest segment of the population living in the project area? Does this income group lack access to the resources required to upgrade its standard of living?

11. *Empowerment:* Will the project enhance the organization and consequent leverage of the beneficiary group? Will it give it greater access to, and control over, productive resources? Will it help the beneficiary group to restructure its economic and social relationships with other groups in the population?

12. *Cooperative activity:* Will the project achieve only limited outreach by focusing on individual participants or does it seek a broader involvement of the local population through more cooperative ventures? Is the project expected to stimulate a group or community process of decisionmaking rather than reinforce hierarchical relationships among beneficiaries?

13. *Distribution of benefits:* Will the project generate higher income, improved services, and/or more productive assets for the intended beneficiary group? Will it yield an equitable distribution of benefits among the project population? Will it narrow economic and social gaps that exist within the beneficiary group or community?

14. *Non-discrimination:* Is the project equally responsive to the needs, aspirations, and activities of all sub-groups in the beneficiary population? Are women equal partners with men in the design, control, and implementation of the project and in the sharing of its benefits?

15. *Local input:* Has the beneficiary population committed resources to the project as a complement to outside assistance? Does this commitment include funds, materials, services, time, etc.? Does the commitment demonstrate a sufficient dedication to the success of the project?

16. *Participant education:* Is there an educational component or element in the project? Will participation in the project enhance the beneficiaries' understanding of their environment, their relationship to it, the causes of their poverty, and their capacity to induce change? Does the project contain a self-evaluation mechanism and provide an opportunity for critical reflection? Will lessons learned be shared with other communities and organizations?

# Glossary

| | |
|---|---|
| ADF | African Development Foundation |
| AID | Agency for International Development/*Administration for International Development (proposed)* |
| APDF | *Asian and Pacific Development Foundation (proposed)* |
| CIDA | Canadian International Development Agency |
| DCA | Development Cooperation Administration |
| DCC | Development Coordination Committee |
| ECA | Economic Cooperation Administration |
| ESF | Economic Support Fund |
| GAO | General Accounting Office |
| GNP | Gross national product |
| IAF | Inter-American Foundation |
| IBRD | International Bank for Reconstruction and Development (World Bank) |
| IDA | International Development Association |
| IDB | Inter-American Development Bank |
| IDCA | International Development Cooperation Administration |
| ISDI | Inter-American Social Development Institute |
| IMF | International Monetary Fund |
| LDC | Less developed country |
| MDB | Multilateral development bank |
| MIT | Massachusetts Institute of Technology |
| MSA | Mutual Security Agency |
| NGO | Non-governmental organization |

| | |
|---|---|
| North | First World |
| NSC | National Security Council |
| OECD | Organization for Economic Cooperation and Development |
| OMB | Office of Managment and Budget |
| OPIC | Overseas Private Investment Corporation |
| OTA | Office of Technology Assesment |
| PACT | Private Agencies Collaborating Togeather |
| PVO | Private and voluntary organization |
| RDF | Regional development foundation |
| SAL | Structural adjustment loan (or lending) |
| SIDA | Swedish International Development Authority |
| South | Third World |
| TCA | Technical Cooperation Administration |
| TW NGO | Third World non-governmental organization |
| UN | United Nations |
| UNCTAD | United Nations Conference on Trade and Development |

# Bibliography

African Development Bank. *Agreement Establishing the African Development Bank,* Revision #2. 17 May 1979.

Agency for International Development. "Approaches to the Policy Dialogue." *AID Policy Paper.* Washington, DC, December 1982.

Agency for International Development. *Blueprint for Development: The Strategic Plan of the Agency for International Development.* Washington, DC, undated.

Agency for International Development. *Implementation of "New Directions" in Development Assistance.* Report to the House Committee on International Relations on Implementation of Legislative Reforms in the Foreign Assistance Act of 1973, 22 July 1975. Washington, DC: U.S. Government Printing Office, 1975.

Agency for International Development. *The PISCES II Experience* (Vol. II). Washington, DC, December 1985.

Agency for International Development. "Private and Voluntary Organizations." *AID Policy Paper.* Washington, DC, September 1982.

Agency for International Development. "Recurrent Costs." *AID Policy Paper.* Washington, DC, May 1982.

Agency for International Development. [Public Notice No. 1, revised] *Statement of Organization, Function, and Procedures: Information Guidance.* Undated.

Agency for International Development. *The Targeted Aid Amendment.* Report to the Congress: Implementation of Section 128 of the Foreign Assistance Act of 1961, as amended. Washington, DC, June 1983.

Arnold, Stephen H. *Implementing Development Assistance: European Approaches to Basic Needs.* Boulder, CO: Westview Press, 1982.

Arnson, Cynthia, and William Goodfellow. "OPIC: Insuring the Status Quo." *International Policy Report.* September 1977 (Vol. III, No. 2).

Asian Development Bank. *Basic Documents: Agreement Establishing the Asian Development Bank.* Undated.

Asian Development Bank. *Questions and Answers.* Manila, April 1982.

Ayres, Robert L. *Banking on the Poor: The World Bank and Poverty.* Cambridge, MA: MIT Press, 1983.

Babb, Tony. *Organization and Structure of AID.* Task Force Report for the Administrator. Washington, DC: Agency for International Development, October 1977.

Bandow, Doug. "The Agency for International Development," in *Mandate for Leadership II,* Stuart M. Butler; Michael Sanera; and W. Bruce Weinrod, eds. Washington, DC: The Heritage Foundation, 1984.

"A Bank for All Seasons: A Survey of the World Bank." *The Economist.* 4 September 1982.

Bartlett, Bruce. "Barber Conable at the World Bank: New Hope for World Economic Growth," *Backgrounder:* The Heritage Foundation, 4 April 1986.

Baum, Warren C., and Stokes M. Tolbert. "Investing in Development." *Finance and Development.* December 1985.

Baum, Warren C. "The World Bank Project Cycle." *Finance and Development.* December 1978.

Bello, Walden; Kinley, David; and Elinson, Elaine. *Development Debacle: The World Bank in the Philippines.* Institute for Food and Development Policy, 1982.

"The Brandt Report." *The New Internationalist.* No. 104, October 1981.

Breslin, Patrick. *Development and Dignity: Grassroots Development and the Inter-American Foundation.* Rosslyn, VA: Inter-American Foundation, 1987.

Brookings Institution. *Interim Report: An Assessment of Development Assistance Strategies.* Washington, DC, 6 October 1977.

Bryant, Coralie, and Louise G. White. *Managing Development in the Third World.* Boulder, CO: Westview Press, 1982.

Bryant, Coralie. "Organization Impediments to Making Participation A Reality: 'Swimming Upstream' in AID." *Rural Development Participation Review.* Spring 1979.

Burke, E.M. "Citizens' Participation Strategies," *Journal of the American Institute of Planners,* September 1968.

Butler, Stuart M.; Sanera, Michael; and Weinrod, W. Bruce, eds. *Mandate for Leadership II: Continuing the Conservative Revolution.* Washington, DC: The Heritage Foundation, 1984.

Cernea, Michael M. *Measuring Project Impact: Monitoring and Evaluation in the PIDER Rural Development Project—Mexico.* World Bank Staff Working Paper #332. Washington, DC: World Bank, 1979.

Chambers, Robert. *Rural Development: Putting the Last First.* Harlow, Essex: Longman Scientific & Technical, 1983.

Chicago Council on Foriegn Relations. "Attitudes of the American Public and Selected Opinion Leaders Related to Foreign Policy." Chicago: 1983.

Church, Frank. "A Farewell to Foreign Aid: A Liberal Takes Leave." Address in Opposition to the FY 1972 Foreign Assistance Act. 29 October 1971.

Church, Frank. "Farewell to Foreign Aid: Why I Voted No." *The New Republic.* 13 November 1971.

Churchill, Anthony A. "Involvement of NGOs in Water, Urban, PHN, Education and Agricultural Projects." World Bank Office Memorandum. 11 April 1986.

Clausen, A. W. *Address to the Board of Governors.* (24 September 1980) Washington, DC: World Bank, 1980.

Commission on International Development. *Partners in Development.* Report of the Commission, Lester B. Pearson, Chair. Praeger Publishers, 1969.

Commission on Security and Economic Assistance. *A Report to the Secretary of State,* Department of State, Washington, DC, 1983.

Congressional Research Service. *Towards an Assessment of the Effectiveness of the World Bank and the Inter-American Development Bank in Aiding the Poor.* Washington, DC, 10 March 1978.

Contee, Christine E. *What Americans Think: Views on Development and U.S.-Third World Relations.* A Public Opinion Project of InterAction and the Overseas Development Council. 1987.

Council on Foreign Relations and the Overseas Development

Council.  *COMPACT for African Development.*  Report of the Committee on African Development Strategies.  December 1985.

Crane, Barbara, and Jason L. Fincle.  "Organizational Impediments to Development Assistance:  The World Bank's Population Program."  *World Politics.*  Princeton University, 1981.

Department of Treasury.  *United States Participation in the Multinational Development Banks in the 1980s.*  Washington, DC: U.S. Government Printing Office, 1982.

Development Alternatives, Inc.  *Final Report:  The Development Impact of Private Voluntary Organizations:  Kenya and Niger.*  2 February 1979.

*Development Issues:  U.S. Actions Affecting Developing Countries.*  Annual Report of the Chairman of the Development Coordination Committee. Washington, DC: 1983.

Dichter, Thomas W.  *Demystifying 'Policy Dialogue'.*  Norwalk, CT: Technoserve, 1986.

Esteva, Gustavo.  "Development: Metaphor, Myth, Threat."  *Development:  Seeds of Change.*  1985 (No. 3, pp. 78–79).

Fagence, Michael.  *Public Participation in Planning.*  Elmsford, NY: Pergamon Press, 1978.

Fordwor, Kwame D.  "Some Unresolved Problems of the African Development Bank."  *World Development.*  1981 (Vol. 9, No. 11/12).

"Foreign Aid:  What's in It for You?"  *AID Highlights,* USAID, Winter 1987 (Vol. 4, No. 1).

Freeman, Linda.  "The Political Economy of Canada's Foreign Aid Programme."  Prepared for the Canadian Political Science Association. University of Guelph, Ontario. June 1980.

General Accounting Office.  *Changes Needed to Forge an Effective Relationship Between AID and Voluntary Agencies.*  Washington, DC, 27 May 1982.

General Accounting Office.  *Donor Approaches to Development Assistance:  Implications for the United States.*  GAO/ID–83-23. Washington, DC, 4 May 1983.

General Accounting Office.  *Political and Economic Factors Influencing Economic Support Fund Programs.*  Report to the Chairman, Committee on Foreign Affairs, House of Representatives.  GAO/ID-83-43. Washington, DC, 18 April 1983.

George, Susan.  *How the Other Half Dies:  The Real Reasons for World Hunger.*  Montclair, NJ: Allenheld, Osmond and Co., 1977.

George, Susan.  *Ill Fares the Land:  Essays on Food, Hunger, and*

*Power.* Washington, DC: Institute for Policy Studies, 1984.

Goodell, Grace. "Conservatism and Foreign Aid." *Policy Review.* Winter 1981–82.

Gran, Guy. *Development By People.* New York, NY: Praeger Publishers, 1983.

Hayter, Teresa. *The Creation of World Poverty: An Alternative View to the Brandt Report.* London: Pluto Press, 1982.

Hayter, Teresa, and Catharine Watson. *Aid: Rhetoric and Reality.* London and Syndey: Pluto Press, 1985.

Hellinger, Douglas, and Diane Soles. "The Debt Crisis: Where Does Responsiblity Lie?" *Food Monitor.* Fall 1987.

Hellinger, Douglas. *Testimony before the House Appropriations Subcommittee on Foreign Operations on the Development Assistance Role of PVOs.* (13 May 1981).

Hellinger, Stephen, and Thomas Kelly. "Breaking Out of the Foreign Aid Morass: How to Do More with Less." *Ripon Forum.* January 1980 (Vol. XVIII, No. 1).

Hellinger, Stephen. "Checking Out the World Bank." *New Internationalist.* November 1978.

Hirschman, Albert O. *Getting Ahead Collectively.* Elmsford, NY: Pergamon Press, 1984.

Independent Commission on International Development. *North–South: A Program for Survival.* A Report of the Commission, Willy Brandt, Chairperson. Cambridge: MIT Press, 1980.

Independent Group on British Aid. *Real Aid: A Strategy for Britain.* Report of the Group, Charles Elliot, Chair. London, 1982.

Interfaith Action for Economic Justice. *Policy Notes.* 86-12. Washington, DC, 1986.

International Bank for Reconstruction and Development, *Articles of Agreement,* as amended effective 17 December 1965, Washington, DC.

International Bank for Reconstruction and Development. *By-laws,* as amended through 26 September 1980, Washington, DC.

International Council of Voluntary Agencies. *Guidelines for Improving the Quality of Projects in the Third World Funded by Non-governmental Organizations.* Approved by Governing Board on 5 October 1984.

International Council of Voluntary Agencies. *Suggested Guidelines on the Acceptance of Government Funds for NGO Programmes.* Approved by Governing Board on 15 March 1985.

International Development Association. *Articles of Agreement,* effective 24 September 1960, Washington, DC.

International Development Association. *By-laws,* as adopted on 8 November 1960, Washington, DC.

International Development Cooperation Agency. *1983 Annual Report: Development Issues, U.S. Actions Affecting Developing Countries.* Washington, DC, February 1983.

International Development Cooperation Agency. *United States Trade and Development Program: FY 1984 Congressional Presentation.* Washington, DC.

International Fund for Agricultural Development. *Reaching the Rural Poor—IFAD's Approach.* Paper for International NGO Workshop on Multilateral Development. 3 December 1984.

Interreligious Task Force on U.S. Food Policy. *Hunger.* Washington, DC, March 1983 (No. 32).

Jackson, Tony, and Deborah Eade. *Against the Grain.* Oxford: Oxfam, 1982.

Korten, David C., and Filipe B. Alfonso, eds. *Bureaucracy and the Poor: Closing the Gap.* West Hartford, CT: Kumarian Press, 1981.

Lappe, Frances Moore; Collins, Joseph; and Kinley, David. *Aid as Obstacle: Twenty Questions About Our Foreign Aid and the Hungry.* Institute for Food and Development Policy, 1980.

Lewis, Jerry. "The Trouble With the World Bank." *The Wall Street Journal.* 18 September 1981.

Libby, Ronald T. "International Development Association: A Legal Fiction Designed to Secure an LDC Constituency." *International Organization.* Undated.

Lissner, Jorgen. *The Politics of Altruism.* Lutheran World Federation, Department of Studies, 1977.

Madison, Christopher. "The Days of McNamara-Style Expansion at the World Bank May Be At an End." *National Journal.* 15 August 1981 (Vol. 13, No. 33).

Madison, Christopher. "Exporting Reaganomics—The President Wants to Do Things Differently at AID." *National Journal.* 29 May 1982 (pp. 960–964).

Mashek, Robert W. *The Inter-American Foundation in the Making.* Rosslyn, VA: The Inter-American Foundation, 1981.

Mashek, Robert. "Overall Observations on Selected AID, IDB, and IBRD Projects." Memorandum to International Division, Office of Management and Budget. 27 October 1977.

Mattingly, Cheryl; Peattie, Lisa; and Schon, Don. *Urban Practice in the Bank: Notes Toward a Learning Agenda.* MIT, April 1984.

McPherson, M. Peter. "Administrator's Message to Employees: State of the Agency." Washington, DC: Agency for International Development, 2 March 1984.

McPherson, M. Peter. "AID's Legislative Process." Memorandum for the Executive Staff. Washington, DC: Agency for International Development, 19 August 1981.

Michanek, Ernst. *Role of Swedish Non-Governmental Organizations in International Development Cooperation.* Swedish International Development Authority (SIDA), April 1977.

Minear, Larry. "Reflections on Development Policy: A View from the Private Voluntary Sector" in *Private Voluntary Organizations as Agents of Development,* ed. Robert F. Gorman. Boulder, CO and London: Westview Press, 1984.

Minear, Larry. "Some Non-Governmental Reflections on IFAD." Draft paper.

"Mobilizing Finance for Development: A Conversation with Moeen A. Qureshi, Senior Vice-President, Finance, of the World Bank." *Finance and Development.* September 1984.

Morawetz, David. *Twenty-five Years of Economic Development.* Washington, DC: The World Bank, 1977.

Morris, Jay. "Decentralization of Project Responsibility." Memorandum. Washington, DC: Agency for International Development, undated.

Morss, Elliot R., and Victoria A. Morss. *U.S. Foreign Policy: An Assessment of New and Traditional Development Strategies.* Boulder, CO: Westview, 1982.

Netherlands Organization for International Development Cooperation. "Information About Novib." The Hague. Undated.

Newman, Barry. "In Indonesia, Attempts by World Bank to Aid Poor Often Go Astray." *The Wall Street Journal.*

Norwegian Agency for International Development. *NORAD and Non-Governmental Organizations: Guidelines for Support to Activities in Developing Countries.* Oslo, May 1983.

O'Regan, Fred; Walker, Eric G.; Hellinger, Douglas; Bendavid-Val, Avrom; and Hellinger, Stephen. *Public Participation in Regional Development Planning: A Strategy for Popular Planning.* Washington, DC: The Development GAP, 1980 (Paper No. 3).

O'Regan, Fred; Hellinger, Stephen; and Hellinger, Douglas. *The African Development Foundation: A New Institutional Approach to U.S. Foreign Assistance to Africa.* Washington, DC: The Development GAP, March 1982.

Office of Technology Assessment. *Continuing the Commitment: Agricultural Development in the Sahel.* OTA–F–308, Washington, DC: U.S. Government Printing Office, August 1986.

Office of Technology Assessment. (U.S. Congress) *Grassroots Development: The African Development Foundation.* Washington, DC: U.S. Government Printing Office, 1988.

Organization for Economic Cooperation and Development. *Compendium of Aid Procedures.* Paris, 1981.

Payer, Cheryl. *The World Bank: A Critical Analysis.* New York and London: Monthly Review Press, 1982.

Payer, Cheryl. "The World Bank and the Small Farmer." *Monthly Review.* November 1980.

Phelps, Timothy M. "An Aid Plan Gone Awry." *Newsday.* 26 May 1987.

Pine, Art. "Clausen Holds World Bank's Course." *The Wall Street Journal.* 13 May 1982.

Pronk, Jan. "Opening Address." NGO Workshop on Official Development Assistance and Public Opinion in the North. Geneva: United Nations Non-Governmental Liason Service, 1-4 December 1982.

Rau, Bill, and Susan Roche with Fantu Cheru and Maghan Keita. *Working for the Food of Freedom.* Washington, DC: Africa Faith and Justice Network, 1988.

*Report of the Committee on International Relations: To Amend the Foreign Assistance Act of 1961 with Respect to the Activities of the Overseas Private Investment Corporation.* Washington, DC: U.S. Government Printing Office, 1977.

*Report of the Presidential Commission on World Hunger.* Draft for Commissioner's Use. Washington, DC, 22 October 1979.

Rich, Bruce M. "The Multilateral Development Banks, Environmental Policy, and the United States." *Ecology Law Quarterly.* 1985 (Vol. 12, pp. 681–744).

Rupesinghe, Kumar. "The Effects of Export-oriented Industrialization in Sri Lanka." *The Ecologist.* 1985 (Vol. 15, No. 5/6, pp. 246–256).

Ruppe, Loret Miller. *Testimony before the House Foreign Affairs Committee.* (8 February 1984).

Sanford, Jonathon, and Margaret Goodman. "Congressional Oversight and the Multilateral Development Banks." *International Organization.* Undated.

Schmidt, Elizabeth; Blewett, Jane; and Henriot, Peter. *Religious Private Voluntary Organizations and the Question of Govern-*

*ment Funding: Final Report.* Maryknoll, NY: Orbis Books, 1981.

Schoultz, Lars. "Politics, Economics and U.S. Participation in Multilateral Development Banks." *International Organization.* Summer, 1982 (Vol. 36, No. 3).

Sierra Club. *Bankrolling Disasters: International Development Banks and the Global Environment.* Washington, DC, September 1986.

Smith, Brian H. "U.S. and Canadian PVOs as Transnational Development Institutions" in *Private Voluntary Organizations as Agents of Development,* ed. by Robert F. Gorman. Boulder, CO and London: Westview Press, 1984.

Smith, William E.; Lethem, Francis J.; and Thoolen, Ben A. "The Design of Organizations for Rural Development Projects—A Progress Report." World Bank Staff Working Paper #375. Washington, DC: World Bank, March 1980.

Sommer, John G. *Beyond Charity: U.S. Voluntary Aid for a Changing Third World.* Overseas Development Council: Washington, DC, 1977.

Sommers, William. "Rescuing AID: It is Time for AID to Make a Strategic Retreat—Into the Department of State." *Foreign Service Journal.* May 1982.

*Sweden's Policy for International Development Co-operation.* Extracts from the Budget and Finance Bill for Fiscal Year 1981/82. Ministry of Foreign Affairs, 1981.

"Taking Up the Running: A Survey of the World Bank." *The Economist.* 23 September 1986.

Tendler, Judith. *Inside Foreign Aid.* Baltimore, MD: Johns Hopkins University Press, 1975

Tendler, Judith. *Turning Private Voluntary Organizations into Development Agencies: Questions for Evaluation.* Washington, DC: Agency for International Development, April 1982.

Task Force on International Development. *U.S. Foreign Assistance in the 1970s: A New Approach.* Report to the President. 4 March 1970.

U.S. Congress. *Foreign Assistance Act of 1961,* as amended.

U.S. Congress, House of Representatives. *AID's Administrative Management Problems in Providing Foreign Economic Assistance. Hearing before the Legislation and National Security Subcommittee,* 97th Congress, 1st Session, 6 October 1981. Washington, DC: U.S. Government Printing Office, 1981.

U.S. Congress, House of Representatives. *A Bill to Amend the*

*Foreign Assistance Act of 1961 with Respect to the Activities of the Overseas Private Investment Corporation,* H.R. 9179, 95th Congress, 1st Session. Washington, DC: U.S. Government Printing Office, 19 September 1977.

U.S. Congress, House of Representatives. *The Future of the Multilateral Development Banks. Hearings before the Subcommittee on International Development Institutions and Finance held jointly with the Subcommittee on International Trade, Investment, and Monetary Policy.* (15, 17, and 22 June 1982.)

U.S. Congress, House of Representatives. *The Future of the Multilateral Development Banks. Report of the Subcommittee on International Development Institutions and Finance.* November 1982.

U.S. Congress, House of Representatives. *Overseas Private Investment Corporation Amendments Act of 1977: Report of the Committee on International Relations,* H.R. 9179, 95th, Congress, 1st Session, 7 October 1977. Washington, DC: U.S. Government Printing Office, 1977.

U.S. Congress, House of Representatives. *U.S. Participation in the International Development Association. Hearings before the Subcommittee on International Development Institutions and Finance of the Committee on Banking, Finance, and Urban Affairs.* 29 February and 1 March 1984.

U.S. Congress, House of Representatives. *U.S. Peace Corps Congressional Presentation: Fiscal Year 1985.* (1 February 1984).

U.S. Congress, House of Representatives. Proceedings and Debates of the 99th Congress, 1st Session. *Congressional Record.* Vol. 131, No. 174–Part II (16 December 1985).

U.S. Congress, House of Representatives. *Report.* Foreign assistance and Related Programs, Appropriations Bill 1981 (24 July 1980).

U.S. Congress, House of Representatives. *Rethinking United States Foreign Policy Toward the Third World. Hearings before the Committee on International Relations and its Subcommittee on International Development,* 95th Congress, 1st Session, 4 August, 12 October and 1 November 1977. Washington, DC: U.S. Government Printing Office, 1977.

U.S. Congress, Senate. *Reorganization Plan No. 2 of 1979. Hearing before the Committee on Governmental Affairs,* 96th Congress, 1st Session, 1 May 1979. Washington, DC: U.S. Government Printing Office, 1979.

U.S. Congress, Senate Committee on Governmental Affairs. *U.S. Participation in the Multilateral Development Banks,* 96th

Congress, 1st Session. Washington, DC: U.S. Government Printing Office, 1979.

van de Laar, Aart. *The World Bank and the Poor.* Boston: Martinus Nijhoff Publishing, 1980.

van der Heijden, Hendrick. *Development Impact and Effectiveness of Non-Governmental Organizations: The Record of Progress in Rural Development Co-operation.* International Symposium, Royal Tropical Institute, Amsterdam, 30 September–4 October 1985.

Viorst, Milton, ed. *Making A Difference: The Peace Corps at Twenty-Five.* New York: Widenfeld & Nicolson, 1986.

Wasserstrom, Robert F. "The World Bank and World Poverty." *The Christian Science Monitor.* 25 June 1984.

"Why Clarence Long is Fighting World Bank Aid." *Euromoney.* April 1978.

World Bank. *IDA in Retrospect: The First Two Decades of the International Development Association.* Oxford University Press, 1982.

World Bank. *Project Completion Report on the Nicaragua Urban Construction Project.* 1983.

World Bank. *Project Completion Report on the Second Guatemala Urban Construction Project.* 1984.

World Bank. *Rural Water Supply and Sanitation: Possibilities for Collaboration with Non-Governmental Organizations, Part One: Africa.* Water Supply and Urban Development Department, Technical Note. January 1985.

Yudelman, Sally. *Hopeful Openings: A Study of Five Women's Development Organizations in Latin America and the Caribbean.* West Hartford, CT: Kumarian Press, 1987.

# Index